The Hidden Magic of Walt Disney World

PLANNER

A Complete Organizer, Journal, and Keepsake for Your Unforgettable Vacation

SUSAN VENESS AND SIMON VENESS

adamsmedia

Avon, Massachusetts

Published by
Adams Media, a division of F+W Media, Inc.
57 Littlefield Street, Avon, MA 02322. U.S.A.
www.adamsmedia.com

ISBN 10: 1-4405-2810-1
ISBN 13: 978-1-4405-2810-1

Printed in China.

10   9   8   7   6   5   4   3   2   1

Library of Congress Cataloging-in-Publication Data
is available from the publisher.

This publication is designed to provide accurate and authoritative information with regard to the subject matter covered. It is sold with the understanding that the publisher is not engaged in rendering legal, accounting, or other professional advice. If legal advice or other expert assistance is required, the services of a competent professional person should be sought.
—From a *Declaration of Principles* jointly adopted by a Committee of the American Bar Association and a Committee of Publishers and Associations

Many of the designations used by manufacturers and sellers to distinguish their product are claimed as trademarks. Where those designations appear in this book and Adams Media was aware of a trademark claim, the designations have been printed with initial capital letters.

The following are registered trademarks of The Walt Disney Company: Adventure-land, Audio-Animatronics, Disney's Animal Kingdom Park, Epcot, Fantasyland, Frontierland, Indiana Jones Epic Stunt Spectacular!, Magic Kingdom Park, Main Street, U.S.A., Mickey Mouse, Tomorrowland, The Twilight Zone Tower of Terror, Walt Disney World. Universal Studios is a registered trademark of Universal Studios, Inc.

Maps by Joe Comeau/copyright © F+W Media, Inc.
Interior photos by Ben Haass.

This book is available at quantity discounts for bulk purchases.
For information, please call 1-800-289-0963.

Dedication

*To dreamers and doers everywhere,
who carry on Walt Disney's tradition
of great storytelling.*

Acknowledgments

We'd like to recognize the help and encouragement of the following in the production of this book:

First, our families for their nonstop support, and especially our boys' uncomplaining ability to tramp around the parks time and time again! And to photographer Ben Haass for sweating over hours of picture-taking.

On a professional level, we are indebted to former Disney Manager of Entertainment Gene Columbus for his example of great storytelling, and to longtime Disney historian and all-around good guy Jim Korkis, whose fabulous book, *The Vault of Walt*, makes inspiring reading. We would also like to thank Disney's Todd Heiden, Carole Munroe, and Darrell Fry for their help in our research, along with Kal David (the voice of Sonny Eclipse!) and Imagineer George Wilkins, Disney's former Director of Music.

Finally, for the hard work of all the people at Adams Media—thanks!

Contents

8   Introduction

10   How to Use this Book

CHAPTER 1

19   The Adventure Begins: Planning and Practicalities

21   Choosing a Ticket

23   Weather

24   Crowds

24   Traveling with Children

26   Special Needs

27   Disney for Seniors

28   Using Fastpass

30   Disney's PhotoPass

30   Special Occasions

31   App Happy

32   Useful Phone Numbers

34   Arriving in Orlando

CHAPTER 2

41   Staying in the Story: Accommodations

43   The Benefits

45   The Resorts

46   Value Resorts

50   Moderate Resorts

59   Deluxe Resorts

77   Deluxe Villas

84   Campground

86   Onsite Non-Disney Resorts

88   Outside the World

CHAPTER 3

97 Where the Magic Begins: Magic Kingdom

98   Practical Information

99   Main Street, U.S.A.

105   Adventureland

113   Frontierland

120   Liberty Square

127   Fantasyland

141   Tomorrowland

149   Parades, Tours, and Events

153   Holidays at Magic Kingdom

CHAPTER 4

161 A World of Discovery: Epcot

162   Practical Information

162   Future World

181   World Showcase

208   Parades, Tours, and Special Events!

CHAPTER 5

225 Movie Magic: Disney's Hollywood Studios

226   Practical Information

226   Hollywood Boulevard

229   Echo Lake

235   Streets of America

240   Commissary Lane

241   Pixar Place

242   Mickey Avenue

244   Animation Courtyard

246   Sunset Boulevard

252   Tours and Special Events

253   Holidays in Hollywood Studios

CHAPTER 6

257   Nature Tells Its Own Tale: Disney's Animal Kingdom

258   Practical Information
258   The Oasis
259   Discovery Island
263   DinoLand U.S.A.
270   Asia
276   Rafiki's Planet Watch
278   Africa
282   Camp Minnie-Mickey
284   Parades, Tours, and Special Events
285   Holidays at Animal Kingdom

CHAPTER 7

289   Enhancing the Story: Water Park Fun and More

290   Typhoon Lagoon
295   Blizzard Beach
300   ESPN Wide World of Sports Complex
301   Disney Golf
304   Walt Disney World Speedway
305   Disney's Wedding Pavilion

CHAPTER 8

308   The World by Night

309   Downtown Disney
316   Disney's BoardWalk
318   Dinner Shows
321   And There's More...!

CHAPTER 9

324 **Discovering Dining**

325 Character Meal Line-Up

327 Resorts

339 Downtown Disney

348 Index

Introduction

···

The magic is in the story; if you don't know the story,
you're just taking another ride.

WELCOME TO THE HAPPIEST PLACE ON EARTH: Walt Disney World! No other vacation destination is as magical as the world Walt Disney and his Imagineers created, where every detail has been designed to tell an all-encompassing story.

Some of the stories are obvious while others may remain elusive, even to repeat visitors. So how will you find them? *The Hidden Magic of Walt Disney World Planner* will guide you around the parks, resorts, and restaurants with an eye toward enhancing your appreciation for the immense creativity that lies at the very heart of the magic—and it provides ample room for you to add your own stories.

You'll also find plenty of practical information that will help make planning for your vacation as easy as possible. This info, combined with maps of the Magic Kingdom, Epcot, Disney's Hollywood Studios, and Disney's Animal Kingdom, will allow you to fully experience the story unfolding around you.

Sprinkled throughout the guide are Reality Check and Rookie Mistake features to help you avoid pitfalls that could take away from your vacation experience. Knowing in advance where these trip-ups occur ensures that you can immerse yourself in the magic without worrying about unexpected bumps in the road. Also, each theme park chapter includes the story behind every attraction and restaurant, and includes icons that help you choose which attractions are most suitable for your family or group (learn what these icons mean in the How to Use This Book section, coming up next). You'll also find more than 100 brand new Hidden Magic gems that you can look for as you are touring—and photos that give you a peek at some of the Hidden Magic you'll be looking for.

But the real magic comes from the memories you make—and in the course of the book you'll find plenty of room to record all of the magical moments you experience, info on all the Hidden Magic that you come across, and—most important—space to write the story of your own visit. You'll also find handy pockets to tuck away little treasures, planning lists, receipts, photographs— all the precious mementos that will remind you of your trip—resulting in a keepsake you'll treasure forever.

How to Use
This Book

Having a Disney trip in the works is a thrilling prospect, and you're probably tempted to flip straight to the theme parks chapter for a full breakdown of all the fun that's in store. But trying to work out what attractions are suitable for *your* family if you don't know Expedition Everest from Kilimanjaro Safaris can be a vexing business. And that's where this section comes in. As you work your way through the *Planner*, you'll see icons next to each ride, hotel, and restaurant that will tell you everything from how much a meal costs to which attractions are most suitable for youngsters. Take a few moments to review our ratings system so that these icons are familiar to you when you see them. After all, the more info you have right up front, the more you can focus on what's really important: the magic!

Is It Worth It? Ratings

Disney vacations never seem to last long enough, so you will want to make the most of the time you have in each park. While all of the attractions and shows are worth experiencing, you would need a month to see it all, so you will have to be somewhat selective about how you spend your time, and choose which attractions are most suited to your group. The good news is that, over the years, we've developed a tried-and-tested ratings method that will help you decide if a particular attraction is a must-try. Look for the following icons throughout the book:

⭐ an attraction that is miss-able

⭐ an attraction that's worth experiencing if you have time

⭐ an attraction that's worth making time for

⭐ an attraction that is not to be missed! Make sure you add these attractions to your story.

Note: The 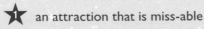 and 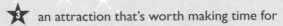 attractions will draw the biggest lines, so focus on experiencing these first. You can get a Fastpass (see Chapter 1) for many of these rides so be sure to take advantage of this option.

The Scare Factor

Walt Disney World isn't just for kids and there are some rides that may be scary for someone in your group. To avoid any unpleasant surprises for less adventurous riders, we add a "Scare" rating for each ride or show that may have some scare factor, especially for a particular age group. But keep in mind that there may be exceptions; after all, you know your child or yourself best! Look for the following icons:

- 😊 will only worry young children or exceptionally timid adults
- 😐 has the ability to scare many young children and a few adults
- ☹️ will scare most young children and some adults
- 😮 means major scare factor

Disney Dining Ratings

Dining is a big part of your vacation experience, whether you're simply taking the time to enjoy a meal together or celebrating a special event. Disney's vast array of choices may be overwhelming, but don't worry, you'll find the following icons that rate the restaurants by price, what meals they serve, the type of service they provide, and a rating of the restaurant's overall quality, to help you narrow down the best selections:

Overall Quality Ratings

★ Poor

★★ Fair

★★★ Good

★★★★ Excellent

★★★★★ Gourmet

Price Ratings

$ average meal costs under $10

$$ average meal costs between $10–15

$$$ average meal costs between $15–$20

$$$$ average meal costs between $20–$25

$$$$$ average meal costs $25–plus

Service Ratings

🍴Ⓑ serves breakfast

🍴Ⓛ serves lunch

🍴Ⓓ serves dinner

🍴CS offers Counter Service

🍴TS offers Table Service

🍴TS2 takes two Table Service credits

Note: All restaurants will be on the Disney Dining Plan, unless specified "Not DDP."

Motion Discomfort Ratings

There are several attractions within the theme parks that may cause motion discomfort in susceptible guests. Below you'll find the icons for each category and a breakdown of the rides—and their triggers—that could be a problem. As a reminder for those who may wish to avoid certain attractions, the following ratings are included next to each attraction that may cause discomfort:

 CATEGORY ONE: includes attractions that can be slightly disorienting visually, some giving the sensation of movement without actual movement.

 CATEGORY TWO: includes attractions that involve some physical movement, of a mild variety. Most can be viewed prior to riding.

 CATEGORY THREE: includes attractions with a definite physical sensation: weightlessness, stomach-dropping sensation, or intense feeling of motion.

 CATEGORY FOUR: includes the attractions that are known to be uncomfortable for most susceptible (and some nonsusceptible!) guests. They include extreme physical sensations, some including visual disorientation as well.

CATEGORY ONE (slight visual disorientation)	
MAGIC KINGDOM	**Buzz Lightyear's Space Ranger Spin**—section where visuals spin around you.
EPCOT	**Soarin'**—slight sensation of motion due to onscreen visuals.
	The Seas with Nemo & Friends—bubble room seems to spin around you.
	Universe of Energy—short movie segment that mimics flying, with steep, banking turns.

DISNEY'S HOLLYWOOD STUDIOS	**Muppet*Vision 3-D**—3-D experience.
	The Great Movie Ride—very short segment where visuals seem to spin around you.
DISNEY'S ANIMAL KINGDOM	**It's Tough to Be a Bug!**—3-D experience.

☄2 CATEGORY TWO (some motion or spinning, not intense)

MAGIC KINGDOM	**Splash Mountain**—short drops, big final drop (Category Three for some guests).
	Dumbo—slow spinning ride.
	The Magic Carpets of Aladdin—slow spinning ride.
	Prince Charming Regal Carousel—slow spinning ride.
	Astro Orbiter—moderate spinning ride.
EPCOT	**Mission: Space green team**—very slight simulator motion; tipping and slight bumps, accentuated by visuals (Category Three for some guests).
	Test Track—high-speed banked turn (Category Three for some guests).
	Maelstrom—moderate drop.
	Sum of All Thrills (noninversion)—moves, but does not twist upside down.
DISNEY'S HOLLYWOOD STUDIOS	None
DISNEY'S ANIMAL KINGDOM	**TriceraTop Spin**—slow spinning ride.
	Kilimanjaro Safaris—bumpy jeep ride.

③ CATEGORY THREE (intense motion or disorientation)

MAGIC KINGDOM	**Big Thunder Mountain Railroad**—tight turns, quick drops.
	Space Mountain—fast roller coaster in the dark; quick turns, moderate drops.
	Seven Dwarfs Mine Train—swaying motion, dips and turns.
EPCOT	None
DISNEY'S HOLLYWOOD STUDIOS	**Twilight Zone Tower of Terror**—intense drop sequences.
	Rock 'n' Roller Coaster—fast turns, loops and drops, in the dark.
DISNEY'S ANIMAL KINGDOM	**Expedition Everest**—big drops, disorienting backward element (this portion may be a Category Four for some guests), in the dark.

④ CATEGORY FOUR (strong caution; most intense)

MAGIC KINGDOM	**Mad Tea Party**—intense spinning in two directions simultaneously.
EPCOT	**Mission: Space orange team**—extreme centrifuge spin with visual disorientation.
	Sum of All Thrills (with inversion)—enclosed robotic arm moving in many directions, including upside down.
DISNEY'S HOLLYWOOD STUDIOS	**Star Tours**—bouncy, jerky motion simulator with visual disorientation (Category Three for some guests).
DISNEY'S ANIMAL KINGDOM	**Primeval Whirl**—quick turns, sharp drops, spinning elements.
	Dinosaur—jerky, bumpy dark ride with strobe light effects.

If you are unsure about how you will react to any particular attraction, you may wish to send a trusted family member on the ride first to get an idea of whether or not that attraction is suitable for you.

With an understanding of how the ratings work and armed with knowledge about any attractions you may wish to avoid, let's move on to the practical side of things.

Chapter 1

The Adventure Begins:
Planning and Practicalities

FOR THOSE NEW TO WALT DISNEY WORLD, this is a vacation adventure like no other. For those who have been here before, welcome back—and get ready for even more excitement, as the story continues to get better, year by year.

Like any good story, certain essential elements have to be in place for it all to flow well. But putting the basics together for a Disney vacation can be a daunting prospect, especially for first-timers. If you have visited Walt Disney World in the past you know how much fun is in store, but you have probably also figured out how vital it is to arrive prepared; if you show up without a well-established plotline, your tale may end up moving in the direction of a mystery or a drama!

Happily, the planning stages don't have to be mysterious or dramatic. In fact, you may find planning is a lot of fun, and a wonderful prelude to a real thriller, a fairy tale, or even a romance. Knowing what sort of story you would like to write is the first step toward choosing the key components that will allow you to relax and enjoy the experience once you arrive.

Overwhelming as it may seem, there is a logical order to putting together your trip of a lifetime. First, you will need to establish your travel dates. If your dates are flexible, weather and crowds may play a role in your decision. Does it have to be hot to seem like Florida to you, or are you happy to travel during slower times of the year when it's cooler? Special needs or special occasions may factor into the time of year you visit as well.

Next, will you drive to Walt Disney World or will you fly? Do you need to rent a car? You may want the convenience of staying onsite, and Chapter 2 will help you decide which Disney resort is right for you. Once these big decisions have been made it's time to think about the smaller, but often more difficult, choices of which park tickets you will use and any dining reservations you would like to make.

With a little research into your options, the tales you tell when you return from your trip can all end in "happily ever after," and that's what this chapter will help you achieve.

Choosing a Ticket

Advance planning is the key to creating an amazing vacation and an essential part of that planning is choosing the right ticket for visiting the parks. This should be the easy part of planning, though; you know how many days you're visiting for, so you just need tickets for that number of days, right? Unfortunately, that's not the case. While much of your visit is a true fairy tale, the Magic Your Way, or MYW, ticketing system can be a real puzzle.

To work your way through the MYW system, do the following:

1. Choose the number of days (one–ten) that you'll be visiting the Disney parks.
2. Decide if you want "park hopping" (the ability to visit more than one park a day).
3. Decide if you want the Water Park Fun & More option, which adds one admission per day to a choice of Blizzard Beach and Typhoon Lagoon water parks, DisneyQuest Indoor Interactive Theme Park, ESPN Wide World of Sports Complex, and Disney's Oak Trail Golf Course (e.g., if you buy the five-day ticket with Water Park Fun & More, you also get five visits to those "extras").
4. Finally, you can buy a no-expiration option for your tickets if you'd like to save some days for a future visit.

You can also buy annual passes that are a good value if you're likely to visit for twenty or more days in a 365-day period. You can get:

1. An annual pass that covers all four theme parks, park hopping, parking ($15 a day if you aren't a Disney resort guest), special Passholder mailings and newsletters, and special events, and discounts on hotels, dining, and merchandise.
2. A Premium Annual Pass that adds the Water Park Fun & More options.

Note: The costs rise with each option, so it's vital to work out what you want in advance.

Confused? You could certainly be excused for feeling a bit giddy (or even Goofy!) at all the choices. To make it easy, consider the following:

- If you have only one–four days, stick to a straight four-day MYW ticket with no extras.
- If you have five–seven days, buy a four- or five-day ticket with Water Park Fun & More (where your water park visits provide a more relaxing day or half-day from the main parks).
- If you have seven–ten days, get a five- or six-day ticket with Water Park Fun & More.
- If you're considering park hopping, keep in mind that it's not recommended if you're only staying for one–four days or if you're traveling with young children. But if you're staying for five or more days it's worth considering if you think you have the stamina (see the Weather section that follows).

ROOKIE MISTAKES

Don't be among those who arrive at the gates without their tickets and end up in long lines at the ticket booths. Buying in advance is not only more convenient, but you can save money, too, with special discounts on multi-day tickets. In addition to buying direct from Disney at *www.disneyworld .com* (407-939-1289), there are various official brokers offering tickets—and many unofficial ones, too—so stay away from anyone offering re-sales; they are strictly illegal. In addition, many timeshare companies offer "free" tickets if you take their high-pressure tours, which may leave you spending half of your day at the timeshare place waiting for your ticket. Check out the folks at Orlando Attractions if you're looking for a good deal. They also offer periodic special discounts and daily deals; group rates; and great offers for Disney hotels, local condos, and vacation villas. Check them out at *www .OrlandoAttractions.com* or call 1-800-626-7695.

Weather

Whenever you travel, you should always make sure that you know what the weather is going to be like. You don't want to get into the parks and spend the day too hot, or too cold, or dripping wet. When it comes to Florida, you probably know that it's called the Sunshine State and that large parts of the region are swampy. Those are clues one and two as to what to expect weather-wise— it's usually hot and can get pretty wet. Average temperatures for Orlando are 74°F in February, 92°F in July, and 79°F in November, but those figures hide a multitude of sins. It can easily top 100°F in the summer, and in the winter months it occasionally dips below freezing at night. There can be also be 6 inches or more of rain each month from June to September, while June–November is also hurricane season—this isn't usually a concern but big tropical storms can churn up the Florida coasts and bring heavy downpours for several days.

ROOKIE MISTAKES

Remember all this weather advice when you start your packing. Just about everything here is relaxed and informal, so you don't need a suit or cocktail dress unless you're planning dinner at Victoria & Albert's. T-shirts, shorts, and flip-flops are perfectly acceptable in most places—but no swimwear is allowed in the restaurants or parks (aside from children in the water areas).

And then there's the humidity, which can be in excess of 90 percent from late May to late September, and this makes everything feel a lot hotter. A full day in the parks can seem like a commando operation in the jungle, so it's important to slow down, take advantage of air-conditioned attractions, and drink lots of water. Dehydration is the biggest cause of illness in Disney, and high-SPF sunscreens are an absolute necessity.

Not many people pay attention to this, but it's vital in the hottest months: The best two parks for avoiding overheating are Epcot and Disney's Hollywood Studios, which have the highest percentage of air-conditioned attractions.

Crowds

You'll have a great time no matter when you plan your trip to Walt Disney World, but you'll likely have more fun if you take your vacation when everyone else doesn't. The crowds in the parks increase steadily through June, peak at July 4, and stay high until mid-August, with another mini-peak for the Labor Day weekend. You'll also find large crowds from the Spring Break period (generally in late March through mid-April) to the week after Easter, and the parks are also packed during the week surrounding Thanksgiving and also during the holiday period ranging from December 20 to January 2.

The ideal times to visit are between Easter and Memorial Day; from early October to mid-November; and (if you don't mind your vacation weather a bit chilly), the first two weeks of December, and early January to late February.

Traveling with Children

Walt Disney World was designed with children firmly in mind, but that doesn't mean that parents can sit back, switch off, and expect everything to run smoothly. This may be a storybook world but it still needs plenty of real-world planning, preparation, and awareness—especially if you're visiting with young'uns in tow.

There's a particular phenomenon around the parks that we like to call the Four O'Clock Meltdown. Around this time of day, many preschoolers (and some older children) decide it's time to go into Bawl Mode. This is due to one of several highly preventable factors:

1. Not having enough to drink during the day. Kids can end up dehydrated and feeling angsty and unable to say why.
2. Parents sticking to a rigid plan that doesn't take unexpectedly long lines and other holdups into account.
3. Sleepiness from being up for the fireworks the previous evening!
4. Overheating due to the fierce summer temperatures and humidity.
5. Just trying to do too much. This can be an exhausting vacation at the best of times and from June to September it can be a real beast.

If your Disney story includes kids, you're well advised to have the following "To Do" list in mind when you set out each day:

1. Bring bottled water (it's cheaper to start with) and refill it at water fountains as often as you need.
2. Make sure you have a small first-aid kit, including baby wipes.
3. Bring a stroller, even if your youngster is a year or so out of it at home—it makes a great emergency nap spot during the day (you can also rent one at all the parks).
4. Bring a change of clothes (or a swimsuit and towel) so kids can splash in the waterplay areas to cool down.
5. Use the Fastpass system as much as possible (see page 28).
6. Be ready to go with the flow if your children find something unexpectedly appealing as a diversion.

But above all else, be flexible! Don't be "That Parent" who marches the family around in military precision from ride to ride. If necessary, take a break in the afternoon and return to your resort to swim or sleep. Everyone will benefit from a little downtime!

Baby Care Centers

All four theme parks have well-stocked Baby Care Centers to help make changing and feeding as easy as possible. These centers provide vital "extras" like Carnation baby formulas (at no charge), spare diapers, sunscreen, and some over-the-counter medications. They are also cool and relaxing, which allows everyone to de-stress when it's hot.

At the Magic Kingdom, the Baby Care Center is next to the Crystal Palace restaurant (turn left at the top of Main Street); in Epcot it is in the Odyssey Center between Test Track and the World Showcase; in Disney's Hollywood Studios it is at Guest Relations just through the main entrance; and in Disney's Animal Kingdom it is to the right of Creature Comforts in Discovery Island. The water parks and Downtown Disney do *not* have Baby Care Centers, but all the restrooms have changing stations.

Use Rider Swap

If you are traveling with a small child who does not meet the ride's height requirement or for whom a particular ride is not suitable, you may need to use Rider Swap for some of the theme park attractions. With this great program, one adult can stay with a nonrider while the rest of the group rides, then another adult can wait with the nonrider while the first adult goes straight to the front of the line for their ride. This allows you to stand in line only once. Simply tell the ride attendant that you would like to use Rider Swap and they will direct you to the correct waiting area. Some locations will require you to have a voucher for the second rider, so be sure to let the attendants know you will be swapping.

If you are traveling with one child who can ride and one who can't, the riding child may be allowed to ride twice, so be sure to ask!

Special Needs

From the hotels to the attractions, few parts of Walt Disney World are not fully handicapped accessible. Wheelchair availability and access is usually good. For hearing-impaired guests, there are assistive listening devices and reflective captioning where a commentary is part of the show. Braille guidebooks are available, rest areas are available for guide dogs, and there are special recordings for blind guests. Disney also has a free accessibility guide for handicapped visitors in all their parks (and online). For disability assistance, call 407-824-4321.

REALITY CHECK

If you're visiting the parks with someone with special needs, stop in at any Guest Relations office with the special-needs person in question, and request a Guest Assistance Card (GAC), which can be tailored to fit their needs. The card doesn't provide front-of-the-line access (which many people believe), but it can make waiting more comfortable.

Disney for Seniors

With so many extended family groups taking advantage of the Disney experience, the story for seniors is also a magical one. Older folks can enjoy things every bit as much as their kids and grandkids, albeit within slightly different parameters.

The parks greatly reward those who take things at a more leisurely pace, stop frequently to admire the architecture and landscaping—and hidden magic—and enjoy the shows as much as the rides. True, there are rides that prove too dynamic for some seniors, but many mature guests get a huge thrill from people watching (especially the children at the many parades), from strolling through Epcot and Disney's Animal Kingdom in particular, and from the fine dining that is a notable aspect of the World these days. Older folks also love the BoardWalk resort area at night, the monorail trip from the Magic Kingdom to Epcot, and classic rides like the Haunted Mansion, Pirates of the Caribbean, Jungle Cruise, Universe of Energy, Soarin', Kilimanjaro Safaris, and the Great Movie Ride. They might also enjoy the animal walking trails in Disney's Animal Kingdom and the nighttime entertainment spectaculars.

Using Fastpass

One of Disney's biggest success stories in recent years was the 1999 introduction of the Fastpass system, which allows guests to bypass the main line for some attractions by getting a separate ticket to return at a specified time.

To use the system, simply go to the Fastpass attraction (listed below by park) and locate the small distribution kiosks. Put your park entry ticket into the machine (one for each member of your party who wants to ride), take the ticket back, and then pick up the timed return ticket that the machine prints out. It will have a one-hour time-slot (say, 2:10 P.M. to 3:10 P.M.) in which to return and join the (much shorter) Fastpass line instead of the stand-by line.

The Fastpass is available for these high-volume rides:

MAGIC KINGDOM
- Peter Pan's Flight
- Space Mountain
- Buzz Lightyear's Space Ranger Spin
- Splash Mountain
- Big Thunder Mountain Railroad
- Jungle Cruise
- Mickey's PhilharMagic
- The Many Adventures of Winnie the Pooh

EPCOT
- Soarin'
- Mission: Space
- Test Track
- Maelstrom
- Captain EO

DISNEY'S HOLLYWOOD STUDIOS
- Star Tours
- Toy Story Mania!
- The Twilight Zone Tower of Terror
- Rock 'n' Roller Coaster

- Voyage of The Little Mermaid
- Indiana Jones Epic Stunt Spectacular!
- Lights, Motors, Action! Extreme Stunt Show
- Muppet*Vision 3-D

DISNEY'S ANIMAL KINGDOM

- Kilimanjaro Safaris
- Dinosaur
- Expedition Everest
- Kali River Rapids
- Primeval Whirl
- It's Tough to Be a Bug!

In 2011, Disney was experimenting with the Fastpass system for character meet-and-greets in the Magic Kingdom, and there's a good chance that this will be extended to all of the really busy character meeting spots around the four parks in the coming years.

ROOKIE MISTAKES

It certainly isn't a secret, but many guests still overlook the Fastpass system even though it is free and easy to use. Some think you can hold only one Fastpass at a time, but you can get one every two hours and immediately after your time slot starts (e.g., if you hold a Fastpass for Buzz Lightyear's Space Ranger Spin in the Magic Kingdom that gives you a 10:30–11:30 A.M. window, you can get another pass at 10:31 A.M.). However, many attractions do run out of Fastpass tickets, sometimes by midday at busy times of the year. To avoid missing out, in each park you should first get a Fastpass for the following attractions:

- Magic Kingdom: Peter Pan (if you have preschoolers in tow; otherwise start with a Fastpass for Splash Mountain or Space Mountain)
- Epcot: Soarin'
- Disney's Hollywood Studios: Toy Story Mania!
- Disney's Animal Kingdom: Kilimanjaro Safaris

Disney's PhotoPass

Every photo taken at Walt Disney World is a special memory that you'll take home as part of your story, but Disney's PhotoPass photographers have a knack for getting just the right shot . . . and then adding a magical surprise!

You'll find PhotoPass photographers, who generally wear a hat and vest, and have a camera around their neck, all around the parks, so just walk up to the first one you see, ask to have your photo taken, and you'll receive a card you can use for the rest of your stay. Every time you see a PhotoPass spot, just hand your card to the photographer.

You can get a new card every day, or use the same one again and again. Select your photos at the end of the day, or save them up and view them for up to a month after your visit. For more about PhotoPass, check out *www.disney photopass.com.*

Special Occasions

Do you have a birthday, anniversary, or other special occasion that coincides with your Disney visit? In that case, there are plenty of ways to celebrate, and while the prices for these special occasions range from free to pretty pricey, the memories you'll take away from the experience will be absolutely priceless.

Take advantage of free birthday badges at City Hall in the Magic Kingdom and Guest Services at Epcot, Disney's Hollywood Studios, and Disney's Animal Kingdom. Cast Members (what the Disney staff are called because they all play a part in "The Show" of theme park entertainment) like to make a fuss over children—and adults!—wearing a birthday badge. For large-scale celebrations, there is a ninety-minute IllumiNations Cruise (to Epcot), with snacks, drinks, streamers, and balloons for up to ten people. You should also look into the kids' birthday parties at Disney's Polynesian Resort, Winter Summerland Mini Golf Course, and Goofy's Candy Company at Downtown Disney. Disney's Pirate Cruise, a two-hour adventure for kids four–twelve, sails from the Grand Floridian, Yacht/Beach Club, Port Orleans, and

Caribbean Beach resorts each day. For info call 407-939-7529; you can book up to 180 days in advance.

REALITY CHECK Yes, you can order birthday cakes at your resort or at Guest Services at the parks! All Disney restaurants offer ready-made 6-inch cakes on demand or something larger if you place your order up to 48 hours in advance (407-827-2253).

App Happy

Today's generation of smartphones and other mobile devices all can access a range of apps that can really help with your time in and around the parks. Look out for the following:

FOR IPHONE, IPOD, AND IPAD:
- Disney World Park Hours (free, by Disney)
- Disney World Wait Times (free, by NKR Innovations)
- Disney World Dining ($1.99, by VersaEdge Software)
- Disney World Park Maps (free, by VersaEdge Software)
- Scott Joseph's Orlando Restaurant Guide (free, by Scott Joseph)
- Hidden Mickeys—Disney World ($1.99, by Healthy Life Labs)
- Disney World Vacation Countdown ($0.99, by Ricky Mills)
- And, for when you are already standing in those lines, try Disney (free, by Disney) for games, characters, videos, and music.

FOR ANDROID:
- Disney World Hidden Mickeys ($1.99, by TimeStream Software)
- Disney World Character Find ($0.99, by Magic Mobile)
- Disney World Wait Times ($0.99, by Phunware)

FOR BLACKBERRY:
- WDW Maps ($2.99, by UPinPoint.com)

Verizon also offers the excellent Mobile Magic application, the only official Disney app, which has park hours, attraction wait times, Fastpass availability, character appearances, games, trivia, and more for $1.99. Text MAGIC to 2777, visit the Verizon Media Store (*www.verizonwireless.com*), or go to the Media Center on your Verizon phone and select Browse & Download. Mobile Magic is in the Travel & Navigation folder. It is being added to more handsets all the time, so check *http://disneyparksmobile.com* for the latest details.

ROOKIE MISTAKES

Disney's pin trading craze, which arrived at the World in 1999, is still going strong. If you would like to give pin trading a try, purchase a few Disney pins (yes, they have to be Disney pins!) at a place like Disney Character Outlet at Orlando Premium Outlets in Lake Buena Vista or the Premium Outlets on International Drive, at a substantial discount, rather than buying them in the parks. You can then trade your less expensive pins for other Disney pins simply by walking up to any Cast Member wearing a lanyard. They'll always trade with you, so don't be shy about asking for the pin you like best!

Useful Phone Numbers

While you're planning your vacation—and even once you're arrived at the parks—having the right phone number for all the different Disney departments can be a real boon, especially when it's busy. Here is a list of the must-have numbers:

DEPARTMENT	PHONE NUMBER
Guest Information	407-939-6244
Hotel Reservations	407-939-7429
Vacation Packages	407-939-7675
Tickets	407-939-1289
Group Reservations	407-828-3318
Dining	407-939-3463
Theme Parks Lost & Found	407-824-4245
Blizzard Beach Lost & Found	407-560-5408
Typhoon Lagoon Lost & Found	407-560-6296
Passholder Info & Bookings	407-827-7200
Tours	407-939-8687
Golf	407-939-4653
Fishing, Tennis, Watersports	407-939-7529
Cirque du Soleil	407-939-7600
Planet Hollywood	407-827-7827
House of Blues (box office)	407-934-2583
Special Needs Department	407-934-7639
Weather	407-824-4104
Weddings	407-828-3400

Room reservations and vacation packages can also be booked online at *www.disneyworld.com.*

Arriving in Orlando

Your first taste of the magic that comes from a Disney vacation is likely to begin once you have disembarked from your plane and arrive in one of Orlando International Airport's four satellite arms that feed into the main terminal.

It is a spacious, clean, and ultra-efficient airport that takes pride in its high customer satisfaction ratings and is a great arrival point for the area. There is even a "ride" to start with—you need to take the shuttle tram to the main terminal to collect your baggage and link up with ground transportation.

The airport is split into an A and a B side, and you need to know the correct one for your baggage pickup on Level 2 (and for the check-in desk for your return flight).

ON SIDE A, YOU'LL FIND:

- Air Canada
- Air Transat
- Alaska
- American
- CanJet
- JetBlue
- Southwest
- SunWing
- Virgin America
- WestJet

ON SIDE B, YOU'LL FIND:

- AirTran
- Continental
- Delta
- Frontier
- Spirit
- Sun Country
- United
- US Airways

And what's a Disney story without your first ride? Disney's Magical Express. . . .

If you arrive by plane and are picking up a rental car, *don't* follow signs for Orlando when you leave the airport (unless you are genuinely staying downtown). Follow signs for the South exit and take Highway 417, the Central Florida GreeneWay, west. For most Disney resorts, take Exit 6 and follow the signs. For the Animal Kingdom Lodge, All-Star resorts, Pop Century, and the new Art of Animation resort, take Exit 3. You will need $2–3 in tolls on the GreeneWay. A taxi will cost around $50 one-way.

Disney's Magical Express

If you're flying into Orlando International Airport and are staying "on-property," be sure to take advantage of Disney's Magical Express, a free shuttle service to your Disney resort. With this service, your luggage is "magically" transported directly to your room, which means minimum hassle during your journey.

Once you arrive at your home airport check in using the special luggage tags you will receive after booking. When you arrive in Orlando, head straight for the Magical Express transportation center, located on the B side of Level 1 at the airport, bypassing the luggage return completely.

Just be sure to ask for this service when booking through a travel agent or if booking online. Or call 407-939-6244 with your reservation number.

At the end of your stay, you will receive a transportation notice advising you of the pickup time and place for your motor coach ride back to the airport. Onsite guests can then use the Resort Airline Check-in Service, which allows you to receive your return boarding pass and check luggage at your hotel.

And speaking of hotels . . . you'll learn all about accomodations in the next chapter.

Write Your Own Story

Write Your Own Story

Write Your Own Story

Write Your Own Story

Write Your Own Story

Chapter 2

Staying in the Story:
Accommodations

IF THE THEME PARKS REPRESENT the story's main plot, Disney's twenty-one resorts are the supporting characters, providing the essential backup to all that's in store and offering an exciting foretaste of the overall style and artistry involved. And, in truth, there is no better way to fully immerse yourself in the magic of Walt Disney World than by staying in an onsite hotel, surrounded by the creativity 24/7. It is more expensive than an equivalent resort elsewhere, but the sheer convenience and ambience of accommodation Disney-style is impossible to beat.

Each hotel, of course, has a unique story to tell. They come in majestic, luxury style and modest-but-fun budget fashion; they feature epic adventure and relaxed, laid-back vibes; they offer rustic charm and cutting-edge glamour; they travel around the globe for inspiration and draw from local, homegrown ideas; they look to the land and the sea; and for members of the armed forces they even come in Shades of Green, an accommodation section set aside specifically for guests serving in the military.

But, most of all, they all feature the work of the Imagineers, the engineering artists Walt Disney charged with ensuring guests are immersed in his tale from start to finish.

ROOKIE MISTAKES

Guests new to the Disney experience may wonder what, exactly, is this "Imagineer" they keep hearing about? Simply put, this slightly mythical creature is a combination of engineer and imaginative creator; someone who can think in the realms of imagination but work in reality, making the "unreal" real. In the beginning, they were Walt's trusted animators and movie designers. Today, they are skilled college graduates, master musicians, brilliant graphic artists, intrepid adventurers, incurable dreamers, architects of the imagination, and creators of wonder.

The Benefits

Style? Check. Convenience? Check. Fun? You bet!

There is a huge range of additional benefits when you stay onsite, almost all of which are exclusive to the Disney hotels.

Staying at a Disney resort ensures entry to the parks at all times, even when the parking lots are closed to new visitors and the "Park Full" signs are displayed. It also provides an extensive free transport system as well as free parking at the four main theme parks.

At check-in you are provided with a Resort ID card, which you can use for almost all purchases in the parks, shops, and restaurants; you also benefit from Dining Priority, which allows you to make reservations for any onsite restaurant up to 180 days in advance plus the length of your stay (for example, if you're staying for seven days, you can book 187 days ahead of time; just call 407-939-3463 or visit *www.disneyworld.com*). Staying onsite also allows you access to Priority Golf, with the best tee times reserved for resort guests (you can book up to 90 days in advance at 407-939-4653 or online).

You should also take advantage of the refillable mugs at resorts which, for a one-time cost, you can refill for free at your hotel's self-service café. There is also free package delivery to your hotel for anything you buy at the parks or Downtown Disney.

In addition, all resorts have in-room or group babysitting and eight of the nine deluxe resorts have supervised kids' activity centers and dinner clubs (for an hourly fee), usually open until midnight. And, of course, there is Mickey on call—the chance to start every day with a wake-up call from the Big Cheese himself!

Finally, the *big* bonus is the Extra Magic Hours privilege, giving you entry into one of the parks one hour early each day or for three hours after the official park closing, providing hours of extra fun, often with much smaller crowds. Disney posts Extra Magic days on their monthly calendars on *www.disneyworld .com*, but beware, selected days can change without notice.

Dine 'n' Plan

In 2005, Disney introduced the Dining Plan—another bonus only available for onsite guests who book a vacation package that includes the dining plan—which allows you to budget for most of your meals and realize a small savings on what you might otherwise spend. Depending on which dining plan you choose, most or all of your Disney dining will be paid for in advance. To use this plan, all members of the party must book for the full duration of their stay, and you must include park tickets.

ROOKIE MISTAKES   Disney offers the Dining Plan as a free incentive to book during some of the quiet times of the year. This makes the restaurants much busier year-round, so you want to book well in advance for many table-service meals; you could be out of luck otherwise.

There are three separate plans you can choose from: Quick Service, the standard Dining Plan, and a Deluxe Plan.

- **Quick Service:** offers two counter-service meals and two snacks per person per day, and one refillable resort mug per person. Counter-service meals provide one entrée or combo meal, one dessert, and one nonalcoholic drink; one juice, one entrée or combo meal, and a drink at breakfast.
- **Disney Dining Plan:** offers one table-service meal, counter-service meal, and snack per person per day. Table-service meals consist of an appetizer, entrée, dessert, and nonalcoholic drink; and a juice, entrée, and drink *or* a full buffet for breakfast.
- **Deluxe Dining Plan:** offers three meals (either table- or counter-service) and two snacks per person per day, plus one refillable resort mug per person.

Keep in mind that gratuities and alcoholic drinks are not included, and an 18 percent gratuity is automatically added for parties of six or more. All of these plans work with the "Key to the World" card provided at check-in, which monitors your daily usage, while every meal receipt details the meals you have remaining.

REALITY CHECK

There are two high-cost accommodation packages that include the Deluxe Dining Plan: the Premium Package, which adds recreation, theme park tours, and admission to the Cirque du Soleil show *La Nouba*; and the Platinum Package, which includes spa treatments, unlimited child care, and reserved seating for Fantasmic!

Dining Plans are valid for Character Meals, Dinner Shows, Signature Restaurants, and In-room Dining. One table-service meal is required per person for each character meal (two at Cinderella's Royal Table in the Magic Kingdom); two for the Signature options, which include our favorites—Jiko, at Animal Kingdom Lodge; and California Grill, at the Contemporary Resort—and In-room Dining or pizza delivery. Dinner Shows also require two table-service credits per person. Children must order off the children's menu at all times.

The bottom line? You'll need to do a lot of pre-planning and you'll probably eat too much, too! Unless it's a free perk it may not be something you want to include.

ROOKIE MISTAKES

Be aware, only those staying at a Disney resort may use the swimming pools, and then only at the resort where they are staying or its "sister resort."

The Resorts

So, now that you know the benefits of staying in the story, let's take a look at the options themselves. Disney classifies them as the Value, Moderate, and Deluxe Resorts; then the Deluxe Villas (Disney Vacation Club properties); and the campground of Fort Wilderness. Disney also divides the year into Value, Regular, and Peak seasons, and into standard or preferred rooms (a preferred room will have a better view).

REALITY CHECK | Disney Vacation Club is a high-quality vacation ownership program with flexible resort choices around the world, plus signature Family Adventures. It features a points-related annual membership with signature service and a no-pressure sales experience.

Value Resorts

ALL-STAR RESORTS

All-Star Sports: 407-939-5000

All-Star Music: 407-939-6000

All-Star Movies: 407-939-7000

Park transportation: By bus

The All-Star Sports, Music, and Movies resorts opened in 1994 and have provided a huge boost for more budget-minded families who still want the excitement of staying onsite. And, even though the rooms are a little bit smaller, these resorts still offer you a great way to be immersed in the Disney experience without breaking the bank.

The architecture—officially "high-tech modernism"—is less story-oriented than other Disney resorts but the amenities are still impressive and the fun, larger-than-life styling—including oversized icons like a giant jukebox (Music), massive helmets (Sports), and huge *Toy Story* characters (Movies)—are a big hit with kids and they remain a popular family choice today.

Each All-Star complex is subdivided into five sections with a central check-in, two themed pools, a pool bar, food court, guest laundry, video arcade, gift shop, and children's play areas. Most rooms feature two double beds, with a handful offering a king bed. The three resorts break down as follows:

All-Star Sports consists of five sections: Touchdown! (which has a football theme), Hoops Hotel (basketball), Surf's Up! (surfing), Center Court (tennis), and Home Run Hotel (baseball). The story is sports, with details like palm trees arranged to look like a basketball team at tipoff and a courtyard that resembles a football field.

All-Star Music highlights the musical styles of Broadway musicals, calypso, jazz, country, and rock 'n roll, and the pools are shaped like a guitar and a grand piano. Top hats, musical notes, and an oversized marquee complete with chorus line dancers add to the façade at Broadway, while giant amplifiers, speakers, microphones, and a neon-lit, oversized jukebox highlight the **Rock Inn**. Unlike the other two All-Star resorts, the Music resort also offers family suites (in the Jazz and Calypso sections) that sleep up to six, with two bedrooms, two full baths and a kitchenette.

All-Star Movies areas are themed as *101 Dalmatians*, *The Love Bug*, *Fantasia*, *Toy Story*, and *The Mighty Ducks*. Guests can "skate" into the *Mighty Ducks'* hockey rink–themed pool or join Sorcerer Mickey as he directs a liquid symphony at the *Fantasia* pool, which features a children's play area.

REALITY CHECK | Most rooms accommodate four guests and a crib, and Disney is strict about this. **Port Orleans Resort–Riverside** can take an extra child on a trundle bed, but for larger groups you need to choose a deluxe suite, a **Fort Wilderness** cabin, or the suites at **All-Star Music** and the **Art of Animation Resort**.

POP CENTURY RESORT

407-938-4000

Park transportation: By bus

Originally meant to cover each decade of the twentieth century, the tongue-in-cheek **Pop Century Resort**—which opened in 2003—ultimately covers the 1950s to the 1990s, using larger-than-life icons and well-known phrases that shout from the rooftops (like "DooWop!" and "The Most" for the '50s; "Peace, Man!" and "Can you dig it?" for the '70s).

The four sections are spread along **Hourglass Lake**—which was initially intended to link to the other half of the resort (1900s–1940s) via the **Generation Gap Bridge**—using the **Classic Hall** for check-in, dining (a busy, four-part food court), and the bus stop.

There are 2,880 compact rooms (260 square feet) with two double beds or one king bed, a table and chairs, vanity area with separate bathroom, wall safe, voice mail, and data port. The complex has the **Bowling Pool**, **Hippy Dippy Pool** with **Petals Pool Bar**, and **Computer Pool**.

HIDDEN MAGIC

Take a closer look at the pool deck around the **Bowling Pool** and you'll spot the triangular lane markings seen on bowling alleys everywhere. At the **Bowling Pool**, the laundry looks like a bowling shoe storage bin. In the '90s, an equipment building appears to be a giant stack of computer floppy disks.

Disney's Imagineers really had some fun with **The Wall** in **Classic Hall**, which features a memory lane of wall-mounted shadow boxes displaying memorabilia from the various periods, including a Betty Crocker cookbook, 1960s postcards, 8-track tapes, Cabbage Patch Dolls, and an early cellular phone.

The **Everything Pop** food court is another riot of visual gags and period memorabilia, including classic 1970s video game tables and giant Rubik's cubes. It also has an excellent food range, with a bakery, grill, ethnic counter, pizza/pasta station, a grab-and-go, and "Mom's Night Out" dinner specials.

Like other All-Star resorts, the theme is only skin deep but it's all done with a terrific sense of humor.

HIDDEN MAGIC

The giant Big Wheel icon can accommodate a child rider weighing up to 877 pounds (or so says the sticker). That matches the stickers affixed to the original Big Wheel that designated a "recommended child weight." Cute, huh?

DISNEY'S ART OF ANIMATION RESORT
Park transportation: By bus

Opening in the summer of 2012, this is the "lost half" of the Pop Century development, re-imagined as four creative journeys into animated movies *The Lion King*, *The Little Mermaid*, *Cars*, and *Finding Nemo*, with 1,120 two-room family suites sleeping up to six and 864 sea-inspired standard rooms with *Little Mermaid* décor, which sleep four.

This may become the most appealing of all the Value resorts, with a greater depth to the themes as well as the appeal of the suites, which feature separate bathrooms, a master bedroom, and three separate sleeping areas in the living room, including the "Inovabed," that transforms from a large dining table to a bed.

The Lion King courtyard places visitors in Simba's savanna, *Cars* brings guests into Radiator Springs, a huge King Triton oversees the *Little Mermaid* under-the-sea courtyard (look for the chance to sing along with Sebastian here!), and young children will enjoy hanging with Marlin and Nemo amid amusing pop-jet fountains in the *Finding Nemo* wing.

The main pool is flanked by a handy pool bar and there are also two quieter pool areas, ideal for younger children. The rest of the planned amenities include an arcade, retail location, and interior airline check-in stations. The animated food court will feature a grab-and-go market, bakery, grill, pizza station, and specialty counter.

REALITY CHECK

Need something to do for the evening but want a less hectic time than the parks? Look for the "Movies under the Stars" program, which is now featured at most Disney resorts. Simply head to the pool area (or the campfire area at Fort Wilderness) and enjoy a classic Disney movie in open-air style.

Moderate Resorts

Need to add more elbow-room and style? Well, step on up to one of the three Moderate-level accommodations and enjoy larger rooms, deeper themes, and extra amenities like pool slides, fishing, boat tours and rentals, more restaurant choices, and live entertainment.

CARIBBEAN BEACH RESORT

407-934-3400

Park transportation: By bus

With Walt Disney World's big expansion in 1988 and '89, Disney urgently needed to increase their hotel offerings, so the Imagineers started thinking big. The seaside motif is a powerful one and the Caribbean provided the ideal inspiration. Built in six island "villages" grouped around **Barefoot Bay**, the Caribbean Beach Resort borrows heavily from traditional Caribbean, with white-sand beaches, lively "markets," and the lilting sounds of steel drums. The six islands are an eclectic bunch, comprised of **Jamaica**, **Barbados**, **Trinidad North**, and **Trinidad South**, plus smaller **Aruba** and **Martinique**, but your story begins at the **Custom House**, where the atmosphere of arriving in a Caribbean hideaway is unmistakable, with its porte-cochére and colonial conservatory décor.

The central amenities are provided in the **Old Port Royale**—aptly named for the Jamaican shipping center of Port Royal, the seventeenth century center of Caribbean commerce, and home of pirates from all over the world. Here, you'll find **Shutters** restaurant (see Chapter 9), the evocatively themed **Market Street food court**, a video arcade, **Calypso Trading Post**, and **Calypso Straw Market**.

ROOKIE MISTAKES

Don't spend all your time traveling from the furthest reaches of the resort. If you want a room closest to **Old Port Royale**, ask for **Trinidad North**, **Martinique** (blocks 24, 25, or 26), **Jamaica** (block 45), or **Aruba** (block 51).

For a quick meal, the outdoor-themed **Market Street** is hard to beat. Continuing the story of bustling Port Royal, it offers a grab-and-go market, pizza and pasta shop, bakery, hamburger shop, deli, and **Bridgetown Broiler**.

The imaginative **Fuentes del Morro** pool—around which the resort is grouped—is themed like a colonial-era Spanish fortress and is loosely based on Castillo de San Felipe del Morro in San Juan, Puerto Rico, and Castillo de los Tres Reyes Magos del Morro in Old Havana. This pool boasts a zero-depth-entry pool with two water-slides and water cannons, plus a water play structure for younger. Add in the **Banana Cabana** pool bar and two hot tubs and you have a blissful Caribbean retreat! This is also the place for children four–twelve to pick up the pirate-themed **Bayou Pirate Adventure** cruise (see info later in this chapter) for two hours of story-tellin' and treasure-searchin' (lunch provided) in best Jack Sparrow fashion. Call 407-939-7529 to book. Each "island" also has its own quiet pool.

HIDDEN MAGIC The first two children to arrive at the **Fuentes del Morro** pool in the morning are invited to take part in the daily Pirate defense ceremony, taking up swords to keep marauding buccaneers at bay and ensure the pool is safe for the rest of the day!

Completing the tropical idyll is **Caribbean Cay**, a four-acre island in the middle of **Barefoot Bay** that is linked by bridges to **Old Port Royale** and **Jamaica**. With picnic tables, hammocks, walking paths, and children's play areas, it is a haven-within-a-haven, ideal as a quiet corner to watch the sun go down.

The new pirate-themed rooms of **Trinidad South** feature "buccaneer beds," a skull-and-crossbones curtain room-divider, and other neat décor touches (like the Flying Dutchman etched into the shower wall, dark-wood furniture, and carpeting that looks like wooden decking). All other rooms have a subtle *Finding Nemo* theme. Rooms are a comfortable 340 square feet, with two double beds or a king, and have a safe, fridge, coffeemaker, and hair dryer. The whole resort is linked by its own internal bus service between all the "islands," the **Custom House**, and **Old Port Royale**.

PORT ORLEANS RESORT

Port Orleans Resort—French Quarter: 407-934-5000

Port Orleans Resort—Riverside: 407-934-6000

Park transportation: By bus

Set on the languid **Sassagoula River**, the Port Orleans Resort opened in 1991, followed by neighbor Dixie Landings in 1992, which was subdivided into Alligator Bayou and Magnolia Bend. However, a combination of economic cutbacks and historical-related protests at the use of the word "Dixie" led to a merging of the two resorts into Port Orleans French Quarter (formerly Port Orleans Resort) and Port Orleans Riverside (formerly Dixie Landings).

Unfortunately, all of Dixie Landings' original backstory and much of Port Orleans story was lost with the merge. Prior to the merge it was the story of a town founded in 1702 by the French and embellished by the Spanish. It was based on New Orleans but it wasn't actually New Orleans. It incorporated elements of the 1970 animated classic *The Aristocats* and influences from the 2009 movie *The Princess and the Frog*. Happily, enough of the essential story exists in this historic setting—full of graceful architecture and amusing features—notably around the pool.

You arrive in **Port Orleans Square**, built in the eighteenth century by "the flamboyant Marquis de Sirloin, Pierre Poupon" (see? we said the story was good!), and turn right into **The Mint**, established in 1886 as the financial heart of the "city," hence the reception desks that look like bank tellers' windows.

HIDDEN MAGIC
> See those musical symbols on the grill at each reception desk? They are the first verse of "When the Saints Go Marching In," the classic Mardi Gras song.

The Marquis and his sons, Gaston and Francois (who studied in France and Martinique), were responsible for the architectural style of the burgeoning city, hence the grand marriage of classical European and Caribbean plantation-era style.

Much of the French Quarter's layout is modeled on historic Jackson Square in New Orleans, a former eighteenth century military parade ground turned city hub. You can shop at **Jackson Square Gifts & Desires**—which, according to legend, was the former 1827 theater and opera house named after former Port Orleans resident, "famous actress and singer Maria Garcia Jackson," and run by her daughters Delia and Celia as a dress shop.

The former mansion home of the "Governor" of Port Orleans (with the shuttered arched windows) is found at the corner of **Building Six**, at the junction of Rue D'Baga and Café au Lait Way. Back in the main building is **Scat Cat's Club**, named for the alley cat jazz band leader in *The Aristocats*, and **Sassagoula Floatworks & Food Factory**, reputedly a storage warehouse for all the Mardi Gras floats.

HIDDEN MAGIC | All those Mardi Gras props in **Sassagoula Floatworks** were built by the famous Blaine Kern Studios, the world's leading makers of floats and parade props in New Orleans, who also build the floats for Universal's Mardi Gras Parade.

Follow the "Parade Route" from the square to **Doubloon Lagoon**, where gator musicians play, and where **Scales**, the giant Sassagoula sea serpent, provides a fifty-two-foot water slide! Scales was invented by the nineteenth century settlers to scare children away from playing in the bayou with its gators and snakes, and ultimately became part of the annual Mardi Gras parade.

Find the resort's famous beignets at the bakery, along with a sandwich and salad counter, specialty burgers, and pizzas. **Mardi Grogs** pool bar provides drinks and snacks, and the pool area hosts movie nights in the summer, with Disney films shown in open-air **Beignet Square**.

Port Orleans Riverside is the other "half" of this extensive property, boasting two distinct styles of building, six pools (including the facilities of **Ol' Man Island**), old-fashioned fishin' hole, campfire, and the children's playground.

Legend has it the town was founded in the early nineteenth century by two gentlemen brothers from Port Orleans. Colonel J. C. Peace made his fortune off of his cotton mill, which attracted his brother Everette to the area.

The colonel built a huge antebellum mansion, Acadian House, which led to a new community of Magnolia Bend. Magnolia Bend expanded to add Magnolia Terrace, as entrepreneur Buford Honeyworth III arrived and married the colonel's daughter Sarah, and they established the Sassagoula Steamboat Company. Oak Manor was then built by cotton baron Tanner Franklin and Parterre Terrace for "quite possibly the richest man in all of the nineteenth century South," Edward Baron, another cotton magnate. The settlement continued to grow upstream and the small-scale community of Alligator Bayou was the result, adding a series of rustic cottage buildings that were all raised off ground level in this gator-infested swampland.

Everette Peace was more of a recluse and settled on **Ol' Man Island**, creating his own backwater playground and staying largely hidden from the nearby settlement until he was reunited with his brother in 1857.

Meanwhile, the arrival of the "famed river-steamer" *Dixie Queen* in 1855 provided more substance to the legend, the mighty boat running aground in shallow water and being stuck for some time, leading to the people of Magnolia Bend, Alligator Bayou, and Ol' Man Island renaming their community Dixie Landings. The *Dixie Queen* was eventually pulled free of her unexpected landing and served the area proudly for many years before being destroyed in a thunderstorm when she was hit by lightning. However, her hull was salvaged and the timbers re-used to build the newly famous Boatwright Shop. Founded in 1877 by Frenchman Henri Le Marin, Boatwright's introduced a new style of boat-building especially for the shallow-running **Sassagoula River** and enhanced the Dixie Landings legend for all time.

HIDDEN MAGIC | Colonel Peace's **Acadian House** is a reference to the historical settlers of southern Louisiana, who hailed from Acadia in modern Nova Scotia, Canada. A mix of outcast French immigrants, they brought a unique dialect to the South and gradually corrupted the word "Acadian" to "Cajun." How cool is that?

The year 1855 was apparently a good one for the young town as it also saw the arrival of General George Fulton and his wife Amelia, who opened the soon-to-be-booming **Fulton's General Store**, "the best shopping stop along the

Sassagoula." As business grew with local cotton traders and shippers, Amelia opened the **Cotton Co-Op** for travelers in search of rest and relaxation (and good food and drink!). At least, this was the backstory until it was decided that the realities of the 1800s cotton trade were politically incorrect and should be written out of the story.

Renaming the resort **Port Orleans Riverside** set the scene for a monumental change. The **Colonel's Cotton Mill** food court became the **Riverside Mill & Market**, the **Cotton Co-Op** bar and lounge was turned into the **River Roost Lounge**, and the whole history of Tanner Franklin and Edward Baron was quietly forgotten.

Guests still arrive in the magnificent **Sassagoula Steamboat Company**, where the high-ceilinged lobby/reception area is reminiscent of the elegant travel style of the era. You'll see the "ports of call" along the river displayed for the next "departure," and the reception desks are themed like a steamboat ticketing office. You can shop for gifts and sundries at **Fulton's Market** and play video games in the **Medicine Show** arcade.

Boatwright's Dining Hall remains the fine dining establishment (see Chapter 9) and the **Riverside Mill & Market** is largely the same (apart from the signage), with the huge water wheel still operating a cotton press. Yee-Haa Bob Jackson, a Riverside fixture since 1997, is the prime entertainer at the **River Roost Lounge** with his mix of sing-along and comedy. Choose from five different serving stations at the impressive (but rather hectic) **Riverside Mill**: a bakery and ice cream outlet; grill shop; pizza and pasta station; fresh meat carving station; and a specialty shop, with fresh sandwiches, soups, and salads.

Ol' Man Island is still a mini theme park of watery fun, with a huge free-form pool, rustic "sawmill" water slide, hot tub, kiddie pool, playground, fishin' hole with cane pole fishing (on a catch-and-release basis for a fee), and the **Muddy Rivers Pool Bar** for drinks and snacks. There is also seasonal evening story-telling around the campfire and there are five smaller "quiet" pools split among the main accommodation areas, two in **Magnolia Bend** and three in **Alligator Bayou**.

Children ages four–twelve can also enjoy the real-life pirate stories and fun of the **Bayou Pirate Adventure**, a pontoon boat tour three times a week to track down hidden treasure (with lunch provided). Or try a leisurely carriage ride around the resort, or the bike and surrey bike rentals at **Riverside Levee**.

REALITY CHECK   There aren't many elevators in the **Alligator Bayou** section of **Port Orleans Riverside**, so be sure to let the check-in staff know if this might be a problem for you.

The two main accommodation areas feature either the mansionesque qualities of **Magnolia Bend**—four three-story buildings set among mature decorative gardens full of azaleas and magnolia trees along **Sassagoula River**—or the more rustic charms of **Alligator Bayou**, with sixteen two-story lodges boasting weathered tin or tiled roofs in a more natural, rural setting straight from southern Louisiana. Again, most feature two double beds. The double beds in each **Alligator Bayou** room (all 1,024 of them!) were hand-carved from hickory by a special woodworker from North Carolina whom Disney called in specifically for this resort.

In 2011, Disney announced a big makeover for **Oak Manor** and **Parterre Place**, giving their rooms a "royal" theme courtesy of Princess Tiana (from the New Orleans–located animated movie *The Princess and the Frog*), due to open by March 2012. The new story says Tiana invited her princess friends, including Belle (from *Beauty and the Beast*) and Jasmine (from *Aladdin*), to join her on vacation, which is why the rooms are designed with a more regal touch, including ornate beds that feature headboards with fiber-optic special effects, and gold and crystal accents, plus custom-made coverings and drapes. Other features include bathroom faucets in the shape of Aladdin's lamp and a luggage holder shaped like Sultan the dog that turns into a bench from *Beauty and the Beast*. You can also enjoy artwork and special mementos left by Tiana's royal friends.

REALITY CHECK   Need to wind down after a long day at the park? Take the leisurely free boat service along the **Sassagoula River** to **Downtown Disney** and enjoy the splendid riverside vistas en route or just sail from one part of the resort to the other for a wander around this eye-catching layout.

CORONADO SPRINGS

407-939-1000

Park transportation: By bus

Welcome to the pre–Louisiana Purchase Southwest, Disney style! At **Coronado Springs**, opened in 1997, you can embark on a search for mythical Mayan gold, enjoy the romance of Spanish-Colonial Mexico, and have fun in one of the best-themed pools of any of the resorts.

The story behind this resort is fascinating and twofold. The resort is named for Francisco Vazquez de Coronado, a real and intrepid sixteenth century Spanish explorer who led a famous expedition for the fabled Seven Cities of Gold in 1540. Although he never found the riches he sought, Coronado and his party were the first Europeans to venture into what is now the American Southwest, ranging along the Colorado River into the Grand Canyon, and reaching up into California, northern Texas, and even Kansas.

However, the Disney backstory to the resort is based on events that occurred more than 300 years later, when another (mythical) expedition led by Francisco Valdez, a "distant relation of de Coronado," set out to seek the treasure cities and ended up discovering a mysterious Mayan temple on the shores of Lake Dorado.

HIDDEN MAGIC | Look up to see the doves dancing in the skies above **La Fuente de las Palomas** (Fountain of the Doves). Legend has it that the daughter of one of Francisco Valdez's workers had a beautiful singing voice, and she used to charm the birds with her songs.

Sadly, after a full and extensive archaeological excavation, no trace of gold could be found, and the search was abandoned. But the workers who lived around the excavations decided this made an ideal resort area. The dig site was turned into a recreation center, and the former workers' quarters made ideal guest accommodations. A central "village" of shops and restaurants was added and **Coronado Springs** was born.

REALITY CHECK

Coronado Springs has a large convention center, hence it can get busy at times in the main building. But its landscaped acres are especially soothing to the eye, it's well spread-out, and you may never notice the convention element except in early morning.

The resort is subdivided into three sections, which roughly correspond to Coronado's travels in the southwest: Cabanas, Ranchos, and Casitas. You'll start your journey at **El Centro**, which includes most of the main amenities, including the **Rix Lounge**, **Maya Grill** restaurant (see Chapter 9), grab-and-go **Café Rix**, and **Panchito's Gift Shop**. Outside is the **Laguna Bar**, ideal for a lakeside beverage or two at sunset! You also have the choice of fine dining at the Latin-inspired **Maya Grill** or the **Pepper Mill** market-style food court, which is permanently ready for a fiesta. It offers a Mexican station, grill, pizza and pasta stations, sandwiches, and a bakery/dessert station, plus an espresso bar and kid's station.

Go counterclockwise from **El Centro** to the **Cabanas**, a coastal version of Mexican-style architecture, with modest two-story dwellings with tin roofs and formal pathways. You then encounter the **Dig Site** and the **Lost City of Cibola pool**, the site of Valdez's mythical excavations and now the fun heart of the resort. The **Lost City of Cibola pool area** also features a kids' pool and **Explorer's Playground**, where children can hunt for "treasure," as well as the **Iguana Arcade** and **Siestas Cantina**, where you can go for a poolside drink or light meal.

ROOKIE MISTAKES

Kids should arrive at the **Dig Site** by 10 A.M. to take part in the daily opening ceremony, where they chant to the water gods. Lo and behold, the water cascading down the temple is mysteriously turned on!

Next, you move into the dry, semi-desert regions of the U.S. Southwest at the **Ranchos**, with overtones of the wide, rustic ranchlands and empty streambeds. The landscape features rocky outcrops dotted with pueblo-style adobe architectural motifs, horse hitching posts, stone cornices, and tiled roofs.

Finally, the **Casitas** "village" introduces a more urban setting reminiscent of Santa Fe and Monterey in Mexico. With colorful plazas, fountains, and shaded courtyards, the buildings here are the most imposing and feature the classical elements of colonial and Mission architecture. Each accommodation group has its own quiet pool area and laundry, while the **La Vida Health Club** and **Casa de Belleza** beauty salon are located in the **Casitas**.

ROOKIE MISTAKES If you want your food "to go" at the **Pepper Market** make sure to let the cashier know at checkout and you will avoid the automatic 10 percent gratuity charged on dine-in meals. Feel free to mix and match at each food station, too.

The lobby, reception area, and restaurants are themed to the rich tradition of life on the wealthiest haciendas of the past or at today's finest guest ranches in New Mexico and Arizona, and **Coronado Springs** offers a variety of plush business-style Club Level rooms, with their own reception, guest services, lounge, DVD player, and bathrobes in the rooms.

Deluxe Resorts

While there is plenty of imagination, style, and Disney magic in the Value and Moderate resorts, the story takes a luxurious turn at Disney's Deluxe resorts. These resorts really show how dramatic an all-encompassing theme can be, with the added bonus of a more extensive range of facilities, including spas, kids' clubs, gourmet-quality restaurants, water sports, and sheer eye-catching splendor.

THE CONTEMPORARY RESORT

407-824-1000

Park transportation: To the Magic Kingdom by monorail or boat, or on foot; to Epcot by monorail or bus; and to the other parks by bus. There are also boats to Wilderness Lodge and Fort Wilderness.

Although Walt Disney passed away before the first resort in his World was even started, it's hard not to think of the **Contemporary** as the embodiment of the urban solutions he envisioned for Epcot, even if it never progressed beyond hotel status. This futuristic-looking A-frame building took shape using a new technique called modular construction, whereby the basic framework was created and then the room units, assembled offsite, were slid into place in the main structure.

The Magic Kingdom monorail was built right through its central axis, and more than 40 years later this revolutionary concept is still a novelty. The amount of light allowed in through the two end glass walls was a genuine "Wow!!" moment back in the early 1970s and, even today, if you view either end from outside as night falls, it looks like a gigantic wedge-shaped spaceship.

HIDDEN MAGIC | The **Contemporary's** location close to the **Magic Kingdom's Tomorrowland** points to its connection with the world of tomorrow. In fact, designers initially thought guests would walk into the park that way.

Originally built with two three-story Garden Wings, the north wing was demolished in 2007 to make way for Disney Vacation Club resort **Bay Lake Tower**, which opened in 2009. But, while the resort's central theme was cutting-edge, the aptly named **Grand Canyon Concourse** was also infused with an element of fun, supplied by Imagineer Mary Blair (principal designer of "It's a Small World"). Using the ten-story internal elevator column as her canvas, Blair crafted a six-sided, ninety-foot tall ceramic mural, entitled "The Pueblo Village," a whimsical message of simple delight.

On the west side of Mary Blair's mural, south of the elevator section and facing the monorail, look for the five-legged goat—it was put there to remind us that no man-made work is ever perfect.

The rooms at the **Contemporary** are some of the biggest on Disney property (430 square feet), with a Concierge level featuring an elegant lounge with complimentary snacks and a turndown service.

New in 2011 were a series of unique Health and Wellness suites, featuring eco-friendly bamboo flooring, 100-percent cotton linens, nonallergenic mattresses, rainwater showers, cardio equipment, and organic foods in the concierge lounge.

The **Contemporary** has a superb overview of **Magic Kingdom** and a grandstand seat for Wishes Nighttime Spectacular fireworks. Book the more expensive Magic Kingdom View if you hope to see the park or the fireworks from your room. All guests staying at the **Contemporary** may watch the fireworks from a special fourth-floor viewing balcony, though.

The amenities at this resort are impressive, with eight dining locations, three shops, two pools, tennis courts, a hair salon, fitness center, boat rentals, and a huge games arcade. Keep in mind, however, that the Contemporary doesn't have a kids' club.

Fine dining is available at the superb **California Grill**, **Chef Mickey's**, and **The Wave** (see Chapter 9), while **Contempo Café** provides a smart counter-service choice. **Contemporary Grounds** is the coffee bar, the **Outer Rim** is the lounge bar, and **The Sand Bar** offers drinks and snacks by the pool.

For a leisurely, high-quality breakfast, avoid noisy **Chef Mickey's**. Instead, check out the more imaginative fare at **The Wave**, with a buffet and full à la carte choice.

The Contemporary's marina offers boat rentals, fishing excursions, and **Sammy Duvall's Water Sports Center** has water skiing, tubing, wake boarding, and parasailing. Stay here and you certainly won't be bored!

POLYNESIAN RESORT

407-824-2000

Park transportation: A monorail station is located on the second floor of the **Great Ceremonial House**, while there is also boat transport to the Magic Kingdom. Transport to Epcot is by monorail and bus, and to the other parks by bus.

While the **Contemporary Resort** was taking shape on one side of **Seven Seas Lagoon**, a tropical South Seas paradise was rising on another. Disney's Imagineers went to Hawaii, Tahiti, Fiji, and American Samoa and returned with a true image of the South Pacific, which they used to create **The Polynesian** or **"The Poly"** (as most know it), an all-encompassing Pacific island retreat.

Visitors arrive in the **Great Ceremonial House** (based on the royal ceremonial lodges of Tahiti), where they are greeted with a fond "Aloha" and garlanded with a traditional lei. The tropical outdoor landscaping and water features continue into the central atrium, which provides a lush focal point. From there, you can venture out to one of the eleven Pacific "islands," a series of longhouse-style buildings.

The looming **Nanea Volcano** next to the main pool—based on the spectacular Mauna Loa on Hawaii's Big Island—isn't so much a threat as an invitation to have fun (*Nanea* means "tranquility" in Hawaiian). The mountain features pretend lava flows and occasional steam, plus a fabulous water slide and scenic waterfall—along with occasional shouts of "Look out belo-ha!" You'll also find a separate freeform "quiet" pool (quiet being a relative term in Walt Disney World!), and a boat marina with a variety of rental options, from sailboats and pontoons to speedy two-person Water Mouse boats.

HIDDEN MAGIC

Enter the **Polynesian Resort** lobby and walk back to the elevators on the right-hand side. There you'll find a carved wooden panel hiding a tiki god. Look closely and you'll see he is making a face at you (see photo insert)! As you stroll around, look for tiki gods peeking out of the landscaping, hiding near the rooftops, even posing as a shower at the pool.

All of the rooms at the **Polynesian** feature two queen beds, apart from the **Tonga block**, which has either two queens or one king bed. Décor is suitably tropical, with batik bed canopies, bamboo, and dark wood furniture accents. Concierge level rooms are found in the **Hawaii** and **Tonga longhouses**, with a private lounge in Hawaii offering views of the Magic Kingdom fireworks.

The Poly's dining options are equally rich, with 'Ohana and Kona Café (see Chapter 9), their South Seas dinner show Spirit of Aloha (see page 318), a coffee bar that becomes a sushi counter in the evening, the **Barefoot Pool Bar**, and the counter-service **Captain Cook's Snack Company**, with a full breakfast menu (including signature Tonga Toast), and a grill counter.

HIDDEN MAGIC

The names of ten of the eleven longhouses were changed in 1999 to more properly reflect true South Seas islands. The mythical island of Bali Hai was removed, as was Pago Pago (a town, not an island), Bora Bora, and Moorea. Maui and Oahu were deemed "too much" Hawaii, so they had to go, hence the "new" islands added were Aotearoa (the Maori name for New Zealand), Rapa Nui (Easter Island), Tuvalu, Rarotonga, Nieu, and Tokelau. The Fiji Longhouse is the only original—Tahiti, Samoa, Tonga, and Hawaii have all changed locations.

Health fanatics can take advantage of the 1.5-mile jogging track or head to the neighboring Grand Floridian to use its fitness center. Shopaholics will also enjoy the variety available, from the basic sundries and gifts of **Samoa Snacks** to the grand **Wyland Gallery** with its amazing sea-themed artwork. For kids, the Peter Pan–themed **Neverland Club** is one of the best children's centers (noon–midnight), while **Mona Mickey's Arcade** provides all the electronic fun and games. If you're adventurous you might want to try the daily fishing excursions.

GRAND FLORIDIAN RESORT & SPA

407-824-3000

Park transportation: To the Magic Kingdom by monorail or boat, to Epcot by monorail or bus, and to the other parks by bus.

By the mid-1980s, with attendance growing steadily (and about to increase even more with plans for a third theme park and other additions), Disney chiefs realized they needed to enhance their upscale hotel offerings and tasked the Imagineers with creating a new flagship resort, where a whole new concept was called for—and discovered—in Florida's grand beach hotels of the late nineteenth and early twentieth centuries.

These huge wooden palaces included the likes of the Belleview-Biltmore in Bellaire, the Royal Poinciana Hotel in Palm Beach, and the Palm Beach Inn (renamed The Breakers), which gave the Imagineers their starting point. Hotel del Coronado in San Diego then provided a vivid living example of the style they were looking for. This opulent 1888 stunner was once the largest hotel in the world and is now one of a handful of surviving Victorian wooden resorts.

The Grand Floridian surrounds guests in a Victorian splendor that borrows from Main Street, U.S.A.'s period appeal and raised it several hundred notches with a five-story lobby, classic cage elevator, stained glass domes, chandeliers, and Italian-marble floors. Together with immaculate service, a spa and health club, exceptional dining, marina, and a monorail station, this is a genuine bastion of luxury, albeit with the price to match.

Set around the imposing main building are a series of five "islands" named for the Florida Keys that enhance the laid-back but stylish ambience. Rooms in the four- and five-story "islands" are spacious (440 square feet) and maintain the general Keys motif with Victorian accents. The twenty-five suites are truly indulgent, while Concierge-level accommodations are provided in **Sugar Loaf Key** "island" and the top level in the main building, with separate lounges for each. In addition, two pools, a hot tub, and a white-sand beach all work together to create and enhance the story of a bygone era.

Many guests don't realize they can request specific areas within the big resorts. At the Grand Floridian, the best (non-Concierge) block to ask for is **Sago Cay**, which is close to the main building and the bus stop.

The main building in the Grand Floridian boasts luxury bath and body store **Basin White**, and upscale boutiques **Commander Porter's** and **Summer Lace**; outside is the relaxed **Courtyard Pool** and the **Beach Pool** with water slide, tennis courts, and the **Spa and Health Club**. The **Captain's Shipyard** provides boat rentals and specialty cruises.

Grand Floridian dining includes Disney's swankiest restaurant, **Victoria & Albert's**, elegant **Citricos**, waterfront **Narcoossee's**, the character meals at **1900 Park Fare**, and the **Grand Floridian Café** (see Chapter 9). There is also the quick 24-hour counter-service option of **Gasparilla Grill**, named after Gasparilla Island in southwest Florida, with its neighboring video arcade, while the conservatory-style **Mizner's Lounge** serves a classic afternoon tea (Addison Mizner was a celebrated 1920s Florida architect who pioneered the Spanish Colonial revival style on which the Grand Floridian is modeled).

REALITY CHECK Too tired to go into the park? The terrace outside **Gasparilla Grill** is a great long-distance viewpoint for the nightly Magic Kingdom fireworks, complete with accompanying music.

Kids will also be bowled over by the **Mouseketeer Club** (4:30 P.M.–midnight), **Wonderland Tea Party**, **Pirate Adventure**, and the elaborate (but seriously expensive) **My Disney Girl's Perfectly Princess Tea Party**.

SWAN AND DOLPHIN RESORTS

Walt Disney World Swan Resort: 407-934-3000

Walt Disney World Dolphin Resort: 407-934-4000

Park transportation: To Epcot and Disney's Hollywood Studios by boat, and to the other parks by bus.

While the fast-developing Walt Disney World seemed to have just about everything by the end of the 1980s, there was one area that remained largely unexplored in Disney terms—the convention business, which was quickly becoming a major facet of Orlando life. The area adjacent to Epcot had long been earmarked for more resort development, and one of the aims was a "convention kingdom" that would actively embrace the company's desire for "entertainment architecture," this time provided by architect Michael Graves.

Because it is not owned by Disney, no Disney characters could be used so Graves picked two whimsical animals as the basis for the twin hotels—a swan and a dolphin. The Swan and the Dolphin are meant to be complementary stories, beginning with the Dolphin (the larger, central pyramid-shaped building) being created by an undersea volcanic eruption that left two dolphins sitting on top of the newly-formed "island."

HIDDEN MAGIC | Why do the dolphins look more like fish? They are modeled after the classical image of dolphins on ancient nautical maps and Roman fountains.

Tropical foliage grew on this new island, but the force of the eruption caused the heart of the island to burst open, sending a huge cascade of water pouring down the sides. This waterfall now drops nine stories down the side of the resort, passing through five clamshells before splashing into **Crescent Lake**.

The force of the water carried across to the neighbor island, washing up the sides (note the water-washed landscape and railings between the two hotels) and culminating in the waves on the Swan resort. Two swans awed by the exploding mountain alighted on the raging waters and were magically transformed into statues.

HIDDEN MAGIC

The "black box" in the center of the Dolphin is not an area that was supposed to be removed for a later monorail route, despite what many people believe. It represents the basalt heart of the volcanic mountain that burst out of the rainforest—hence the painted banana leaves on its sides.

While the Swan and the Dolphin are distinctly separate buildings, they effectively operate as one 2,265-room mega-resort. Although they are not Disney-owned, they maintain Disney standards in most instances, although guests do not have charging privileges with their room key throughout the parks, and none of the restaurants at these resorts are included in the Disney Dining Plan.

The dining choices are stellar, though, from the artsy Todd English's **bluezoo** and upscale steakhouse of **Shula's Steak House** in the Dolphin to the fine Italian of **Il Mulino New York Trattoria** and Japanese cuisine of **Kimonos** (see Chapter 9) at the Swan. There are another thirteen cafes, bars, and lounges serving a mix of full-service meals, counter fare, and poolside snacks.

Rooms are bright and spacious, if a touch more corporate these days than their original fun-style décor, while suites can sleep up to ten. A Club Level includes a private lounge, robes in each room, and a concierge staff.

Recreation also covers a huge range, from the extensive **Grotto Pool and Beach**—complete with water slide—to the blissful **Mandara Spa**, tennis courts, jogging trails, paddleboats, basketball court, and another four pools and four hot tubs! For children, the **Camp Dolphin** children's center (ages 4–12; 5:30 P.M.–midnight) is guaranteed fun, and Disney's **Fantasia Gardens** mini-golf (see Chapter 7) is right across the street.

HIDDEN MAGIC

The central green pyramid of the Dolphin looks convincing, with rooms all the way to the top, but the top 80 feet of the structure is hollow, as there was no practical way to use that space. Therefore, the top seven floors of "rooms" are fake.

YACHT CLUB AND BEACH CLUB RESORTS

Yacht Club: 407-934-7000

Beach Club: 407-934-8000

Park transportation: To Epcot and Disney's Hollywood Studios by boat, and to the other parks by bus.

While one big-name architect went to work on the Swan and Dolphin, a second architect was called in for another double-barreled project: the Yacht Club and Beach Club Resorts. Noted East Coast designer Robert A. M. Stern, who redesigned Times Square in New York, was chosen, and it was back to the sea for this Crescent Lake duo, this time even closer to Epcot.

Inspired by America's classical architecture, each resort was given a unique identity. The Yacht Club resembles a rambling, shingle-covered New England seaside resort reminiscent of Newport, Marblehead, and Bar Harbor at the end of the nineteenth century. Nautical style prevails throughout this resort, where guest rooms feature portholes and wicker furniture. The more formal atmosphere is representative of the mansionesque summer "cottages" built by the Vanderbilts and Dukes, surrounding guests with the rich-but-relaxed feel of a seagoing yesteryear that is indulgent but accessible, especially for families.

The Beach Club has a lighter motif, recalling the "Stick Style" cottages and resorts of places like Cape May, New Jersey. Things are more casual at this resort, which has an 1860s wooden cottage style featuring period cabana architecture.

The two clubs share many amenities, including three-acre **Stormalong Bay**, a "New England shipwreck" that is an unarguable hit with families. This shipwreck accommodates a fabulous pool slide, sandy beach, freeform pool, lazy river feature, water jets, and a quiet pool.

The two resorts also offer a heady dining mix, with options ranging from the gourmet **Yachtsman Steakhouse** to the character-meal fun of **Cape May Café** and **Captain's Grille** (see Chapter 9), plus the classic soda-shop style of **Beaches**

& Cream (try the Kitchen Sink—guaranteed to sink any unsuspecting landlubber!), and three bars and lounges.

REALITY CHECK | If you're staying at the Yacht or Beach Club and wondering which park passes you need, bear this in mind: In many cases, it's hard to get kids out of **Stormalong Bay**, so you can save on those Water Park Fun & More options!

You can also enjoy "Movies Under the Stars" each night on the beach and **Lafferty Place Arcade**. Be sure to take advantage of the **Shipshape Health Club**, tennis courts, volleyball, and even a croquet lawn. The marina offers a variety of boat rentals and specialty cruises, including the highly sought-after IllumiNations Cruises to view the nightly pyrotechnics show at Epcot. Kids ages three–twelve can also visit the **Sandcastle Club** (4:30 P.M.–midnight).

Rooms at the Yacht and Beach Clubs are an average of 380 square feet (slightly smaller than the other Deluxe resorts) with French doors that lead to a balcony or patio and full nautical décor. Concierge suites on the fifth floor have their own private lounge and extra amenities, including turndown service.

WILDERNESS LODGE

407-824-3200

Park transportation: To the Magic Kingdom (and Fort Wilderness and Contemporary Resort) by boat; to the other parks by bus.

On a completely new site close to the Magic Kingdom (but not on the monorail), what had started out in the Imagineers' handbook as the Cypress Point Lodge became one of the World's most eye-catching—and story-rich—resorts.

Once again, Disney called on an outside architect and found the perfect match for their homage to national park lodges in Denver's Peter Dominick, who took his inspiration from the rustic style of the American West.

Dominick studied the evocative historic lodges of Old Faithful Inn at Yellowstone National Park, which served as inspiration for the stunning atrium featuring open wood-beamed balconies; the Ahwahnee Hotel (Yosemite); Lake McDonald Lodge (Glacier National Park in Montana); and Timberline Lodge (Mount Hood, Oregon) and came up with his own rich interpretation of the style, stemming from the nineteenth century Arts and Crafts movement, which combined natural materials and traditional craftsmanship. Disney then added a typically compelling backstory.

HIDDEN MAGIC | View the back side of Wilderness Lodge at night and you will see a massive rendition of the resort's mascot, a brown bear, outlined in the building lights—two eyes (skylight windows), the muzzle, and massive arms reaching forward (the two wings of the building). You can see this most easily as you arrive at or depart the resort by boat.

Legend has it that the Wilderness Lodge was founded in 1823 by intrepid (but mythical) explorer Colonel Ezekiel Moreland, a hero of the War of 1812, who was keen to follow in the Northwest tracks of Lewis and Clark. He set up camp in the newly discovered Silver Creek Springs valley and, after making his fortune in the fur trade, returned to St. Louis in 1825. Soon his daughter Jenny and her companion, an Austrian artist by the name of Frederich Alonzo Gustaf, journeyed back to the valley.

The pair built a small lodge near the freshwater spring and gradually attracted more and more visitors. Eventually the lodge grew around the spring, which was incorporated into the main lobby. Other characters and buildings added to the legend—the **Teton Bike and Boat** rental depot was the colonel's original log cabin; the main pool was created by misguided silver prospector Georgie Macgregor (and a lot of dynamite!) in 1852; the hot springs where the colonel survived one bitter winter are now **Fire Rock Geyser** (which manages to erupt on the hour every day from 7 A.M.–10 P.M.); and the fine dining of **Artist Point** restaurant (see Chapter 9) was inspired by Gustaf's work.

Interwoven into the myth is real Native American history and design. The breathtaking eight-story lobby is crafted mainly from lodgepole pine from

Oregon and the hardwood floors (best viewed from the fourth or fifth floor) feature elements from traditional Native creation stories. Two 55-foot-tall totem poles honor the northwest Native American clans, Raven and Eagle, depicting animals popular in the two clans' numerous legends. The towering stone fireplace is also built to resemble the rock strata of the Grand Canyon.

ROOKIE MISTAKES | Don't forget to check your resort's activity guides for special events. Every November (which is Native American Heritage Month), two Native interpreters perform the Blessing of the Four Directions in the Wilderness Lodge's lobby, a ceremony intended to drive out negative energy and purify the resort for the next twelve months.

In simple terms, the resort's standard rooms come in at 340 square feet and feature the lodge's rustic styling. Family-friendly bunk bed rooms feature a queen bed and set of two bunks—much better than the standard two queens arrangement elsewhere.

Suites can sleep up to six while the Villas—the former lodging of railroad workers who moved on to new projects—offer regular studio-style accommodations as well as one- and two-bed suites sleeping up to eight. The **Old Faithful Club** is the hotel's Concierge level, which features a private lounge and extra amenities.

HIDDEN MAGIC | If you're a Disney history buff you should head over to the **Carolwood Pacific Room** in the Lodge Villas. A nod to Walt's obsession with trains and railroads, this mini-museum features two train cars from his original small-scale backyard railway, the Carolwood Pacific Railroad, donated by his family.

Amenities range from the huge freeform **Silver Creek Springs Pool** (complete with waterslide and two hot tubs) and the **Sturdy Branches Health Club and Spa**, to the **Buttons and Bells Arcade** and shopping at **Wilderness Lodge Mercantile**.

Dining is provided by **Artist Point**, the raucous **Whispering Canyon Café** (see Chapter 9), and the quick counter-service establishment **Roaring Fork**. You'll also find drinks and snacks available at the **Trout Pass Pool Bar** and the classic saloon-style **Territory Lounge**. A resort to revel in? You bet!

THE BOARDWALK INN

407-939-5100

Park transportation: To Epcot and Disney's Hollywood Studios by boat, and to the other parks by bus.

The master plan for the Epcot resorts around Crescent Lake was still missing one central element, so Disney again called on Robert A. M. Stern. His newest creation? The BoardWalk Inn! Situated near New England at the Yacht Club and New Jersey at the Beach Club, the BoardWalk Inn is reminiscent of the large-scale experiences found in Atlantic City and Ocean City at the turn of the century. This resort completes a whole lakeside resort district with a single vision of period and style.

The BoardWalk is split into the main inn and the Disney Vacation Club Villas, and the architecture is beautifully presented to show this distinction. Guests for both the inn and villas arrive in the same entry tower and lobby, a graceful 1920s colonial revival décor that immediately establishes the sense of time and place, like stepping into the pages of *The Great Gatsby*, with porches, dormers, lookout towers, and widow's walks spread out throughout the resort.

HIDDEN MAGIC The spectacular 1920 **Illions Carousel** in the center of the lobby is a true scale-model original and comes to life every hour. M. C. Illions and Sons were America's premier manufacturers of full-size carousels in the early twentieth century. Look for the horse with the Hidden Mickeys on it!

To the east of the entry tower is the actual inn, boasting ground-level restaurants that open on to the boardwalk promenade. Behind the waterfront façade, the hotel takes its design cue from more of the rambling colonial revival–style hotels of New England. The Disney Vacation Club portion of the hotel transitions into a lakeside resort town. The building gradually takes on a larger scale as it turns to face a canal, reflecting the early twentieth century American tradition combining classicism with cottage architecture to create the Bungalow style. The historical timeline of the town's development is brought to its conclusion with a nod toward the initial modernism of the early twentieth century.

HIDDEN MAGIC | See the elephant statue over the fireplace in the lobby? That is a model of Elephant Bazaar, or Lucy the Elephant, a sixty-five-foot high tourist attraction built by James Lafferty in Margate City, New Jersey (south of Atlantic City), in 1882. It was saved in 1970 and is a designated National Historic Monument today.

A period country fair has also come to town, setting up "camp" on the outskirts of town. Called **Luna Park** (a famous name from Coney Island history), this is the backstory of the main swimming pool, where the 200-foot long water slide is cunningly disguised as the Keister Coaster ride. Even the resort's convention center has its own place in the theme, a sprawling bracketed Victorian-Gothic-inspired hall, which would have served as the community social and cultural center of a seaside town 100 years ago.

HIDDEN MAGIC | The **Dundy's Sundries** store in the BoardWalk is named for Elmer "Skip" Dundy, who co-created Luna Park in Coney Island with partner Frederic Thompson in 1903.

Standard rooms offer two queens or one king at 380 square feet, with beautiful marble bathrooms and French doors opening on to a balcony or patio. Fourteen delightful two-story garden suites feature private rose gardens, living rooms, loft bedrooms, and hot tubs. The Concierge level adds a private lounge with balcony, ideal for watching the nightly IllumiNations fireworks display from Epcot.

Dining-wise, guests are spoiled for choices with the **ESPN Club** sports bar, **Big River Grille & Brewing Works**, Mediterranean-themed **Kouzzina** by celebrity chef Cat Cora, and the fine seafood of the **Flying Fish Café** (see Chapter 9). Modern retail space is cleverly squeezed into the period façades—notably a **Wyland Galleries** boutique, **Thimbles & Threads**, and **Disney Character Carnival**— while tennis courts, a modern fitness center, bike rentals, two smaller quiet pools, an arcade, and fishing excursions round out a superb entertainment offering. You won't find a kids' club here, but guests can use the Sandcastle Club at the neighboring Yacht and Beach Clubs.

ROOKIE MISTAKES | Anyone who thinks the resorts are only for Disney guests is making one of the biggest errors of their visit. The BoardWalk is open to all, so come out at night and enjoy the live entertainment, with Crescent Lake acting as a brilliant mirror for this eye-catching backdrop.

ANIMAL KINGDOM LODGE

407-938-3000

Park transportation: By bus.

The overwhelming success of the Wilderness Lodge put Peter Dominick at the top of Disney's list for their next project, so it was no surprise when he got the nod to design the first resort associated directly with Disney's Animal Kingdom park.

If Wilderness Lodge was a triumph, the Animal Kingdom Lodge topped it, taking a classic African game lodge design and giving it a sense of awe-inspiring drama. The sheer "Wow!" factor of this hotel is totally breathtaking, incorporating real-life elements of African heritage and wildlife that are the next best thing to going on safari.

HIDDEN MAGIC

Art plays a huge part in the Animal Kingdom Lodge. The amazing sixteen-foot Ijele mask in the lobby is the only one of its kind outside Nigeria, where it is used in ceremonies by the Igbo people.

As far as the story is concerned, the lodge is the result of a geographical quirk, a precious freshwater spring that bubbled up from the dry savanna and provided the basis for a local settlement. It coincided with a nearby *kopje*—an Afrikaans word for a rock outcropping, an ancient volcanic remnant—that afforded the local people the chance to build a *kraal*, or protected enclosure.

As the settlement grew up around the kopje and its life-giving spring, a much bigger kraal was built—the lodge itself, which curves around the central kopje like a gigantic stockade, with four-story fence posts and stakes along the top to keep predators out. Inside, animals could graze in safety and harmony with the local people. Now, you can happily view the wildlife, hear stories of African life, and enjoy the feel of a man-made environment in balance with nature.

A stay at the lodge reveals itself in four stages. First is the Approach, where you drive through the gates, leaving Florida behind to be magically transported to a stylized version of Africa full of tropical plants, native landscaping, and hut-like, low-rise structures. The cunning front elevation of the hotel is forced perspective in reverse, making a six-story building look barely two stories tall at a casual glance.

HIDDEN MAGIC

There are African proverbs sprinkled all around **Kidani Village**. One of the proverbs, located near the pool, is a fitting tribute to Walt Disney, who wisely noted, "It's a small, small world." Notice how each proverb is accompanied by a butterfly, in keeping with a Ghanaian proverb: "Proverbs are like butterflies. Some are caught, some fly away."

The next stage is Arrival, where you pull into the thatched-roof portico and are surrounded by the sights and sounds of sub-Saharan Africa; the artwork, rustic brickwork, and weathered handrails and gateposts, plus the almost subliminal music, are all indicative of the journey beyond our continent.

The breathtaking effect of the Entry is immense. Suddenly, you're surrounded by a dimly lit, four-story lobby of epic proportions. Immense faux-wooden columns support an array of stick-railed balconies, linked from one side to the other by a rough-hewn footbridge at third-floor level. Huge light fittings are disguised as Masai shields and the five-story window at the rear hints at an endless savanna beyond.

Traditional mud construction, wood and earthen floors, a cozy fire pit, natural stone outcroppings, and the original settlement's "spring" are all incorporated into the atrium, where the elemental stream cascades through the hotel and out to the "watering hole" (the main resort pool).

Finally, you come to the Accommodation experience, with 1,307 rooms and suites spread over the resort's 74 acres in two main buildings, the original **Jambo House** and a Disney Vacation Club extension, **Kidani Village**, which has a smaller, more intimate lobby area and even more organic design, plus its own range of amenities, dining, and animal savanna. Guests are free to use the facilities and amenities of both.

There are four savannas in all, covering more than 40 acres with some 200 animals, including zebras, giraffes, ankole cattle, ostriches, blesbok, kudu, wildebeest, impala, and eland, along with multiple viewing areas, all with cultural interpreters from Africa ready to explain the animals' lifestyles and ecological issues.

HIDDEN MAGIC | *Kidani* means "necklace" in Swahili and the plan of the resort does, indeed, look like an open, beaded necklace.

Standard rooms are only 340 square feet but all have balconies, many with a savanna view (for an extra cost) and superb African-themed décor and furniture. The suites and villas (one, two, and three bedrooms) add much more space and have full kitchens.

More than any other resort, though, Animal Kingdom Lodge invites you to explore and enjoy the wide array of activities and features, from romantic dining at **Jiko**, buffet-style **Boma**, and the inventive menu at **Sanaa** (see Chapter 9), to three lounge bars, the mini water park of **Samawati Springs** and **Uwanja Camp** at **Kidani Village**, and a massage and fitness center. Children can enjoy the **Hakuna Matata Playground, Pumbaa's Arcade**, and **Simba's Cubhouse** activity center, and there are also tennis, basketball, and shuffleboard courts.

HIDDEN MAGIC Come out to the Arusha savanna at night and enjoy the clever artificial moonlight projected from the resort's rooftops that adds a special glow to the animal areas and counteracts the effect of neighboring light pollution.

If you decide to stay here don't miss the wonderful array of interactive programs that underline the human dimension of the lodge—sunset and sunrise safari adventures, campfire storytelling, arts and crafts classes, wine tasting, night-vision viewing of the savannas, and even animal tracking. It all adds up to the most compelling and completely immersive resort experience possible, as well as sheer, classic Disney fun!

Deluxe Villas

The advent of the timeshare-based Disney Vacation Club added a whole new strand to the World's accommodation offerings, which are available to regular guests when not occupied by Disney Vacation Club members. They add self-catering elements and extra living space, plus some unique features. The largest villas can accommodate twelve and each new development adds to the rich tapestry of resort themes.

There are currently seven main Walt Disney World Disney Vacation Club properties, plus Hilton Head Island in South Carolina, Vero Beach in Florida, the Villas at Disney's Grand Californian in Disneyland, and the new Aulani Resort in Hawaii.

OLD KEY WEST

407-827-7700

Park transportation: By bus.

The theme of Disney's Old Key West Resort—made up of 761 studios and one-, two-, or three-bedroom homes—takes its cue from the Caribbean-flavored city of Key West, from its bright pastel colors to the wooden boarding and sheer tropical ambience, but this is also a historic setting, based on a turn-of-the-century version of Ernest Hemingway's hangout. Lakes, waterways, and even six holes of the **Lake Buena Vista Golf Course** are all woven through the resort.

ROOKIE MISTAKES The spread-out nature of Old Key West makes having your own car advisable. If you don't have a car, request a room close to Hospitality House in buildings 11–14. It can be a long walk otherwise, although there is an internal bus service.

Meandering paths and a village feel give the resort a sense of community, and the obvious Key West signature touches—the big lighthouse, sandcastle-shaped water slide, and lilting music of Jimmy Buffett—all ensure a more family-friendly version than the real thing (no all-night bar crawls here!), with some of the biggest standard rooms and one-bed villas in the Disney Vacation Club inventory.

Activities include tennis, volleyball, basketball, sauna, and two arcades, as well as bike rentals, boat rentals, and fishing. It can be surprisingly frenzied at times around the main pool and **Hospitality House**, with its **Turtle Krawl** main promenade, main restaurant **Olivia's Café** (see Chapter 9), **Gurgling Suitcase** bar, general store, and snack bar.

DISNEY'S BOARDWALK VILLAS AND THE VILLAS AT DISNEY'S WILDERNESS LODGE

BoardWalk Villas: 407-939-5100

Villas at Disney's Wilderness Lodge: 407-938-4300

Park transportation: By bus, while there is also boat transportation to Magic Kingdom.

The BoardWalk Villas were added in 1996 as part of the original master plan for that resort, and the Wilderness Lodge Villas were added to the Wilderness Lodge resort in 2000. Legend has it they were built by workers on the transcontinental railroad, incorporating railroad memorabilia and artwork, but the workers moved on, leaving the villas for future generations to discover.

The accommodations include studio units with a kitchenette, as well as one- and two-bedroom villas with a full kitchen and extended living space. The rest of the resort facilities are shared with the Wilderness Lodge.

DISNEY'S BEACH CLUB VILLAS

407-934-8000

Park transportation: To Epcot and Disney's Hollywood Studios by boat, and to the other parks by bus.

Two years later, the Disney Vacation Club list expanded again with the Beach Club Villas. Maintaining the nautical Cape May motif, they include studios and one- and two-bedroom villas, plus two elegant side rooms—the drawing room and the breezeway—and a quiet pool.

DISNEY'S SARATOGA SPRINGS RESORT AND SPA

407-827-1100

Park transportation: By bus to all parks, plus there is a bus service around the resort, and bus and boat transport to Downtown Disney.

Disney went all-out for Saratoga Springs, their biggest-ever Disney Vacation Club resort in the style of the upstate New York resort town, which is opposite Downtown Disney and has views over the lake and the Lake Buena Vista Golf Course.

Saratoga Springs, which was a renowned health spa in the nineteenth century, opened a race course for its thousands of visitors in 1863. Because of this, its turn-of-the-century Victorian ambience takes the theme of "Health, History, and Horses." The art and signage mimic Saratoga's grand heritage—which featured magnificent hotels like the Grand Union, the world's largest in 1870—and classic architecture, with ornate shingle roofs, stone chimneys, rotunda-topped rectangular towers, dormer windows, Romanesque columns, and elaborate ornamentation. This sprawling resort is also split into six sections: **The Springs**, **The Paddock**, **Congress Park**, **The Carousel**, **The Grandstand**, and the **Treehouse Villas**.

REALITY CHECK | The extensive nature of Saratoga Springs means you can be a long way from the central facilities. If this is a concern for you (bearing in mind the furthest-away blocks can feel wonderfully remote and secluded), request a room in either the **Springs** or **Grandstand** sections, or, if you prefer a Downtown Disney view, in **Congress Park**.

Congress Park in New York was the historic heart of Saratoga Springs, a beautiful seventeen-acre stretch of gardens, lawns, fountains, the signature carousel, and the historic Canfield House Casino, as well as one of the springs for which the city became famous. Fittingly, **Congress Park** here in Disney was the first section of the resort built and the main check-in area. The gorgeous rotunda-style **Carriage House** features a carousel horse reminiscent of the ones in Congress Park.

The main feature of this resort, though, is the **High Rock Springs Pool**. Named for the original spring in Saratoga that was discovered in 1776 by wounded British army hero Sir William Johnson, the resort pool is a charming mix of cascading streams, hot tubs, zero-depth-entry waters, a water slide, children's splash area, footbridge, and pool bar.

Add to that a state-of-the-art spa, health and fitness facilities, bike rentals, video arcade, jogging trails, basketball, tennis, and shuffleboard, plus another four "quiet" pools and two children's playgrounds, and this stands out as a superbly complete resort—highly reminiscent of its namesake, but without the horse racing!

ROOKIE MISTAKES

It's a mistake to believe there are resort facilities available only to resort guests. The **Saratoga Springs Spa** provides some blissful massages and other pampering for all to enjoy.

Rooms come in studios with kitchenettes that sleep four, and one-, two-, and three-bedroom grand villas, with full kitchens, that sleep up to twelve.

The **Treehouse Villas**, technically part of **Disney's Saratoga Springs Resort and Spa**, are the odd ones out in thematic terms. They were part of an unusual and innovative style that dates back to 1975, when Disney decided to add a more adventurous option tucked away along the Sassagoula River and secluded from just about every other resort type and amenity. For those who enjoyed the Swiss Family Treehouse in the Magic Kingdom, this was the perfect accommodation!

However, the **Treehouse Villas** were actually part of an aborted attempt to build a full-time residential community in Lake Buena Vista, with single family homes, condos, vacation homes, retirement apartments, and a shopping village. It was designed in four themed areas—Golf, Tennis, Boating, and Western. The sixty tree houses and a selection of other villas were built for the golf-themed section but the full plan was quietly abandoned after 1975. From their inception to 2002, the Villas were used for resort guests, occasionally for Disney's college program, and for the imaginative but short-lived Disney

Institute from 1996–2002 (with several of the institute's buildings being rei-magined for Saratoga Springs, notably the **Spa** and **Community Hall**).

All the villas in this section, with the exception of the tree houses, were then torn down to make way for Saratoga Springs, and the tree houses were all but forgotten until 2008. When Disney came to review these 1970s misfits, they found the Villas were in a sorry state but worth salvaging for their won-derfully secluded location.

All sixty were effectively rebuilt from the ground up and given totally modern fittings and furnishings, as well as becoming more eco-friendly within the wetlands area they occupy. Elevated 10 feet off the ground, they all feature three bedrooms and two bathrooms and some gorgeous features, like granite countertops, cathedral ceilings, large wooden decks, and barbe-cue grills.

While not strictly "tree houses," they are still rustic and cabin-style from the outside. They also feature their own quiet pools, but have tight living space for up to nine guests. The other drawback is they are quite a way from the **Saratoga Springs** amenities, so having a car here is highly advisable. There is a bus link to the **Carriage House**, but it can be time-consuming to get to the parks.

DISNEY'S ANIMAL KINGDOM VILLAS

407-938-3000

Park transportation: By bus.

The Disney Vacation Club went for another grand expansion from 2007–2009 with the conversion of the top two floors of the Animal Kingdom Lodge to 134 studios and one-, two-, and grand three-bed villas. The neighboring Kidani Village, also at Animal Kingdom Lodge, then added another 324 units in its own purpose-built wing (see page 76). Kidani Village continues the African lodge décor and ambience of the original Jambo House, on a slightly smaller scale. A big advantage here is the the addition of a second bathroom and the ability to sleep five guests in Kidani's one-bedroom villas.

BAY LAKE TOWER AT DISNEY'S CONTEMPORARY RESORT

407-824-1000

Park transportation: To the Magic Kingdom by monorail or boat (or on foot), to Epcot by monorail or bus, and to the other parks by bus. There are also boats to Wilderness Lodge and Fort Wilderness.

Disney Vacation Club fans were thrilled to learn about this unique development, which opened its doors in 2009, but it was one of the most controversial construction projects in recent Disney history as it involved tearing down the North Garden wing of the Contemporary Resort and altering the distinctive profile of the signature A-frame building.

Instead of standing alone as the pinnacle of 1960s futuristic design, the iconic Contemporary now shares its "space" with another fifteen-story tower building. Viewed from the other side of Seven Seas Lagoon, the two almost appear as one big block. However, architect Charles Gwathmey worked hard to keep the overall view sympathetic to the original, to the extent that Bay Lake Tower features the same striking horizontal lines and vertical sectioning. Even the suspended fifth floor footbridge that connects the two buildings is designed to mimic the smooth lines of the monorail track.

While Contemporary purists will probably never be placated, Bay Lake Tower offers the best views of the Magic Kingdom (albeit at a Disney Vacation Club premium) and has its own top-deck bar, lounge, and open-air viewing deck. Check-in and most facilities are still located in the Contemporary Resort, although the Tower does have its own pool with imaginative water slide, pool bar, community hall, and barbecue pavilion, in addition to the **Top of the World Lounge**—named for the long-closed bar atop the Contemporary.

In the Bay Lake Tower Villas, you'll find the usual mix of studios and one-, two-, and three-bed villas sleeping up to twelve.

Campground

FORT WILDERNESS

407-824-2900

Park transportation: To the Magic Kingdom (and Wilderness Lodge and Contemporary Resort) by boat; to the other parks by bus.

Taking its cue from frontier territory, this wonderfully rustic and rural combination of campground and cabins has been one of the World's best-kept secrets. Named after the former Fort Wilderness on Tom Sawyer Island at Disneyland in California, this campground is firmly dated at 1812 and characters like Davy Crockett still roam the land, exploring and keeping the pioneers safe. There are trading posts and trails, ranches and campfires. "Log cabin" is the architectural motif and "stockade style" is the overriding image.

HIDDEN MAGIC | The tree-trunk trash cans in Fort Wilderness are actually from the long-since-closed Indian Village attraction in Frontierland at Disneyland in California.

Much of the 740-acre site is made up of untouched woodland, canals, and wetland, which gives the resort a natural, peaceful ambience that also helps to maintain the period feel. In keeping with the era, Fort Wilderness also had its own railroad transport service from 1973–77 (you can still see portions of the tracks, notably the former railroad bed and ties behind the 700 loop). Today, guests can try carriage and wagon rides that evoke the feeling of a more gentle age. Fort Wilderness is home to all of Walt Disney World's horses, including the huge Percherons that pull the Main Street Trolley and Cinderella's white carriage ponies often seen at Disney's Wedding Pavilion.

In all, there are 799 sites and 409 cabins. Campsites are all level, paved pads with electric, water, and sewer hook-ups; charcoal grills and picnic tables; air-conditioned comfort stations offering private showers; a coin laundry facility; vending machines; and telephones nearby. Each cabin features more than 500 square feet of air-conditioned living space as well as a private patio deck with a charcoal grill and picnic table. The master bedroom sleeps four with a full-size bed and set of bunks, while the living room sleeps two with a full-size pull-down bed. Despite the 1800s look, the cabins include all modern conveniences like cable TV, DVD player, and telephone.

Provisions can be bought at two **Trading Posts**, while **Crockett's Tavern** offers a saloon-style lounge (drinks, pizza, appetizers) and the **Trail's End Restaurant** (see Chapter 9) is a full-service diner.

ROOKIE MISTAKES

Family pets aren't forgotten here. Fort Wilderness has always been a pet-friendly choice, and dogs have their own "playground" with the **Waggin' Trails Dog Park**, an off-leash play area.

The real draw of the campground, though, is all the fun that guests can have, ranging from horseback riding, fishing excursions, nature trail exploration, and golf cart, bike, and boat rentals to volleyball, tennis, shuffleboard, and the unique **Wilderness Back Trail Adventure**, where you can trundle around the resort on Segway personal transporters. The main pool area features a child-friendly water slide and one of two video arcades, and then there is the **Tri-Circle-D Ranch**, with pony rides for kids.

Finally, there are the nightly entertainment programs. You can roast marshmallows with Disney characters during **Chip 'n Dale's Campfire Sing-along**, which features a fire-lighting ceremony, camp songs, and appearances by Chip and Dale. More importantly, it is open to all Walt Disney World guests—and it's free.

The Hoop-Dee-Doo Musical Review dinner show performs three times nightly while **Mickey's Backyard BBQ** is offered seasonally (see Chapter 8).

Onsite Non-Disney Resorts

The following resorts are in Walt Disney World but they are not owned by Disney. With the exception of the Orlando Hilton Resort, they do not include the Extra Magic Hour perk or other perks offered to Disney resort guests.

SHADES OF GREEN

407-824-3600

Park transportation: By bus.

The ultimate "lone soldier" of all Disney's resort offerings is this hotel expressly for military servicemen and women. The U.S. Department of Defense approached Disney in 1994 with a proposal to lease the former Disney Inn as a permanent resort base for all military personnel. Two years later, the Department of Defense bought it outright and it has remained a source of military R and R ever since, with huge standard rooms (480 square feet), three restaurants, a fitness center, tennis courts, and two pools. Learn more at *www.shadesofgreen.org*.

HIDDEN MAGIC Shades of Green also features the unique "Remember the Fun" walkway, a tribute to guests' experience there. The brick walkway is in the center of the property near the gazebo and displays the names and messages of different military guests.

DISNEY HOTEL PLAZA

While Disney was busy building up its own portfolio of hotels in the 1970s and '80s, another story was quietly being written along Motor Inn Plaza, the road that is now Hotel Boulevard, linking Lake Buena Vista with Downtown Disney.

Here, on land leased from the Disney company, four hotels—the Dutch Inn, Howard Johnson's, Royal Inn, and Travelodge—took shape and became great alternatives to the official hotels, offering ideal location but less of the costs.

HIDDEN MAGIC | The very first building in Walt Disney World to open to the public can be found on Hotel Boulevard. Now the Amateur Athletic Union, it was the official Preview Center in January 1970 and has survived through various usages to the present day.

Today the Dutch Inn has progressed from the Grosvenor Resort to the Regal Sun Resort and now the Wyndham Lake Buena Vista; the Howard Johnson became a Courtyard by Marriott and then a Holiday Inn; the Royal Inn is now the Hotel Royal Plaza; and the Travelodge has become the Best Western.

Three more were added after the opening of the Epcot park—a Hilton hotel (owned by the same company that built the Swan and Dolphin resorts), the Pickett Suites resort (which ultimately became a Doubletree property), and the smart Buena Vista Palace.

There are another seven independent resorts on Hotel Boulevard, just past Downtown Disney, that benefit from free bus transportation to the parks as well as a great location. These hotels include:

- The Hilton Orlando Resort: the only "outside" hotel to benefit from Extra Magic Hours for its guests (407-827-4000, *www1.hilton.com*)
- The Buena Vista Palace (866-397-6516, *www.buenavistapalace.com*)
- The Best Western (407-828-2424, *www.bestwestern.com*)
- The Wyndham Lake Buena Vista (407-828-4444, *www.wyndham.com*)
- The Holiday Inn (407-828-8888, *www.hiorlando.com*)
- The Royal Plaza (407-828-2828, *www.royalplaza.com*)
- The DoubleTree Suites by Hilton Lake Buena Vista (407-934-4000, *http://doubletree1.hilton.com*).

For our money, the Holiday Inn often represents outstanding value here, but you can learn more at *www.downtowndisneyhotels.com*.

WYNDHAM BONNET CREEK RESORT

Here's a story of mystery and perseverance: Back in the mid-1960s, Walt Disney's agents were busy buying up as much Florida land as they could for

'Project X' (the code name for what would become Walt Disney World), using made-up corporation names to hide the fact they were purchasing the land on behalf of Walt. However, there was one parcel of land they couldn't acquire. For reasons that have never been publicly made clear, the owner of 480 acres of prime real estate alongside I-4 simply refused to sell and the parcel of land remained empty and unused until 1993.

Orlando Sentinel reporter Tim Barker then made the discovery the land had been owned, since 1962, before Walt even came along, by a Taiwanese businessman, who died in 1992. His heirs finally decided to sell to a private developer who drew up a master plan for an upscale multihotel resort with a golf course.

Fairfield Resorts bought into the development in 2002 and started the first project, which became the huge timeshare-based Wyndham Bonnet Creek Resort, which was given a Mediterranean theme and boasted 1,594 suites. Hilton Hotels then built a flagship Hilton Hotel as well as the first Waldorf Astoria Hotel to exist outside New York, which both opened in October 2009.

Bonnet Creek is accessible only off Buena Vista Drive but, despite being "on" Disney property for all intents and purposes, the resorts here are not on the Disney transport routes (although they do have their own) and do not benefit from Extra Magic Hours and other perks. Learn more at *www.wyndhambonnetcreek .com*, *www.hiltonbonnetcreek.com*, and *www.waldorfastoriaorlando.com*.

HIDDEN MAGIC | While the Bonnet Creek resorts are inside Disney property, their signage is very different (and much smaller!). Interestingly enough, the resort's name caused Disney to drop the use of Bonnet Creek as the overall title for its Osprey Ridge and Eagle Pines golf courses in 2007.

Outside the World

While Disney does feature a wonderful range of accommodations, there is even more to choose from beyond the boundaries of its World.

You will find every major chain here, from budget-minded Motel 6 to the swanky Ritz-Carlton, and price tends to vary according to proximity to Disney, although there are nearly always good deals available. Dining is usually cheaper and the shopping opportunities much broader. These accommodations basically fall into three main areas: Lake Buena Vista (the area immediately outside Disney and along I-4), International Drive, and Highway 192, which offers the bulk of the budget-choice accommodations, with numerous motels and basic hotel brands.

ROOKIE MISTAKES

It's common to see hotels and villas designated as "just minutes from Disney" but, in some cases, that might be 30 or 40 (or "just minutes by fighter jet!"). Make sure you get a realistic idea of the distance before you book.

A good starting point is the official Visitor Center on International Drive at Austrian Court (*www.visitorlando.com*), the Kissimmee tourist agency (*http://www.visitkissimmee.com*), or the official International Drive website (*www.internationaldriveorlando.com*). For vacation home rentals, try *www.cfvrma.com* and *www.discovervacationhomes.com*. You can also try some of the following hotels:

FOR A BUDGET CHOICE CLOSE TO WALT DISNEY WORLD:
- Galleria Palms Hotel, in Kissimmee at Maingate West, just off Highway 192 (407-396-6300, *www.galleriakissimmeehotel.com*)
- Holiday Inn Maingate East, in Kissimmee (407-396-4222, *www.holidayinnmge.com*)
- Orlando Vista Hotel, in Lake Buena Vista (407-239-4646, *www.ascendcollection.com*)
- CocoKey Water Resort, on International Drive, boasting its own mini water park (877-875-4681, *http://cocokeyorlando.com*)
- Rosen Inn at Pointe Orlando, a long-standing and reliable I-Drive hotel (800-999-8585, *www.roseninn9000.com*)
- Radisson Hotel Lake Buena Vista, just outside the Downtown Disney entrance (407-597-3400, *www.radisson.com*)

FOR A GOOD MID-RANGE CHOICE:

- Holiday Inn Resort Lake Buena Vista, not far from Disney property (407-239-4500, *www.hiresortlbv.com*)
- Monumental Hotel, a converted Crowne Plaza hotel on a quieter part of International Drive (877-239-1222, *www.monumentalhotelorlando.com*)
- Embassy Suites International Drive South, in the heart of International Drive (407-352-1400, *www.embassysuitesorlando.com*)
- Rosen Centre Hotel, right next to the I-Drive Convention Center (800-204-7234, *www.rosencentre.com*)
- Palisades Resort, a great value condo-hotel in a quieter part of Highway 192 (321-250-3030, *www.palisadesresortorlando.com*)
- Floridays Resort, family-friendly condo-hotel on International Drive (866-797-0022, *www.floridaysresort.com*)

FOR A GREAT DELUXE EXPERIENCE:

- Rosen Shingle Creek Resort, off Universal Boulevard behind International Drive (407-996-9939, *www.shinglecreekresort.com*)
- Hyatt Grand Cypress, in a quieter part of Lake Buena Vista (407-239-1234, *http://grandcypress.hyatt.com*)
- Gaylord Palms Resort, a massive, Florida-themed creation in Kissimmee (407-586-2000, *www.gaylordpalms.com*)
- Bohemian Hotel, a lovely boutique-style hotel in the Disney-created town of Celebration, just off Highway 192 (407-566-6000, *www.celebrationhotel.com*)
- The Peabody Orlando, a superb mix of convention and leisure resort on I-Drive (407-352-4000, *www.peabodyorlando.com*)
- Grande Lakes Resort, a combination of upscale J. W. Marriott and Ritz-Carlton, in its own 500-acre reserve between I-Drive and Kissimmee (407-206-2300/2400, *www.grandelakes.com*)

And now, with a full understanding of the practical side of things, let's move on to where the real magic happens!

Write Your Own Story

Write Your Own Story

Write Your Own Story

Write Your Own Story

Write Your Own Story

Write Your Own Story

Chapter 3

Where the Magic Begins: Magic Kingdom

WELCOME TO THE MAGIC KINGDOM, where wondrous stories can be found at every turn! They are stories of fantasy, science fiction, history, and adventure. But there is far more to it than that. The stories here are multifaceted and, like a timeless novel, they have layers of meaning just waiting to be discovered. The moment you enter the park you step into a fantasy world, a movie set, and a historical timeline come to life.

From the standpoint of movie-making, the first story involves entering the park and becoming part of the "show," with the credits rolling by in the upper story windows along Main Street. Disney movies are the basis for most of the attractions, and all of the attendants are known as Cast Members. Another aspect of the story is told through the subtle "world exploration" you take, starting in small-town America, moving into Europe, the American West, the Caribbean, the Middle East, and finally into the future, when space travel is common.

There is also a factual story in Magic Kingdom, with small references to the Imagineers, designers, and creators scattered throughout the park. The atmosphere is filled with history and patriotism, themes that were extremely important to Walt, and while the fanciful side is at the forefront, many of the locations represented are based on real places.

But the most important stories here are the ones you make, sparked by the vast imagination and all-encompassing storytelling Disney Imagineers have taken to the level of a fine art.

Practical Information

In keeping with the idea that everything in Walt Disney World has a story, we could tell you a tale of frenzied queries, hidden treasures, imaginative transportation, wounded warriors, and wet diapers, but it's simpler just to say: Guest Relations is to the far right of the turnstiles; locker, wheelchair, and stroller rentals are to the left of Guest Relations; and First Aid and the Baby Care Center are located between Casey's Corner and Crystal Palace.

ROOKIE MISTAKES You're finally here and you can't wait to get into the park! In all the excitement it's easy to forget where you parked. Pause for a moment before you board the tram and take a digital photo of your row number. Then, simply delete it when you get back to your car.

Main Street, U.S.A.

Welcome to "hometown America," an idyllic place that tugs at the heartstrings for the simpler time it represents. Horse-drawn carriages are still used, but motorcars have made an appearance, and the gentle flame of the gas lamp gives way to the wonders of the electric light bulb. The myriad of small details that make up Main Street tell an important part of the story, indicating when and where you are. Here, you're standing on the edge of a new era, when all things are possible.

The town's functional elements of **City Hall**, the **Main Street Fire Department**, and the **Barber Shop** are on the left, and the entertainment venues of **Town Square Theater** and **Tony's Town Square Restaurant** are on the right.

All of Magic Kingdom is a show, and the host of that show is, of course, Mickey Mouse. You can meet him at **Town Square Theater**, along with Minnie Mouse and (until late 2012/early 2013) the Disney Princesses. Go backstage for some one-on-one time as Mickey and Minnie prepare for their next show. You can even reserve time with Mickey by using the Fastpass machines to the left of **Tony's Town Square**.

Just a few doors down from the fire house is the **Harmony Barber Shop**, harkening back to a time before beauty salons, when there was one hairstyle for men, and it was mighty short! This barber shop keeps up with the times though, and some wacky styles come out of here (think glitter and washable hair paint!). For a very special memento, toddlers can get a My First Haircut certificate when Disney gives their locks their very first trim.

As you make your way down Main Street take a look at the upper story windows, where the town's businesses advertise their wares. While this adds to the story of a bustling community, those names you see are the designers and Imagineers who created Walt Disney World. The work those designers did are alluded to in the "business" they own.

HIDDEN MAGIC Town Square's fire house doesn't see much action, but it performs an important function just the same. As **Fire House 71**, it points to the year Magic Kingdom opened (1971).

FLAG RETREAT CEREMONY

Each day at 5 P.M. the **Main Street Philharmonic band** strikes up a medley of patriotic music and this beautiful ceremony honoring veterans and the American flag is played out. Sign up at City Hall to be chosen as the day's veteran or military special guest. Take a brief moment to let today's special guest know you're grateful for their service. It means a lot to them to hear it.

HIDDEN MAGIC Notice how Main Street's light fixtures progress from gas lamps near the Emporium to electric lights down by Casey's Corner. You're walking a virtual timeline from the 1800s into the Industrial Revolution.

WALT DISNEY WORLD RAILROAD

Walt Disney had a great love of trains. In designing his idea of a perfect park one of his requirements was that there should be a train encircling it, with its main station at the very front. Magic Kingdom's train does just that. There are three trains, named for Walt, his brother Roy, and Roger Broggie, Disney legend, mechanical wizard, and train buff. The ride makes a great midday break, with time off your feet.

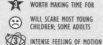

★ MISS-ABLE	★ IF YOU HAVE TIME	★ WORTH MAKING TIME FOR	★ NOT TO BE MISSED!
☺ WILL ONLY WORRY YOUNG CHILDREN	☺ MAY SCARE MANY YOUNG CHILDREN; FEW ADULTS	☹ WILL SCARE MOST YOUNG CHILDREN; SOME ADULTS	☺ MAJOR SCARE FACTOR
↻1 VISUAL DISORIENTATION	〰2 MILD PHYSICAL MOVEMENT	〰3 INTENSE FEELING OF MOTION	〰4 EXTREME PHYSICAL SENSATIONS AND VISUAL DISORIENTATION

Town Square and Main Street Dining

★★ $$$$

It's a "Bella Notte" every night (and lunchtime) as you enter this homage to *Lady and the Tramp*. Tony's Town Square Restaurant is a representation of the restaurant behind which the two famous canines had their romantic engagement in the 1955 movie. You're in a typical Italian trattoria run by Tony, and the Victorian Italianate style is light and airy, wonderful for lunch on a hot day. The original exterior façade is borrowed from the classic-era hotels of Saratoga Springs, which is why it is not as rustic looking as Via Napoli in Epcot. Tony's is a touch overpriced for dinner but still serves up a decent Italian flavor, even if the menu is rather unadventurous.

HIDDEN MAGIC

Slightly confused by the theme of Tony's? That's because it was originally the Town Square Café (sponsored by the Oscar-Mayer wiener company!) and was converted to its Italian theme in 1989. The original design was a happy coincidence though, as the Saratoga Springs architecture it borrowed from was an Italian style called Lombardian.

★★★ $$

Often overlooked by visitors as they scamper from Main Street to Tomorrowland, this Victorian-inspired art nouveau creation, offering classic American salad-and-sandwich fare, is a haven of cool in the summer (especially with sundaes and other desserts!). Actually comprised of two 1890s-era buildings, this restaurant features the nouveau glass-and-mirrors of the main dining room, with its wrought-iron tables and chairs, and the more simple, airy, Victorian feel of the conservatory wing.

CRYSTAL PALACE

★★★★ $$$$$

The Crystal Palace is hugely elaborate, modeled on a series of famous Victorian conservatories, notably San Francisco's 1878 Conservatory of Flowers (which borrowed from the style of the Palm House in Kew Gardens, London, built 30 years earlier) and the New York Crystal Palace, constructed for the 1853 Exhibition and destroyed by fire just five years later. New York's version was inspired by the original "Crystal Palace" in London's Hyde Park, a stunning construction of steel and glass made for the 1851 Great Exhibition that was thought impossible for its time. Sadly, it also burned down, in 1936.

REALITY CHECK Spending all day in the Magic Kingdom? Book a late breakfast seating for Crystal Palace (10:30 A.M.) and you can probably fill up well enough to get through to dinner, thus avoiding having to eat three meals in the park.

Winnie the Pooh and friends lead an ever-eager cavalcade of child-friendly fun here, with plenty of character interaction and enough buffet selections to keep everyone happy. They have great fresh fruit and salad, and delicious hot-carved rotisserie-cooked meats. For breakfast, don't miss Pooh's Breakfast Lasagna; it sounds weird, but it's worth it.

HIDDEN MAGIC The Imagineers backtracked slightly on their timeline for Main Street, U.S.A. with the Crystal Palace, reverting to a mid-Victorian architectural influence. However, its antique style helps make the transition to colonial-era Africa and Asia as you head toward Adventureland. Notice the tactile "signal" as the pavement changes in this area, too. Disney always transitions from one land to another with visual, tactile, and auditory cues. The exception is over at **Tomorrowland Speedway**, which has no audio transition.

 MISS-ABLE   IF YOU HAVE TIME   WORTH MAKING TIME FOR   NOT TO BE MISSED!

 WILL ONLY WORRY YOUNG CHILDREN   MAY SCARE MANY YOUNG CHILDREN; FEW ADULTS   WILL SCARE MOST YOUNG CHILDREN; SOME ADULTS   MAJOR SCARE FACTOR

 VISUAL DISORIENTATION   MILD PHYSICAL MOVEMENT   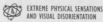 INTENSE FEELING OF MOTION   EXTREME PHYSICAL SENSATIONS AND VISUAL DISORIENTATION

MAIN STREET BAKERY AND PLAZA ICE CREAM PARLOR

$

No Main Street would be complete without a bakery, hot dog vendor, and ice cream shop, hence you can get a worthwhile breakfast (plus pastries and cakes at any time of the day) at **Main Street Bakery** or chill out with a cool sundae at the **Plaza Ice Cream Parlor**.

REALITY CHECK Tired, frustrated, and ready to quit the Magic Kingdom on a hot, busy day? Don't—take the boat over to Fort Wilderness and relax among the quiet, wooded acres while enjoying a crowd-free lunch at Trail's End. Then head back to the Magic Kingdom suitably refreshed!

CASEY'S CORNER

★★ $

Casey's Corner is a wonderful three-way tribute to the baseball of yesteryear, Ernest L. Thayer's 1888 poem "Casey at the Bat," and the 1946 Disney short cartoon based on the poem. Baseball memorabilia lines the walls and outside stands a statue of Casey in the style of a turn-of-the-century tobacco store Indian, a 3-D advertising gimmick of the period. The front of the building is adorned with an elaborate letter "C," the logo of the Cincinnati Reds—the country's first professional baseball team. Casey's was originally Coca-Cola Refreshment Corner, but Imagineer Eddie Sotto did such a fabulous job of Main Street, U.S.A. in Disneyland Paris that it was retrofitted to the Magic Kingdom in 1995. Drop by and grab a 'dog.

HIDDEN MAGIC Inside the bleachers area of Casey's Corner restaurant is a scoreboard reading Visitors 4, Mudville 2—the fateful score in Thayer's poem when Casey struck out to end the game.

Town Square and Main Street Shopping

CURTAIN CALL COLLECTIBLES

The merchandise is general Disney-ware, but the story puts you in a backstage props area of the **Town Square Theater**, where you'll find a couple of references to the now-extinct Toontown. See that long mirror in the back of the store on the right-hand side? It was originally in **Minnie's Country House**. And that yellow cartoon-style model of a house with screws holding it together (sitting on a high shelf on the left side toward the back) was from **Pete's garage**. Just for fun, notice the locks on the **Tank of Terror**. They're hidden Mickeys.

LE CHAPEAU

This store is owned by **Julia and Nancy Cary**, cousins in the Disney movie *Summer Magic*. Enter the shop from the door nearest Tony's Town Square, where you'll find a phone in a small room on the right, next to the door. Pick up the receiver and you'll discover it's a "party line" from a time when many neighbors shared the same phone line. Stop and listen for a while. You'll hear gossipy conversation, including advice on how to catch a man.

THE EMPORIUM

Every good Main Street has a general store, and the Emporium is Magic Kingdom's. Take a look at the window on the left as you enter the front door, just off the hub area. It reads "Osh Popham," Proprietor. Ossium "Osh" Popham is a character from Disney's 1963 movie *Summer Magic* with Hayley Mills, Dorothy McGuire, and Burl Ives. Ives played Osh, the kindly postmaster in Beulah, Maine, who helps a new family settle in to rural life.

THE EMPORIUM GALLERY

Next to the Emporium is the Emporium Gallery, the town's Victorian clothier with an Edwardian ambience (circa 1901, which, not so coincidentally, is Walt Disney's birth year). Connected to the Gallery are McGregor Sportswear,

 MISS-ABLE
 WILL ONLY WORRY YOUNG CHILDREN
 VISUAL DISORIENTATION

 IF YOU HAVE TIME
MAY SCARE MANY YOUNG CHILDREN; FEW ADULTS
MILD PHYSICAL MOVEMENT

 WORTH MAKING TIME FOR
WILL SCARE MOST YOUNG CHILDREN; SOME ADULTS
 INTENSE FEELING OF MOTION

 NOT TO BE MISSED!
 MAJOR SCARE FACTOR
 EXTREME PHYSICAL SENSATIONS AND VISUAL DISORIENTATION

Disney Clothiers ready-to-wear, Main Street Fashion and Apparel, and Hall of Champions, the town's athletic club, which was established in 1884.

HIDDEN MAGIC If you think those faces in the mural along the back wall of the Emporium Gallery must mean something, you would be right. They are the Imagineers who designed and created the gallery.

Adventureland

Adventureland calls to mind the classic childhood tales of *Swiss Family Robinson*, *The Jungle Book*, *In Search of the Castaways*, and *Aladdin*, filled with high-seas peril, pirate battles, and travel to exotic lands. There is a promise of adventure around every corner, and if you really want to immerse yourself in the story, you can even join up with Captain Jack Sparrow and become an honorary pirate. More than any other land in the Magic Kingdom, Adventureland retains the artistry of classic Imagineering at its finest. Disney legends, including Marc Davis, Claude Coats, and Yale Gracey, designed and created the attractions here (with the exception of the Magic Carpets of Aladdin, which came much later), making them timeless favorites and direct links to the style of storytelling Walt Disney loved.

SWISS FAMILY TREEHOUSE

This walk-through experience gives a glimpse into the coolest part of being shipwrecked: you get to live in a tree house. The story comes from *The Swiss Family Robinson* by Johann David Wyss, which was subsequently made into a Disney movie in 1960, in which the Robinson family is en route to New Guinea. When pirates pursue them and the ship is engulfed in a storm, the family is shipwrecked and washed up onto an uninhabited island, where they carve out a life for themselves until they can be rescued.

Apparently the Robinson family wanted for nothing (they even had grapes!), and their tree house is filled with conveniences, both invented by the family and salvaged from the ship. The thrill factor is low, but you'll get a little exercise climbing stairs for a glimpse of the family's newfound home. There is rarely any wait here.

HIDDEN MAGIC | The Robinson family in the book was chased off course by pirates, resulting in their shipwreck on the island. Is it any coincidence Swiss Family Treehouse is just down the way from Pirates of the Carribean? We don't think so!

THE MAGIC CARPETS OF ALADDIN

   FOR THOSE UNDER 6

From a practical standpoint, this fairground-style ride takes some of the load off of Dumbo's back. As part of the story, you're flying along with Aladdin and Jasmine over the marketplace in Agrabah. Jewels are scattered throughout the pavement below you, while above you the magic lamp is a reminder of the Genie who made Aladdin's wishes come true. Not only can you make your carpet rise and fall, you can also make it tip from front to back for an even greater sense of flight. It's great fun—and it's very real—for young children.

THE ENCHANTED TIKI ROOM (TROPICAL SERENADE)

Through the inspiration of a small mechanical bird, Walt Disney's idea for an attraction filled with singing animatronic parrots took flight. Initially intended to be a show inside a restaurant, it became a stand-alone attraction: the Enchanted Tiki Room, in Disneyland, renamed Enchanted Tiki Birds starring in the Tropical Serenade when the attraction came to Magic Kingdom. Over the course of time it underwent a few incarnations, and has now returned to the original show.

  MISS-ABLE   IF YOU HAVE TIME   WORTH MAKING TIME FOR   NOT TO BE MISSED!

 WILL ONLY WORRY YOUNG CHILDREN   MAY SCARE MANY YOUNG CHILDREN; FEW ADULTS   WILL SCARE MOST YOUNG CHILDREN; SOME ADULTS   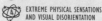 MAJOR SCARE FACTOR

VISUAL DISORIENTATION   MILD PHYSICAL MOVEMENT   INTENSE FEELING OF MOTION   EXTREME PHYSICAL SENSATIONS AND VISUAL DISORIENTATION

Jose, Michael, Pierre, and Fritz (parrots from Mexico, Ireland, France, and Germany respectively) host the show from their perches high in the rafters, and after waking up the "glee club" they launch into "In the Tiki Tiki Tiki Tiki Tiki Room," a song so insidious it will haunt your dreams long after "It's a Small World" has given up.

The birds trade gentle ribbings between singing, whistling, and requesting applause for their efforts. An enchanted fountain begins to sparkle and spout and a chorus of female parrots descends on its "bird-mobile," warbling "Let's All Sing Like the Birdies Sing," while Jose encourages the audience to join them.

The Tiki Room comes alive as orchids launch into "The Hawaiian War Chant," and before you know it a storm breaks out and the tiki gods take up the chant, beating their drums in anger at the celebration going on around them. This is your cue to get up and go . . . if you haven't already.

Visitors either love it or hate it, but one thing is certain—that infernal song will be hanging around in your head for days to come. That said, the air conditioning here is a welcome relief in summer.

REALITY CHECK | With all those free badges Disney hands out, it is not realistic to expect preferential treatment from Cast Members on your special day. Let their good wishes be enough, and if some extra magic comes your way consider it a wonderful bonus!

JUNGLE CRUISE

Essential Information: Fastpass

The Jungle Navigation Company is offering one heck of a tour, cruising the Amazon, Congo, Nile, and Mekong rivers. While your skipper may impart small snippets of useful knowledge, for the most part the jokes just keep coming, even if you can't quite tell if they're funny or not.

★ POOR	★★ FAIR	★★★ GOOD	★★★★ EXCELLENT	★★★★★ GOURMET
$ UNDER $10	$$ $10–15	$$$ $15–$20	$$$$ $20–$25	$$$$$ $25+

 BREAKFAST   LUNCH   DINNER   COUNTER SERVICE   TABLE SERVICE   TABLE SERVICE (TWO CREDITS)

At the start of this story, you arrive at a 1930s British outpost, board your tour boat, wave goodbye to the passengers on shore, and head off for a three-week journey that starts in the Amazon River, where the main feature (okay, the only feature) is the giant butterflies. Transition past Inspiration Falls into Africa and the Congo River, where the pygmy party your skipper is expecting has abandoned their boats, fearing the giant cobra across the river. Further into the jungle, gorillas have trashed your skipper's camp, but there is no time to stop. You're about to enter the Nile.

African elephants cooling themselves in the river are curious about your arrival, and it isn't long before you come across a variety of wildlife, including a pride of lions enjoying fresh black and white striped lunchmeat (the humble zebra, feeder fish of the savanna).

Lean far to the right as you pass Schweitzer Falls (a takeoff on Albert Falls; get it? Albert . . . Schweitzer?) and you'll veer toward the back half of a crashed airplane, presumably belonging to the expedition party you passed earlier who were fleeing the business end of a raging rhino.

When hippos menace *your* boat, the skipper threatens them with a less-than-convincing gun. Moving on, evidence of restless natives abounds, and suddenly you come upon a war party waiting in ambush! Be sure to duck!

You enter Cambodia after your narrow escape, floating along the Mekong River into a creepy temple that lies in ruins due to an earthquake. Tigers, snakes, spiders, and crazy monkeys make their home here. You'll want to get your camera ready, not for them, but for the Indian elephant families playing just beyond. These pachyderms are pranksters; watch out for the little squirts!

Just before your journey ends you meet the jungle native and shrunken head dealer, Chief Na-Me. Listen closely and you may hear him say something that sounds suspiciously like, "I love disco!" If you have grand dreams of being a Jungle Cruise skipper yourself someday, try your hand (for a small fee) at **Shrunken Ned's Junior Jungle Boats**, on the right-hand side as you exit the attraction.

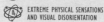

HIDDEN MAGIC

When Magic Kingdom's Jungle Cruise was conceptualized, the shrunken head salesman's name from the Disneyland version (Trader Sam) was slated to be changed. The name had not yet been decided when practice for the attraction began. The line on the script the skippers would eventually use simply indicated you were meeting "Chief (Name)." One skipper misunderstood the intent and called him Chief Na-Me. And that has been his Na-Me ever since.

PIRATES OF THE CARIBBEAN

In creating Pirates of the Caribbean, Imagineer Marc Davis referred to documented accounts of real-life pirate activities, then made them humorous. The attraction is another classic blend of Marc Davis's inspired wit and Claude Coats's brilliant staging.

HIDDEN MAGIC

Before you enter the line, check out those lava rocks to the left of the entry. The biggest one sure does look like a skull, doesn't it (see photo insert)? Creepy!

The time is the 1700s, the place is the West Indies, and you're entering the Spanish fort, El Castillo—Torre del Sol (based on Fort San Felipe del Morro in San Juan, Puerto Rico). The citadel is dim and dank, just perfect for a pirate takeover. Wind your way through abandoned hallways, where the skeletal remains of imprisoned pirates (and the sounds of the living trying to tunnel out!) can be found, then board your boat for a float down the river and into the town nearby.

But wait. All is not well here! Your first clue comes when you approach a waterfall, where the image of Davy Jones, rightful captain of the ghost ship *The Flying Dutchman* from the popular *Pirates of the Caribbean* movie series, asks if you are brave, or just foolish. Pass into a darkened area where a disembodied voice issues the eerie warning that "dead men tell no tales." All doubt about the danger of this voyage is removed when you come upon a beach littered with the skeletons of pirates who met their fates at the end of a sword.

Just beyond, another skeleton braves a raging storm on the deck of his wrecked ship, and while his disaster has already struck, yours is just about to begin. After a short drop through raging waters, you find yourself in the middle of a battle being waged between Captain Barbossa and soldiers in the fortress. Barbossa demands they turn over Captain Jack Sparrow, who he believes is hiding in the town.

None of the townspeople can (or will) comply with the demand, so the pirates take over, plundering, pillaging, and making an unholy mess of things. Being of a scurvy nature, their revelry turns to boozing, and before you can say Jack Sparrow they're creating drunken mayhem while the town burns.

Jack, who has been sneaking his way through town, takes refuge in a cask where an exceptionally inebriated reveler, who just happens to be holding a map, has flopped down for a rest. Captain Jack pops up out of the barrel, spies the map, and looks upriver with intense curiosity. He knows something you don't!

Locked in the town's jail, a band of contemptible comrades tries to tempt a mangy mutt who has the keys to their cell in his mouth, but Rover is having none of it. The pirates' luck has run out, but just across the way Captain Jack Sparrow has hit the jackpot, sitting like a prince amid his treasures, singing "Yo ho, yo ho, a pirate's life for me!" This is classic Disney Imagineering at its finest, a must-see attraction of the first order.

HIDDEN MAGIC When you enter the gift shop, look for a key hanging on a Chinese vase, just to the left of the exit leading to the restroom (it's on a shelf near the ceiling). Then search for a medallion stuck to another vase, on another high shelf just to the left of the entry into the Pirates League. Both are original props from the *Pirates of the Caribbean* movie series.

 MISS-ABLE
 WILL ONLY WORRY YOUNG CHILDREN
VISUAL DISORIENTATION

 IF YOU HAVE TIME
MAY SCARE MANY YOUNG CHILDREN; FEW ADULTS
MILD PHYSICAL MOVEMENT

 WORTH MAKING TIME FOR
 WILL SCARE MOST YOUNG CHILDREN; SOME ADULTS
INTENSE FEELING OF MOTION

 NOT TO BE MISSED!
 MAJOR SCARE FACTOR
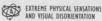 EXTREME PHYSICAL SENSATIONS AND VISUAL DISORIENTATION

CAPTAIN JACK'S PIRATE TUTORIAL

Captain Jack and his first mate Mack are looking for new recruits for the *Black Pearl*, and young swashbucklers can try their hand at sword fighting to prove their worth in this delightful street show, performed several times daily outside Pirates of the Caribbean. Young buccaneers are given the pirate oath and a certificate that prove they're now honorary pirates, but that still doesn't mean they can pillage their way through the park.

Adventureland Dining

TORTUGA TAVERN

   (SEASONALLY)

The advent of *Pirates of the Caribbean: On Stranger Tides* marked a makeover for this counter-service option opposite its namesake ride. Formerly the rather ho hum El Pirata y El Perico (The Pirate & Parrot), it is now the slightly-more-appetizing pirate-themed tavern, under the ownership of Angelica Teach (Blackbeard's daughter) and boasting several themed touches from the fourth film in the Pirates movie franchise. Look for the ledger listing the crews of both the *Black Pearl* and *Queen Anne's Revenge* and bullet holes in the walls, indicative of some rowdy pirate behavior!

> **HIDDEN MAGIC**
>
> In the courtyard between Tortuga Tavern and Pecos Bill's, look for bullet holes in the wall going up the stairway (see photo insert). There's been foul play hereabouts!

While Tortuga Tavern now looks better, the food is still the same perplexing Mexican fare. When was the last time you saw pirates chowing down on tacos and burritos?

ALOHA ISLE AND SUNSHINE TREE TERRACE

$

Popular Aloha Isle, home of the soft-serve Dole Whip—which has something of a cult following among Disney fans—is here too. It's just pineapple-flavored yogurt, but oh, is it delightful on a hot day! Sunshine Tree Terrace is a quick-service option for ice cream, slushies, and coffee drinks.

Adventureland Shopping

THE PIRATES LEAGUE

Young'uns can "Yo-Ho Yo-Ho" all day, outfitted as a first mate or an empress. Jack Sparrow and his crew have set up a recruitment base, located in the office of the East India Trading Company (really a room off the gift shop, to the left of the attraction's exit). Young recruits are given a pirate name, made-up and outfitted as a member of the crew, issued the pirate oath, and allowed to participate in a daily Adventureland Pirate Parade. Ransom must be offered if you want 'em back (and no, you can't leave 'em there for free).

MAGICAL MERCHANDISE

Find all the toys, clothing, and accessories a good pirate needs at **Pirates Bazaar**; **Island Supply** carries hats, apparel, and jewelry; and **Agrabah Bazaar** features clothing, costumes, and Aladdin merchandise.

HIDDEN MAGIC When you reach the intersection where Adventureland becomes Frontierland, look for a signpost giving you directions to the nearby attractions (it's to the left as you're facing Splash Mountain). Originally it pointed to the Ghastly Mansion, but someone has crossed that word out and scribbled "Haunted" above it (see photo insert)!

  MISS-ABLE   IF YOU HAVE TIME   WORTH MAKING TIME FOR   NOT TO BE MISSED!

 WILL ONLY WORRY YOUNG CHILDREN / MAY SCARE MANY YOUNG CHILDREN; FEW ADULTS / WILL SCARE MOST YOUNG CHILDREN; SOME ADULTS / MAJOR SCARE FACTOR

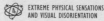 VISUAL DISORIENTATION / MILD PHYSICAL MOVEMENT / INTENSE FEELING OF MOTION / EXTREME PHYSICAL SENSATIONS AND VISUAL DISORIENTATION

Frontierland

Frontierland tells the story of the American west, with its dusty boots set firmly in the 1800s when the likes of Davy Crockett and Daniel Boone ventured into the wilderness and helped carve out a new country. A sturdy horse and thick shoe leather were still the main modes of transportation, but travel by train was becoming popular, paddlewheel boats plied the waterways, and if a boy had access to some logs, a bit of rope, and a river—well, he could get just about anywhere.

Here in Frontierland the horses are a bit scarce, but the trains always run on time, rafts are plentiful, and if you spend some time along the riverbank and listen closely you may hear Mark Twain telling stories from the deck of the *Liberty Belle* riverboat. However you choose to explore the frontier, pay attention to the tales it tells. It is the stuff of legend, and you'll want to experience it all.

SPLASH MOUNTAIN

Essential Information: 3 feet, 4 inches; no expectant mothers; Fastpass

Splash Mountain brings the rascally critters from Uncle Remus's stories in Disney's animated movie *Song of the South* to life in this log flume journey through Chickapin Hill, where mischievous Br'er Rabbit makes his home. Sit two by two in your hollow log as you float along a gentle (and not so gentle!) Georgia river, following Br'er Rabbit as he outwits his would-be captors, Br'ers Fox and Bear.

HIDDEN MAGIC | Where does the word "Br'er" come from? It is believed to have its origin in Gullah, a language sometimes used by slaves in the American South, which combines English and various African dialects. "Br'er" is the Gullah word for "brother."

Two short lift hills take you to the top of the briar patch where Rabbit makes his home, then a short drop down Slippin' Falls reveals scenes from two of Uncle Remus's stories, *The Tar Baby* and *Br'er Rabbit Runs Away*. Fox and Bear have hatched a plan to capture Rabbit when he leaves home to escape his troubles, only to find more trouble in a rope trap set by Fox, who has a hankering for rabbit stew. Rabbit convinces Bear he can make "a dollar a minute keeping the crows out of the cornfield" by trading places in the rope trap.

Shortly before the next drop the dastardly duo have been outsmarted again, having been led to Rabbit's "laughing place," a beehive that is far more amusing to Rabbit than it is to Bear! But tension rises with the next drop, as the story and the scenery darken. Music becomes chaotic, water jumps from one side of the river to the other, and the runaway's luck finally runs out.

Tied up and facing a boiling stewpot, Rabbit begs not to be thrown into the briar patch, but that's exactly where he is about to go . . . and so are you! Vultures await your demise (this is your signal to hang on tight!), but don't worry; it all ends happily, with a thrilling five-story splashdown before Br'er Rabbit's friends break into a rousing rendition of "Zip-A-Dee-Doo-Dah," giving him, and you, a grand welcome home.

BIG THUNDER MOUNTAIN RAILROAD

Essential Information: 3 feet, 4 inches; Fastpass

In this story, you are in the small Southwestern town of Tumbleweed during the gold rush, heading into abandoned Big Thunder Mining Co. Equipment is scattered around, but this excavation's luck seems to have run out. The local Indians who named the mountain for the sound the area's flash floods make, warned that the mountain should not be disturbed, but the lure of gold was too strong for the prospectors to resist. Disaster ensued in the form of a drought, at which time self-proclaimed rainmaker Cumulus Isobar was called upon. And boy, did he ever make it rain!

 MISS-ABLE WILL ONLY WORRY YOUNG CHILDREN VISUAL DISORIENTATION   IF YOU HAVE TIME MAY SCARE MANY YOUNG CHILDREN; FEW ADULTS MILD PHYSICAL MOVEMENT WORTH MAKING TIME FOR WILL SCARE MOST YOUNG CHILDREN; SOME ADULTS INTENSE FEELING OF MOTION NOT TO BE MISSED! MAJOR SCARE FACTOR EXTREME PHYSICAL SENSATIONS AND VISUAL DISORIENTATION

Board an ore car, enter the mine shaft, and begin your ascent (clank, clank, clank) through an interior cavern dripping with stalactites as a flash flood pours down on either side when you crest the hill. Suddenly, your train becomes a runaway! As you turn and zig-zag your way through the mine remember to wave to the 'possums as you streak up a hill and travel into Dave V. Jones Mine, finally getting a breather as you clank up another hill with a great view of the flooded town. But your breather doesn't last for long! You then make a sharp bank down to where the track goes crazy, and before you know it you're in the middle of a smelly mine full of loose rocks with more floodwaters pouring above your head. The train then descends out of the mine into a couple of sharp lefts, then you crest a small hill, worry about the dinosaur skeleton on the right, make a sharp left, another gentle left, and it's over.

Whew! You made it back safely! Did you catch a glimpse of Cousin Elrod in his floating bathtub as you streaked through town?

ROOKIE MISTAKES Find yourself in Frontierland during a parade? Use the boardwalk along the river to avoid fighting your way through parade watchers if you need to get to the other side of the park.

TOM SAWYER ISLAND

Enter American author Mark Twain's stories of *The Adventures of Tom Sawyer* and *The Adventures of Huckleberry Finn*. Tom, Huck, and Joe Harper run away to uninhabited Jackson Island to escape the cares of the world and live like pirates, and here in Magic Kingdom you can escape the crowds on just such a retreat, including the river raft ride that gets you there.

Dock at **Tom's Landing**, where you have the choice to head right toward Aunt Polly's and that unpainted fence of hers, or left toward the Ambush Cave. Tom rarely chose the "right" direction, but you may want to as most visitors to the island will veer left. Start at **Old Scratch's Mystery Mine** ("Old Scratch" was

Southern slang for the devil, so think carefully about whether you want to enter his domain). Listen for bats dipping and diving, just as they did when Tom and his love interest Becky got lost in a cave. Further in, a wealth of gems sparkles in the walls, recalling the treasure Tom and Huck would find, buried by Injun Joe.

When you reach the end of Old Scratch's mine you're near **Injun Joe's Cave**, which Becky's father ordered sealed once the children found their way home, thus sealing Injun Joe's fate. The cave was opened again, only to find Injun Joe starved to death, but don't worry; it's unlikely his ghost haunts these underground caverns anymore. Go on in. It'll all be fine!

Pass by **Poor Ole Jim's Shack** on your way to the **Barrel Bridge**. (In Mark Twain's story, Jim was a slave belonging to Miss Watson, sister to Widow Douglas.) Then head over to **Aunt Polly's**, the home of Tom's kindly aunt who took him in when his mother died. Her house is just beyond, and it's a good place to pull up a rockin' chair and "set a spell" (meaning take a load off your weary feet).

Round the corner and drop in at **Harper's Mill**. Joe Harper was one of Tom's bosom buddies who accompanied Tom and Huck when the boys decided to run away. The mill was named for Joe's father. Then wave at Old Scratch again as you move on toward **Potter's Mill**, which refers to Muff Potter, drunkard and friend of Injun Joe, who was falsely accused of murdering the town's physician, Dr. Robinson. But Tom knew the truth, and stood up in court to reveal Injun Joe as the culprit.

Pass by **Huck's Landing** and on to **Superstition Bridge**, which transitions you from Tom Sawyer Island to **Fort Langhorn**, in part named for the fort in the Disney movie *Tom and Huck*, but also a tribute to Mark Twain's real name, Samuel Langhorne Clemens.

Follow the path to the left, to **Pappy's Fishing Pier** and into the fort, seeking out **Rifle's Roost**, where the soldiers seem to have a keen interest in those trainloads of passengers that whiz by every now and then. Go ahead, take a shot! You can make a quick getaway through the escape tunnel if need be.

River Pirate Ridge is a reminder of what might befall the unwary when traveling the **Rivers of America**, and finally, **Indian Territory** represents the end of the island and also the end of *The Adventures of Huckleberry Finn*.

          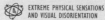

MISS-ABLE | IF YOU HAVE TIME | WORTH MAKING TIME FOR | NOT TO BE MISSED!
WILL ONLY WORRY YOUNG CHILDREN | MAY SCARE MANY YOUNG CHILDREN; FEW ADULTS | WILL SCARE MOST YOUNG CHILDREN; SOME ADULTS | MAJOR SCARE FACTOR
VISUAL DISORIENTATION | MILD PHYSICAL MOVEMENT | INTENSE FEELING OF MOTION | EXTREME PHYSICAL SENSATIONS AND VISUAL DISORIENTATION

COUNTRY BEAR JAMBOREE

Enter the frontier-style meeting hall and it immediately becomes obvious the show is not being performed for trappers and traders, it's being performed for—and by—the bears who would have been trapped and traded! The floor is covered in claw marks left by the woodland patrons and portraits on the wall give you a hint about the actors here. Even the trophy heads on the wall—Buff the buffalo, Max the deer, and Melvin the moose—are part of the show.

As the curtain rises, Gomer strikes up a tune on the piano and your bear host Henry welcomes you to an evening of backwoods entertainment. Henry first introduces the Five Bear Rugs, the most homespun country band you'll ever see. Then you're pulled into the story, as Wendell and Henry pick out a three-chord tune, Liver Lips McGraw plucks the steel guitar in honor of his true love, Henry and Wendell gently implore Momma not to whup "little Buford," and Trixie chimes in with a tender tale of heartbreak and woe. In addition, the heartbroken bears Bonnie, Bubbles, and Beulah lament their bad luck (seems all the guys that turn them on turn them down). Flirtatious Teddy Beara has a broken heart too, but at least she gets to sit on a pretty swing when she makes her entrance.

It's all knee-slappin' funny until the real star of the show, Big Al, takes his solo. And his song is definitely not of the humorous variety. Al's got problems, no doubt about that!

Reminiscent of the wonderfully social porch gatherings in the hills of the Southern states, the Country Bear Jamboree is hand-clappin,' foot-stompin' merriment, and a cool break on a hot day.

HIDDEN MAGIC The Country Bear Jamboree concept was one of the last things Walt Disney saw before his untimely death in December 1966. Walt loved the humorous idea of "these musical bears," so when the project they were initially intended for—a Mineral King ski resort in California—fell through, Imagineers Marc Davis, Claude Coats, and X. Atencio kept the idea alive, in Walt's memory, and brought the bears to Magic Kingdom in 1971.

 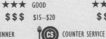

Dining in Frontierland

PECOS BILL TALL TALE INN AND CAFÉ

★★ $ 🍴(L) 🍴(D) 🍴(CS)

Boasting "the tastiest eats and treats this side of the Rio Grande," this Western-themed saloon is owned by Pecos Bill, the larger-than-life character from American folklore. His tall tales were first immortalized around cowboy campfires, then in storybook form, before becoming a segment in Disney's animated *Melody Time* movie in 1948.

The saloon is packed with mementos left by Bill's cowboy friends, from Jim Bowie and Davy Crockett to Zorro—all roads led to the saloon, it seems!—even if the timescale is wildly suspect. The story maintains that Bill opened the restaurant in 1878, but Crockett and Bowie died at the Alamo in 1836. Nearly all of Pecos Bill's friends in the Café were also featured in Disney films or TV:

- Johnny Appleseed in the 1948 animated classic *Melody Time*
- Railroad engineer Casey Jones (who actually died in a 1900 train wreck) in *The Brave Engineer* cartoon in 1950
- Davy Crockett in the 1955 live-action movie *King of the Wild Frontier* (compiled from TV programs)
- Paul Bunyan in a 1958 animated short
- Zorro in a 1950s Disney TV series
- Kit Carson in the 1977 movie *Kit Carson and the Mountain Men*
- Freed slave and railroad builder John Henry in a 2000 animated short
- Annie Oakley in the 2004 movie *Hidalgo*
- Jim Bowie in the 2004 major Disney movie remake of *The Alamo*

The only one of Bill's friends not to appear in a Disney film or program? Wild Bill Hickok; his TV series (1951–58) aired on CBS.

Counter-service Pecos Bill's is a great place for a burger (although it also does wraps, barbecue sandwiches, and salads, too) as it has an extensive topping bar to allow you to customize your meal.

★ MISS-ABLE

😊 WILL ONLY WORRY YOUNG CHILDREN

🌀(1) VISUAL DISORIENTATION

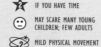
★(2) IF YOU HAVE TIME

🙂 MAY SCARE MANY YOUNG CHILDREN; FEW ADULTS

🌀(2) MILD PHYSICAL MOVEMENT

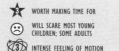
★(3) WORTH MAKING TIME FOR

☹️ WILL SCARE MOST YOUNG CHILDREN; SOME ADULTS

🌀(3) INTENSE FEELING OF MOTION

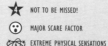
★(4) NOT TO BE MISSED!

😬 MAJOR SCARE FACTOR

🌀(4) EXTREME PHYSICAL SENSATIONS AND VISUAL DISORIENTATION

HIDDEN MAGIC You may start out in the Wild West when you go through the front door of Pecos Bill's, but, if you go right through the back, the theme changes from Western to Mexican as you get closer to Adventureland.

THE DIAMOND HORSESHOE

Essential Information: Not DDP

★★ $ (FOR SUBS AND SANDWICHES) $$$$ (FOR AN OCCASIONAL BUFFET DINNER)

This magnificently authentic early 1800s St. Louis saloon by the Mississippi River is open only at peak periods and, sadly, not for its original purpose. During its heyday it offered the Diamond Horseshoe Revue (and, later, the Diamond Horseshoe Jubilee), a hokey-but-fun Old West stage show featuring dancing girls, comedians, and singers, notably Slue-foot Sue, the first wife of Pecos Bill.

Now a seasonal counter-service option, Diamond Horseshoe serves a fairly standard array of subs and sandwiches and an occasional buffet dinner.

GOLDEN OAK OUTPOST

Essential Information: Not DDP

★ $

Golden Oak Outpost isn't just a quick-bite stop, it's also a nod to Walt Disney's Golden Oak Ranch north of Los Angeles. Movies and television shows with scenes shot at Golden Oak Ranch include *The Mickey Mouse Club*, *Old Yeller*, *The Muppet Movie*, *Little House on the Prairie*, *The Santa Clause*, and *Pirates of the Caribbean: Dead Man's Chest* and *Pirates of the Caribbean: At World's End*. The ranch features settings such as an urban business district, residential and rural backdrops, bridges, barns, cabins, and natural vistas. Frontierland's Golden Oak Outpost is a good representation of the ranch's rustic set style and serves sandwiches, flatbreads, and chicken nuggets.

★ POOR	★★ FAIR	★★★ GOOD	★★★★ EXCELLENT	★★★★★ GOURMET
$ UNDER $10	$$ $10–15	$$$ $15–$20	$$$$ $20–$25	$$$$$ $25+
BREAKFAST	LUNCH	DINNER	COUNTER SERVICE	TABLE SERVICE	TABLE SERVICE (TWO CREDITS)

Shopping in Frontierland

FRONTIERLAND PIN TRADING

The proprietor at this pin trading station is "Texas" John Slaughter, trail boss. "Texas" John Slaughter was a quiet Civil War veteran, cattleman, and Texas Ranger who served as sheriff in Cochise County and later as Arizona state representative. In his role as sheriff he was tasked with cleaning up the lawlessness in Tombstone, Arizona. Disney also produced *Texas John Slaughter*, a television Western series, in the 1950s and '60s. Check out **Big Al's** for Western-wear, coonskin caps, and toys.

BRIAR PATCH GIFT SHOP

You don't have to be thrown into the Briar Patch, as Br'er Rabbit was, to see the home he makes there. Simply visit the Briar Patch gift shop, and take a look at the vignettes along the back wall. Br'er Rabbit's most curious possession is the black and white picture of *Whistler's Mother* in his sitting room. In this instance *Whistler's Mother* is wearing bunny ears! Find **Splash Mountain** souvenirs here.

Liberty Square

Colonial America is faithfully recreated in Liberty Square, with its box-like red brick buildings trimmed in white, and you could be forgiven for thinking you've entered the pages of a historical novel set in Williamsburg, Virginia, during the founding of the country. The atmosphere here is exceptionally convincing, in part due to the fact that some of the details replicate historical icons every United States citizen can quickly identify. The Liberty Bell here is cast from the same mold as the original bell in Philadelphia, and you may recall seeing pictures of the Liberty Tree in your school textbooks, hung with lanterns to signify the thirteen original colonies.

 MISS-ABLE

WILL ONLY WORRY YOUNG CHILDREN

VISUAL DISORIENTATION

 IF YOU HAVE TIME

MAY SCARE MANY YOUNG CHILDREN; FEW ADULTS

MILD PHYSICAL MOVEMENT

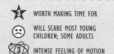 WORTH MAKING TIME FOR

WILL SCARE MOST YOUNG CHILDREN; SOME ADULTS

INTENSE FEELING OF MOTION

 NOT TO BE MISSED!

MAJOR SCARE FACTOR

EXTREME PHYSICAL SENSATIONS AND VISUAL DISORIENTATION

In fact, Liberty Square is so accurate, you'll even find a nod to the realities of colonial life immortalized in the pavement here. That brown gravelly pavement that winds through the area represents the sewage the good citizens of yore threw into the streets.

The area is small; in fact, the smallest in Magic Kingdom. But the stories here are immense, telling the tale of the human qualities of bravery and a drive for independence that led to a proud new nation.

THE HALL OF PRESIDENTS

The time period here is 1787 (notice the address on the front of the building) and the hall is built in the style of the historical meeting houses in which a new nation's independence was forged. While this may be a great place for a nap for some visitors, the level of detail here is extraordinary, right down to period-accurate stitching in the presidents' clothing.

The show begins with a key phrase from the preamble to the United States Constitution—"We the people"—and then moves on to tell the nation's story, from the signing of the Declaration of Independence through the Civil War, Emancipation, Western settlement, and on to other great American accomplishments. Then the curtain raises on a roll call of every United States president in the order they served, from George Washington to Barack Obama, who speaks to the endurance of the American Dream. Notice how the presidents react to each other's comments, with nods of the head and whispered comments.

The Hall of Presidents is a masterpiece of audio-animatronic technology and a long-awaited realization of the attraction Walt Disney was passionate about creating before his death. His work on the concept took a detour when the time available to create attractions for the 1964 World's Fair in New York did not allow for the full roll call of presidents, instead resulting in the attraction **Great Moments with Mr. Lincoln**, which would find its way to Disneyland.

★ POOR	★★ FAIR	★★★ GOOD	★★★★ EXCELLENT	★★★★★ GOURMET
$ UNDER $10	$$ $10–15	$$$ $15–$20	$$$$ $20–$25	$$$$$ $25+

 BREAKFAST   LUNCH   DINNER   COUNTER SERVICE   TABLE SERVICE   TABLE SERVICE (TWO CREDITS)

LIBERTY SQUARE RIVERBOAT

This gentle steamboat ride in a circle around **Tom Sawyer Island** tells the story of Samuel Clemens (a.k.a. Mark Twain) as he makes his 100th voyage on the riverboat. Throughout the ride, Clemens describes the journey, mentioning each place you pass and telling personal anecdotes about them. **Beacon Joe**, the leadsman who marks the channel to show if it's safe, sings the depth readings throughout your journey, and you can hear his analysis of the river conditions (by the way, did you know "mark twain" is a leadsman's call that indicates the water is two fathoms deep?). There is some danger from river pirates, but if you listen closely you can hear them as they carouse in **Wilson's Cave Inn**, so you're safe. For now.

Part of Liberty Square's story and Frontierland's story overlap here at the river. It is perfectly plausible that you would see a riverboat from New York's Hudson Valley in the American West. Neat little detail, hey?

HIDDEN MAGIC On the left side as you pass **Alligator Swamp**, you'll see a rustic cabin where a settler is fishing while his faithful dog helps from his perch in the boat. Watch the dog's tail each time a fish jumps.

HAUNTED MANSION

Welcome, foolish mortals, to this creepy Dutch-Gothic home in **New York's Hudson Valley**, where there is room for one more ghost—and you could be it! The Haunted Mansion is classic Disney storytelling at its finest, and the ride is a beautiful blend of designers Marc Davis's and Claude Coats's respective desires for a humorous theme and a dark theme. As you ride through this attraction, bear in mind it was originally meant to be a walk-through exhibit. Aren't you glad it isn't?

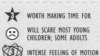
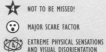

Prior to a 2011 makeover, there was no official backstory for the Haunted Mansion other than a loose assembly of vignettes that pointed toward an ill-fated bride and groom. Now the story is clear: That lonely bride waiting for the return of her seafaring groom is really a five-time bride waiting for her next victim!

As you near the front of the house, you will have the choice to go directly into the mansion or detour through the graveyard (choose the latter!). **Grandpa Marc** has pride of place as the first headstone, and rightfully so as he is a reference to **Marc Davis**, one of the primary Imagineers for the Haunted Mansion. **Francis Xavier** is next, referring to **X. Atencio**, who wrote "Grim Grinning Ghosts," the mansion's theme song.

The order in which you see the tombs hints at the order in which you will see their counterparts inside the mansion. First you'll see the composer's tomb, designed as a Ravenscroft organ, which plays a traditional version of the Haunted Mansion song when you touch the instruments on one side and a rather eerie version on the other side. At the end of the **Library tomb**, **Prudence Pock**, poetess, is having a bit of trouble finishing her latest ode. As you watch her ghostly pen writing, shout out the answer if you know the final word.

Master Gracey, resting under the central headstone, was the original homeowner until he made the wrong choice for a bride. Master Gracey is named in honor of Imagineer Yale Gracey, who created most of the illusions in Haunted Mansion. Next, that large stone coffin is the final resting place of the **Sea Captain**, the mariner whose portrait you see inside the Haunted Mansion just before you enter the line for the ride.

HIDDEN MAGIC

That's not Master Gracey swinging by his neck just before you leave the stretch room, it's the Ghost Host! Notice he says you can get out of the chamber "his way," just before you see him dangling high above you.

When you enter the mansion the first thing you come across is a changing portrait, setting the stage for the ghoulish goings-on. Proceed into the

---

★ POOR	★★ FAIR	★★★ GOOD	★★★★ EXCELLENT	★★★★★ GOURMET
$ UNDER $10	$$ $10–15	$$$ $15–$20	$$$$ $20–$25	$$$$$ $25+

 BREAKFAST   LUNCH   DINNER   COUNTER SERVICE   TABLE SERVICE   TABLE SERVICE (TWO CREDITS)

gallery (stretch room) where you are greeted by your Ghost Host. You'll also meet some of the mansion's former residents, whose quirks are revealed as the room stretches.

The gallery opens to a dark, cobwebby hallway where you board your **Doom Buggy**. Pass through a hallway of changing pictures into the library, where busts of ghost writers seem to watch your every move. A ghostly presence becomes obvious in the music room (you can see its shadow on the floor), then your doom buggy proceeds upstairs and down a hallway where skeletal hands are busy prying the lid off a coffin. Phantom sightings are increasing!

Enter the séance room, where **Madame Leota** conjures up apparitions, and as you move on, you enter a grand ballroom filled with haunts, some celebrating a birthday, others waltzing, dueling, knitting, and going about their afterlives. Move on to the attic where you meet the bride and her progression of grooms through their wedding portraits. Notice the gifts; each time the bride marries she moves up the social ladder and the wedding gifts get better.

HIDDEN MAGIC | What was the inspiration for the new "ghostly bride" story? When you are in the stretch room look at the picture of the woman holding a rose while sitting on a headstone. Notice how she doesn't seem particularly upset about the ax in George's skull? It was this detail that inspired the idea of a five-time, unremorseful bride.

Go out the window and down the slope of the roof, where a host of apparitions have taken the celebration into the family graveyard, and Madame Leota urges you to "hurry back." Beware, those hitchhiking ghosts are about to prove that you have symbolically become one of them!

REALITY CHECK | Lots of children are afraid of the dark rides, including Haunted Mansion. One way to deal with their fear is to give them a small light-up toy that they can use to vanquish the scary stuff. Works like a charm with most kids!

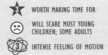

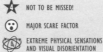

Dining in Liberty Square

LIBERTY TREE TAVERN

★★★ $$$$$

Welcome to late 1700s Boston for this full-service adventure into America's founding fathers' fare. The colonial ambience is a combination of period home and museum, with a rich sprinkling of antiques throughout the six main dining rooms. Look for a full alphabetized list of the Sons of Liberty, located on the back wall in the small room to the right of the entry.

The tavern offers a modern interpretation of the fare our New England predecessors enjoyed, with an à la carte lunch and fixed-fee family-style feast at dinner. The tavern features reliable, plentiful comfort food, and offers you a cool haven at lunchtime.

REALITY CHECK

It's ironic the Magic Kingdom boasts three restaurants with "tavern" in the name. According to our dictionary, a tavern "is a place of business where people gather to drink alcoholic beverages." Yet this is the only Disney park that doesn't serve alcohol! A person could feel hard-done by with taverns, taverns everywhere, but not a drop to drink. Pop over to one of the Magic Kingdom resorts if you would like a libation.

COLUMBIA HARBOUR HOUSE

★★★ $

Welcome to a quaint eighteenth-century inn situated in the port of a small Boston community. The nautical theme is carried throughout the building, which has a slightly mysterious air as the various sections are dedicated to either ghost ships or ships famously lost at sea. The fare features sandwiches, salads, soups, fried fish, and shrimp, with a couple of good vegetarian choices. It is all fresh, with portions large enough to share.

★ POOR	★★ FAIR	★★★ GOOD	★★★★ EXCELLENT	★★★★★ GOURMET
$ UNDER $10	$$ $10–15	$$$ $15–$20	$$$$ $20–$25	$$$$$ $25+
(B) BREAKFAST	(L) LUNCH	(D) DINNER	(CS) COUNTER SERVICE	(TS) TABLE SERVICE	(TS2) TABLE SERVICE (TWO CREDITS)

HIDDEN MAGIC

There is no Columbia Harbour in the United States, but there is a Columbia Point in Boston, hence its geographical basis is firmly in the Beantown area. "Harbour" (with the "u") would have been the correct spelling in the eighteenth century. It was only with the publication of Webster's 1806 dictionary that the American spelling of the word officially became "harbor."

SLEEPY HOLLOW REFRESHMENTS

$

The story is obvious here. You're in the small town of Sleepy Hollow from Washington Irving's tale "The Legend of Sleepy Hollow". Inspiration for the building comes from Irving's home, Sunnyside, in Tarrytown, New York. Here you'll find funnel cakes, ice cream, and beverages.

Shopping in Liberty Square

YE OLDE CHRISTMAS SHOPPE

You can tell Ye Olde Christmas Shoppe harkens back to colonial times because it's got all those extra e's in the name. Find the expected Christmas decorations and gifts here. **Heritage House** features Early American–themed gifts, and **Yankee Trader** has household items.

HIDDEN MAGIC

Look for a sign in the shape of a book on the corner of Ye Olde Christmas Shoppe (see photo insert). It advertises voice lessons by Ichabod Crane. Now look directly across the street and you'll see Sleepy Hollow Refreshments. Coincidence? Not a chance!

★ MISS-ABLE
😊 WILL ONLY WORRY YOUNG CHILDREN
🔄 VISUAL DISORIENTATION

★ IF YOU HAVE TIME
😊 MAY SCARE MANY YOUNG CHILDREN; FEW ADULTS
🌀 MILD PHYSICAL MOVEMENT

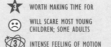
★ WORTH MAKING TIME FOR
😣 WILL SCARE MOST YOUNG CHILDREN; SOME ADULTS
🌀 INTENSE FEELING OF MOTION

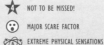
★ NOT TO BE MISSED!
😲 MAJOR SCARE FACTOR
🌀 EXTREME PHYSICAL SENSATIONS AND VISUAL DISORIENTATION

Fantasyland

Fantasyland is in the midst of a grand medieval tournament, with colorful tents, flags flying, jousting matches and horse competitions, visiting royalty, and even a rather raucous tea party, presided over by the comforting presence of both **Cinderella Castle** and the **Beast's Castle** (the latter of which opens in late 2012).

The stories in Fantasyland come from old Germanic folklore, "cleaned up" for Victorian sensibilities by the Brothers Grimm and later translated into English. Here, Disney tells its version of these classic tales, adding beloved characters of modern childhood memory.

HIDDEN MAGIC In the mural scene inside Cinderella Castle, where the prince has placed the glass slipper on Cinderella's foot, you'll find two Disney Imagineers (see photo insert). The man standing to the far left is John Hench, and the man directly behind the prince is Herbert Ryman.

"IT'S A SMALL WORLD"

★2 ★4 (UNDER 6)

As you walk through the line, look for world icons such as the **Eiffel Tower**, **Parthenon**, **Leaning Tower of Pisa**, and the **Taj Mahal** in the mural along the back wall. Unity is represented by the silver, white, and gold coloring, with no distinction according to country; this color choice subtly asks you to immerse yourself in the ride's lesson and to start thinking of the world's population as "similar," not "different." During your gentle float through the attraction, six regions of the world are represented by cheerful animatronic dolls, each with the icons and costuming of their homeland. You are viewing them as if through the eyes of a child, where everything is bright, colorful, and unaffected.

Pass under a bridge and you find yourself in **Europe**. Germany and drummers from England are the first to greet you, then England, Scotland (can you hear the bagpipes?), and Ireland come up on the left and Spain, Portugal, and France are on the right. The Netherlands and Italy are next (on the left) and finally, Austria and Switzerland make their appearance on the right.

Follow the story into **Asia** as you pass under a bridge, and come up on the Middle East and India on the left and Russia, Japan, and China on the right. Another transition bridge brings the story to **Africa**, where North Africa is represented on the left and Sub-Saharan Africa on the right. Notice how the colors on the left are "hot" colors, indicative of the desert, while those on the right are lush greens and bright yellows you would find in the jungle.

Next you'll journey to **Central** and **South America** as you pass under another transition bridge. The colors cool down in Antarctica on the left, while Mexico, the Andes, and Peru pulse with heat on the right. When you reach the **Rainforest** the colors are muted, dark, and mysterious; notice this is the one place where only animals are present.

Soft tropical colors reign as you transition into **The Islands**, with Hawaii on the left, Fiji on the right, Australia and Easter Island just beyond (on the left), and French Polynesia and New Zealand on the right. Your final transition bridge takes the story to the **Finale**, a celebration of unity as all countries come together in joyful companionship. As your boat lines up for unloading, take a look at the various signs and see if you can memorize a few ways to say "goodbye" in different languages.

The song may grate on your nerves, but the message is uplifting and young children adore this attraction.

REALITY CHECK

All that money you see in the water below you as you pass through "It's a Small World" fittingly goes to charities such as Give Kids the World and Kids Miracle Network, helping make wishes come true for children with life-threatening illnesses. Make a wish and make a wish come true!

⭐ MISS-ABLE

😊 WILL ONLY WORRY YOUNG CHILDREN

🔄 VISUAL DISORIENTATION

⭐ IF YOU HAVE TIME

😊 MAY SCARE MANY YOUNG CHILDREN; FEW ADULTS

🔄2 MILD PHYSICAL MOVEMENT

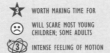

⭐ WORTH MAKING TIME FOR

😟 WILL SCARE MOST YOUNG CHILDREN; SOME ADULTS

3 INTENSE FEELING OF MOTION

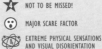

⭐ NOT TO BE MISSED!

😲 MAJOR SCARE FACTOR

EXTREME PHYSICAL SENSATIONS AND VISUAL DISORIENTATION

PRINCE CHARMING REGAL CAROUSEL

 (UNDER 5)

Cinderella used to own the carousel, but **Prince Charming** took possession of this fairground-style attraction in 2010. As part of the ongoing celebration, the story is that you're involved in medieval competitions. Notice how the horses are galloping, rather than walking or trotting, and some are wearing gear that might be used in jousting and other competitive matches. While the horse with the golden ribbon was never intended to be **Cinderella's horse** (being less elaborate than others, and with no symbol that ties it directly to Cinderella), it was a myth started by Cast Members and has since become part of the established story.

> **REALITY CHECK**
>
> You overdid it and now you have a screaming, crying child on your hands, and he or she is wailing like a siren right in the middle of Main Street. What's a parent to do? Stop, breathe, and remember there are dozens more just like yours all over the parks right now. This is your cue that it's time for a break from the overwhelming input, so either leave the park for some time in your resort pool or seek out the water play areas or quiet spots in the park.

DREAM ALONG WITH MICKEY

Showing on the **Castle Forecourt Stage** up to six times daily, this high-energy show featuring Mickey and his friends is an uplifting celebration of the power of believing in your dreams. But Donald is skeptical until Mickey shows him that "dreams really do come true."

First, Minnie believes in her dream of being a princess, and Snow White, Cinderella, Aurora, and their princes arrive. Goofy believes in his dream of being a pirate and Peter Pan, Wendy, Captain Hook, and Mr. Smee show up. But amidst all the sword fighting and adventure, Maleficent takes the stage and says she has a dream to share. And it's not a pleasant one!

This Disney villain changes dreams into nightmares, but Mickey and his pals enlist the audience in asserting that dreams *do* come true, and, with your help, succeed in vanquishing the evil fairy, Captain Hook, and Mr. Smee. At the end of the story, Donald finally understands the power of positive thinking and a grand celebration takes place, complete with fireworks and a feeling that anything is possible, if you only believe.

REALITY CHECK Fantasyland is undergoing a major transformation as the celebration expands to include the **Beast's Castle** and **Belle's charming little town**, as well as the seaside where Ariel makes her home. And while there has always been a circus present at the festival, the **Big Top** offerings are now even bigger. The pages of this new part of the story will begin to open in late 2012 and into 2013.

UNDER THE SEA—VOYAGE OF THE LITTLE MERMAID
(opening in late 2012)

 (UNDER 7)

Board your clam-mobile and head toward the seashore, where you meet **Scuttle**, who tells you that this ride is the story of how **Ariel** became a human. Plunge into an undersea grotto, where the little mermaid swims above you singing about her treasures. As you round the corner, there she is, wishing she could be where the people are. But Sebastian reminds Ariel her home is under the sea, where a colorful "hot crustacean band" has the whole kingdom flipping their fins in joyful celebration.

Flotsam and **Jetsam** segue into the next scene, where **Ursula** convinces poor unfortunate Ariel to give up her voice in return for legs. A bit of watery black magic happens, and the next scene allows you to eavesdrop on **Eric** and Ariel as their rowboat floats under the stars and Eric seems ready to kiss the girl.

Ursula's evil plan is thwarted, Ariel gets her voice back, the undersea creatures join **King Triton** in celebrating the marriage of Ariel and Eric, and the happy bride is now firmly a part of the human world.

 MISS-ABLE   WILL ONLY WORRY YOUNG CHILDREN   VISUAL DISORIENTATION

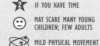 IF YOU HAVE TIME   MAY SCARE MANY YOUNG CHILDREN; FEW ADULTS   MILD PHYSICAL MOVEMENT

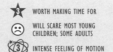 WORTH MAKING TIME FOR   WILL SCARE MOST YOUNG CHILDREN; SOME ADULTS   INTENSE FEELING OF MOTION

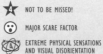 NOT TO BE MISSED!   MAJOR SCARE FACTOR   EXTREME PHYSICAL SENSATIONS AND VISUAL DISORIENTATION

It's a gentle retelling of the popular movie, perfect for young children but with enough whimsy that even adults can appreciate its enchanting charm.

SCUTTLE'S SCAVENGER HUNT

As you make your way toward Ariel's adventure, Scuttle invites you to scan the seashore in search of treasures from the human world in this interactive game. Ariel already has all the thingamabobs she needs, but who knows? Maybe you'll find something that will make her collection complete.

MAD TEA PARTY

As you wait for your turn, you can see that this attraction is mad (using the British term for "crazy") and that it's a tea party, but the story may seem a bit elusive as the floor rotates one way and riders make their cups spin another way. If you guess that the ride has to do with the scene from *Alice in Wonderland* where the **Mad Hatter** is throwing a very merry unbirthday party, you would be right. And just as Alice has issues with size, you too have shrunk down so small that you can fit in a teacup! Even the poor, tea-drunk mouse makes an appearance as he dizzily pops up from the center teapot. Although your journey doesn't take you anywhere, a bit of magic occurs here: Notice when you exit your tea cup that you suddenly find yourself transported to Walt Disney Whirled. (Groan!)

THE MANY ADVENTURES OF WINNIE THE POOH

 (UNDER 6)

That cuddly old bear gets into all sorts of mild mishaps, and here you are drawn into a re-telling of A. A. Milne's gentle tale, *Winnie-the-Pooh and the Blustery Day*, also adapted into an animated short by Walt Disney Productions in 1968. The story here starts before you enter the boarding area and, if

you're a parent, you'll be pleased to know youngsters will be happily occupied by scenery and pre-schooler–appropriate interactive puzzles and hands-on distractions featuring Pooh-bear and his friends, that make the time waiting in line pass quickly. Even adults in the right frame of mind will find them amusing. Traveling in your honey pot, the story begins in the **Hundred Acre Wood** as Gopher wishes you a Happy Winds-day, while Piglet, Pooh, and little Roo are blustered about on a gusty gale. Poor Owl isn't having much fun, lamenting his ruined home as you travel through the destruction. But even amid the chaos, nothing keeps our friend Tigger down for long! He invites you to bounce along with him, and you spring along to Pooh's house together, to warn the tubby cubby there are honey-stealing Heffalumps and Woozles about.

It's a stormy night for Pooh, both weather-wise and in his dreams, as your honey pot enters a cartoony circus of mischief-makers while rainwater builds around you. Suddenly, your honey pot begins to float on the rising flood, with each of Pooh's forest friends bobbing along with you. Finally, the sun comes out, a hero's celebration ensues, and Pooh is the happiest of all, landing smack in the middle of the honey tree.

ROOKIE MISTAKES

Don't forget to wash your hands often or bring a small bottle of hand sanitizer to the parks. Not only will your hands be gripping the same railings and ride restraints that thousands of other hands have touched, but the trend toward interactive lines provides even more opportunity for germy encounters.

MICKEY'S PHILHARMAGIC

Essential Information: Fastpass

In the shadow of **Cinderella Castle** stands the **Royal Concert Hall** (notice the crowns decorating the exterior), home to the **PhilharMagic Orchestra** under the

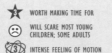
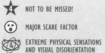

★ MISS-ABLE	★² IF YOU HAVE TIME	★³ WORTH MAKING TIME FOR	★⁴ NOT TO BE MISSED!
☺ WILL ONLY WORRY YOUNG CHILDREN	☺ MAY SCARE MANY YOUNG CHILDREN; FEW ADULTS	☹ WILL SCARE MOST YOUNG CHILDREN; SOME ADULTS	☹ MAJOR SCARE FACTOR
↻ VISUAL DISORIENTATION	↻² MILD PHYSICAL MOVEMENT	↻³ INTENSE FEELING OF MOTION	↻ EXTREME PHYSICAL SENSATIONS AND VISUAL DISORIENTATION

leadership of Mickey Mouse. This is where **Cinderella** and **Prince Charming** might enjoy a concert, but today you are among the special guests. Posters reveal that several Disney characters have a musical sideline when they're not working as actors.

As you enter the theater you can hear Goofy making preparations for the show. Predictably, he makes a mess of it, and just to add to the chaos Minnie Mouse announces the orchestra is missing. Put your 3-D glasses on as the curtain rises on a napping Donald, who is awakened and told to get ready for the show. He ignores Mickey's orders not to tamper with the sorcerer's hat, just as Mickey ignored Yen Sid's orders in *Fantasia*, and you can guess what will happen next!

HIDDEN MAGIC | The sorcerer in the "Sorcerer's Apprentice" segment of *Fantasia* is named Yen Sid, which is "Disney" spelled backward. The Imagineers occasionally use that technique with character names in the attractions, too.

Donald sets up the orchestra, but when he is cruel to a little flute that only wants to spread love and joy by playing the theme song for *The Mickey Mouse Club*, the whole orchestra turns on him. In a great magical swirl of instruments and flying duck, Donald finds himself, minus the hat, in the company of **Lumiere** from Disney's *Beauty and the Beast*, inviting him to "be our guest." As his dinner dances around him, Donald spies the hat and attempts to retrieve it.

With a crash, he arrives in a room full of bucket-carrying brooms from *Fantasia* (you know you're going to get wet, don't you?), where he angers a giant Momma broom by being mean to one of her little broomettes. He is washed away on a bucket-load of water, into the undersea realm of *The Little Mermaid*. Gems and jewels are everywhere as Ariel wishes she could be "part of their world." With an electrifying kiss, Donald, who is still trying to retrieve the hat, swims up toward the sun, where the future *Lion King*, Simba, brags about his destiny in a kaleidoscope of exuberant savanna celebrations until poof! With a sprinkling of pixie dust Tinker Bell and Donald are soaring over London, where Peter Pan and the hat are perched on the hands of Big Ben's clock tower.

Peter Pan and Tink tell Donald, "you can fly," and he's off on a wondrous journey—not to Neverland, but to Agrabah. Aladdin promises his lady-love Jasmine that he can show her the world, but instead it's Jasmine who shows (and gives) Donald the hat, which has touched down on Aladdin's magic carpet.

Just when Donald thinks the nightmare has finally ended, that pesky bird Iago knocks the hat off Donald's head. Donald dives after it, and as he spins into another vortex, Mickey appears, snatches the hat, puts it on his own head and saves the day. The world is right again as Mickey conducts the orchestra in a rousing finale, with a surprise ending (especially for poor Donald!).

The graphics in this story are incredible, but this cinematic experience really highlights the role music plays in making Disney movies so memorable.

PETER PAN'S FLIGHT

Essential Information: Fastpass

To get into this story, all you need to do is board your flying pirate ship, think happy thoughts, and off you go to **Neverland**! The classic tale of a boy who refuses to grow up unfolds before you as you fly through the Darling children's bedroom, out the window, and over the cityscape of nighttime London. Below you are **Big Ben** and **Tower Bridge**, and as you fly into the night look for Peter Pan and the children's shadows against the moon.

Next, you bank to the left, soaring past **Volcano Island** and the **Lost Boys' campfire**, but beware! **Mr. Smee** and **Captain Hook** take aim, firing a cannonball at your ship! It's a near miss as you round the corner toward **Mermaid Lagoon**, swing by an **Indian powwow**, and then it's on to **Skull Island**!

But all is not well. Wendy and the boys have been captured, and the poor girl is being forced to walk the plank while Peter Pan fights Captain Hook, with a hungry crocodile waiting nearby. With a bit of luck and some excellent

  MISS-ABLE
  WILL ONLY WORRY YOUNG CHILDREN
  VISUAL DISORIENTATION

IF YOU HAVE TIME
MAY SCARE MANY YOUNG CHILDREN; FEW ADULTS
MILD PHYSICAL MOVEMENT

WORTH MAKING TIME FOR
WILL SCARE MOST YOUNG CHILDREN; SOME ADULTS
  INTENSE FEELING OF MOTION

  NOT TO BE MISSED!
  MAJOR SCARE FACTOR
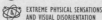 EXTREME PHYSICAL SENSATIONS AND VISUAL DISORIENTATION

sword fighting, Peter Pan takes over the ship, rescues the children, and Hook is left to deal with a pair of wide-open crocodile jaws.

 HIDDEN MAGIC See that barrel just outside the exit for Peter Pan's Flight? It reads "Fire Chief W. Ray Colburn Lost Boys Fire Brigade," and is a reference to Ray Colburn, fire chief for more than thirty years for the Reedy Creek Improvement District (Disney's privately owned "government" that oversees Walt Disney World).

PRINCESS FAIRYTALE HALL

(opening in late 2012)

 ★ ★(UNDER 7)

Princesses Aurora, Tiana, Cinderella, Rapunzel, and others are holding court, and you are invited to be their special guest. Young girls can't resist interacting with their favorite princess at this meet-and-greet, and adults will find it surprisingly emotional when their little princess has her turn. Bring your camera and an autograph book!

 ROOKIE MISTAKES Don't use a regular pen for character autographs. A fat pen or a marker is easier for the characters to hold. And remember, they can sign your T-shirt or hat, but only if you're not wearing it.

MAURICE'S COTTAGE

 ★ ★(UNDER 7)

Visit Belle's small provincial town, where her quaint cottage holds an enchanting secret. In *Beauty and the Beast*, Belle, held captive by the Beast, uses a magical hand mirror and sees her ailing father wandering lost in the woods, which convinces the Beast to allow her to go to her father's aid. He gives her the mirror to remember him by. Here in the cottage you step through a similar

 ★ POOR $ UNDER $10   ★★ FAIR $$ $10–15   ★★★ GOOD $$$ $15–$20    ★★★★ EXCELLENT $$$$ $20–$25   ★★★★★ GOURMET $$$$$ $25+

(B) BREAKFAST   (L) LUNCH   (D) DINNER   (CS) COUNTER SERVICE   (TS) TABLE SERVICE   (TS2) TABLE SERVICE (TWO CREDITS)

magical mirror in Maurice's workshop and are transported to the library in the **Beast's Castle**, where Belle and Lumiere host **Enchanted tales** with Belle, an interactive retelling of the story of *Beauty and the Beast*.

SEVEN DWARFS MINE TRAIN

(opening in late 2012)

  (UNDER 7)

This story begins in the cottage of the **Seven Dwarfs**, then it's off to work you go! Your visit occurs during the time when **Snow White** is keeping house for her industrious little friends, whose workday is just beginning.

Take a ride in a rickety mine train over hill and valley, along trails and through tunnels, on your way to the mine where "a million diamonds shine." Part dark ride, part coaster, your train car swings back and forth as you trundle along, accompanied by music from the animated movie. The Seven Dwarfs dig, dig, dig their way through their day, then you all return to their comfy cottage where Snow White greets you in happy celebration.

STORYBOOK CIRCUS

(opening late 2012 through 2013)

Technically a part of Fantasyland, Storybook Circus follows through on the celebration theme, but with a modern twist. In this part of the story, a traveling circus has come to town, complete with interactive games, flying elephants, stunt planes, and even a child-sized train that's blowing off a little steam.

DUMBO THE FLYING ELEPHANT

  (UNDER 6)

The circus has joined the celebrations going on in Fantasyland, and the star of the show, **Dumbo the Flying Elephant**, is no longer embarrassed about his jumbo-sized ears but instead revels in the happiness they can bring . . . and

 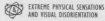

he's giving rides! A flock of storks similar to the one who first delivered Dumbo to his loving mother cheer you on as you soar above the fairgrounds.

While the twin Dumbo rides are standard carnival fare, the element of fantasy is strong for children, making it classic family fun.

BARNSTORMER HOSTED BY THE GREAT GOOFINI

Essential Information: 3 feet

Goofy has begun a traveling stunt plane business, presumably after his previous crop dusting venture in Toontown failed. Today he's offering you the chance to take an airplane ride so wacky it could only be piloted by "The Great Goofini" himself. If the banner advertising Goofini's style of flying doesn't scare you off, you're in for a flight like no other!

This is perfect "my first coaster" territory, with small hills, tight turns, and a feeling of flying that is quite convincing. It's terrific fun for youngsters, but even older kids and adults will find it packs a speedy little wallop!

CASEY JR. ROUNDHOUSE

Casey Jr. is the tender engine tasked with the job of hauling circus cars, some filled with animals, in the 1941 Disney movie *Dumbo*. He's here at the festival today with his live cargo still in their cars. And they're just spittin' to get out!

Kids love the spontaneous freedom of water play, and Casey's is the place to be when they need a cool-down on a hot day.

Dining in Fantasyland

CINDERELLA'S ROYAL TABLE

★★★ $$$$$

Cinderella welcomes you as her very special guests at a royal banquet held inside Cinderella Castle. The festival going on in Fantasyland is also being celebrated by Cinderella and her friends in sumptuous, regal style. The banquet is laid out in a lavish ballroom where medieval regalia abounds, from the stained glass windows to the banners and servers' costumes.

The story here is all-encompassing, from the special welcome and photo opportunity with Cinderella in the **Grand Hall,** to the "show" that introduces each princess in turn and then includes tableside visits from **Jasmine, Snow White, Aurora,** and **Belle.** Children find it enthralling and even some adults are bowled over by the detail, which includes a wand or princely sword for every diner, occasional appearances from the **Fairy Godmother,** and a photo package per group of four.

Cinderella's will take a big chunk from your wallet, and the food may not match up to the price. But where else can you dine in a castle (without visiting Europe!). Dinner is possibly the best value, with a choice of six entrees, including prime rib and pan-seared salmon.

ROOKIE MISTAKES More than any other restaurant, Cinderella's Royal Table and the Princess Storybook meals (at Epcot) book up fast. Unless you are staying at the Grand Floridian (which holds several reservation times aside specifically for their guests), you are unlikely to find any openings during your visit. Plan well in advance.

 MISS-ABLE
 WILL ONLY WORRY YOUNG CHILDREN
 VISUAL DISORIENTATION

 IF YOU HAVE TIME
 MAY SCARE MANY YOUNG CHILDREN; FEW ADULTS
MILD PHYSICAL MOVEMENT

 WORTH MAKING TIME FOR
WILL SCARE MOST YOUNG CHILDREN; SOME ADULTS
INTENSE FEELING OF MOTION

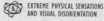 NOT TO BE MISSED!
 MAJOR SCARE FACTOR
 EXTREME PHYSICAL SENSATIONS AND VISUAL DISORIENTATION

PINOCCHIO VILLAGE HAUS

★★ $

Dive into the story of the little wooden puppet here, with a series of intricately themed rooms that offer murals, stained glass windows, and decorative effects, all in an alpine village setting that borrows heavily from the opening sequence of the movie. Each room is dedicated to a *Pinocchio* character, from **Gepetto** and **Jiminy Cricket** to **Figaro** and **Cleo**, while the main dining area represents a tavern and **Stromboli's** puppet show arena, complete with an interior "puppeteer's balcony." The **Monstro** room overlooks the "It's a Small World" loading area and the serving area is designed like an exterior courtyard that links back inside to the seven different rooms, providing a neat central point.

Sensibilities toward healthier dining find their most drastic effect here, where the totally uninspired former fare has been replaced by a much fresher counter-service version, with pizza, pasta, salad, subs, and chicken nuggets. The one drawback is this is one of the busiest restaurants in the park and it can feel frenzied much of the time.

GASTON'S TAVERN (opening late 2012 through 2013)

$$  (EXPECTED)

Yes, it's that "tavern" word again. Gaston's Tavern, which will offer counter-service only, is expected to be a typical nineteenth-century French inn, packed with rustic detail. Look for plenty of visual gags surrounding the rather bombastic movie fall guy **Gaston**, including his favorite chair and a fountain in the courtyard outside.

BE OUR GUEST RESTAURANT (opening late 2012 through 2013)

$$$$$ (AND EXPECTED)

This promises to be a real *Beauty and the Beast* extravaganza, with daytime counter-service and fine dining in the evening. Designed in three parts to look like the Beast's elegant castle (ballroom, art gallery, and West Wing), this could rival Cinderella's for a regal atmosphere and memorable setting. It will feature a "welcome" from **Mrs. Potts** and **Chip** and an interactive **Lumiere** doing the rounds (like Remy at Chefs de France in Epcot). The Imagineers have also hinted there will be snow here year-round—which could be quite a feat in the Sunshine State!

SNACKS AND QUICK SERVICE OPTIONS

$

For snacks and other quick-service options, try **Friar's Nook** (cheese dog, salads), **Storybook Treats** (sundaes, cookies, ice cream), and **Fantasyland Cart,** which peddles popcorn, frozen treats, and drinks. If you haven't had breakfast yet, try the **Enchanted Grove** for muffins and drinks. **Maurice's Amazing Popping Machine** is modeled on the wood chopping invention Belle's father invented, but you'll find popcorn filling his newest creation instead.

Shopping in Fantasyland

BIBBIDI BOBBIDI BOUTIQUE

Cinderella's transformation from a poor country girl to a regal princess is played out here every day, with young princesses having a makeover in preparation for a grand ball (or just a day in the park). There is a salon inside **Cinderella Castle** and at **Downtown Disney**. It's popular, so reserve early.

 MISS-ABLE   IF YOU HAVE TIME   WORTH MAKING TIME FOR   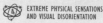 NOT TO BE MISSED!

 WILL ONLY WORRY YOUNG CHILDREN   MAY SCARE MANY YOUNG CHILDREN; FEW ADULTS   WILL SCARE MOST YOUNG CHILDREN; SOME ADULTS   MAJOR SCARE FACTOR

VISUAL DISORIENTATION   MILD PHYSICAL MOVEMENT   INTENSE FEELING OF MOTION   EXTREME PHYSICAL SENSATIONS AND VISUAL DISORIENTATION

MAGICAL MERCHANDISE

Castle Couture carries a wealth of Princess-ware, **Fantasy Faire** has all your PhilharMagic needs, **Hundred Acre Goods** has the obvious Winnie the Pooh merchandise, **Seven Dwarfs' Mine** is the place for Snow White toys and apparel, and **Sir Mickey's** carries hats, gifts, and apparel. Be sure to pop inside and look for the Giant from Disney's *Jack and the Beanstalk*. He's picking up the roof to see if Jack (in this case, Mickey Mouse) is inside.

Tomorrowland

As soon as you enter this part of the story, you're transported to the Earth of the future, when Tomorrowland has become the headquarters for the League of Planets. This is a working city filled with interplanetary beings with all the comforts and conveniences of home, and then some. Phones really are smart, robots deliver your newspaper and scuttle around collecting your garbage, aliens are an important part of the community, and the overriding theme is one of hope and progress.

SPACE MOUNTAIN

Essential Information: 3 feet, 8 inches; Fastpass

Starport Seven-Five (remembering 1975, the year Space Mountain opened) is an intergalactic port buzzing with the comings and goings of Tomorrowland visitors and various cargo transports required to keep a busy town running. This is your chance to blast off in your own space shuttle, but beware; it's dark out there in the cosmos!

The Starport has service to **Lunar stations, Earth stations, connecting systems**, and **Star Gates**, but you can be pretty sure you've booked return service back to Tomorrowland. Walk through the boarding area, settle into your shuttle, and you're off!

★ POOR	★★ FAIR	★★★ GOOD	★★★★ EXCELLENT	★★★★★ GOURMET
$ UNDER $10	$$ $10–15	$$$ $15–20	$$$$ $20–25	$$$$$ $25+

 BREAKFAST LUNCH DINNER  COUNTER SERVICE TABLE SERVICE / TABLE SERVICE (TWO CREDITS)

Remember we said it was going to be dark out there? Once you make the jump to hyper-speed, you won't be able to see much, so hold on tight. You're going to be dodging and dipping and experiencing weightlessness, and if that's not enough to crank up the thrill factor, wait until you hit the vortex near the end of your flight!

In fact, the track is no more aggressive than the average "wild mouse" coaster, but when you experience it in the dark it takes on a thrill level far above its inherent size and speed.

HIDDEN MAGIC

Notice the Earth stations listed on the sign just inside Space Mountain. They are:

- Tomorrowland Station MK-1, the station at Space Mountain: MK-1 refers to Magic Kingdom, where the first Space Mountain was built
- TL Space Station 77: Disneyland's ride, built in 1977
- Discovery Landing Station-Paris: Disneyland Paris's ride is located in Discoveryland
- Ashita Base-Tokyo: Tokyo Disneyland, with "ashita" meaning "tomorrow" in Japanese
- HK Spaceport E-TKT: Hong Kong Disneyland, and a nod to the use of E-tickets when the original Disneyland opened

TOMORROWLAND SPEEDWAY

  (UNDER 6)

This attraction is the odd man out, no longer relevant to Tomorrowland, nor to Fantasyland. When Tomorrowland was built, these slow-moving race cars represented the nation's fascinating with the automobile, and were in keeping with the theme of progress. Now, they're just a great way for children to safely drive a car without worrying about hitting a tree or backing out over the dog.

 MISS-ABLE
 WILL ONLY WORRY YOUNG CHILDREN
 VISUAL DISORIENTATION
 IF YOU HAVE TIME
 MAY SCARE MANY YOUNG CHILDREN; FEW ADULTS
 MILD PHYSICAL MOVEMENT
 WORTH MAKING TIME FOR
 WILL SCARE MOST YOUNG CHILDREN; SOME ADULTS
INTENSE FEELING OF MOTION
 NOT TO BE MISSED!
 MAJOR SCARE FACTOR
 EXTREME PHYSICAL SENSATIONS AND VISUAL DISORIENTATION

HIDDEN MAGIC The speedway has its own brickyard, just like the speedway in Indianapolis! It's just after the first bridge at the start of the race, and a reminder that it used to be the Tomorrowland Indy Speedway.

As part of the story, it could be argued this is an entertainment venue for intergalactic sports enthusiasts. But beware, the line moves even slower than the race cars.

TOMORROWLAND TRANSIT AUTHORITY

Recognizing the importance of "green" before green became popular, and in keeping with the theme of state-of-the-art technology, this brisk people mover is powered by linear induction using electromagnetic energy. Walt Disney was fascinated by transportation of every kind, and here, citizens of Tomorrowland can use the TTA for their commute into and out of the city.

Die-hard Disney fans tend to call it the **WED-Way**, using its former name (WED being Walter Elias Disney's initials), and because of its strange appeal, it has developed a cult following, much in the same way **Dole Whips** and **Epcot's Maelstrom** have done.

WALT DISNEY'S CAROUSEL OF PROGRESS

This attraction may seem out of place here, but the truth is that Tomorrowland evolved around the Carousel of Progress. The land was originally an interpretation of what the future might hold. Today, the carousel stands as the lone reminder of a future that came and went.

When it debuted at the 1964 World's Fair in New York City, the Carousel of Progress (called Progressland for the fair) showed folks how electricity changed the world, decade by decade, and its sponsor was General Electric.

It's a story of advancements in technology and sensibilities, and a celebration of lives made better by ingenuity.

The first scene in this story opens on Valentine's Day as the theater seats turn their way into the new century. John, your host, marvels over twenty-story buildings, movies, and cars as symbols of human progress, chiding those foolish **Wright Brothers** for working on some weird flying machine. **Electricity** hasn't arrived, but with all the modern conveniences it seems life couldn't be much better.

Next, you turn toward Independence Day in the 1920s where **Charles Lindbergh** makes his famous flight across the Atlantic and **Al Jolson** stars in a talkie. Electric plug-in lights have arrived, and so has indoor plumbing. Where there was once just open land, the town is growing up, with a hardware store across the street from John's house.

It's Halloween in the 1940s next, and technology has added refrigeration and dishwashers, and the world has widened due to television. But great advancements are ahead, including a giant leap into the Millennium. In the year 2000 the joy of Christmas is enhanced by ease and convenience, where virtual reality, high-definition television, and voice-activated appliances have made life easier. But there are drawbacks too!

Ultimately, the "great big beautiful tomorrow" they sing of is an ongoing thing, and while we don't know what tomorrow might bring, it's sure to be wonderful!

ASTRO ORBITER

The story here is simple, as is the ride. In the future, everyone gets around in spaceships and this is your chance for a flight. Take the gantry alongside **Rockettower Plaza** to a loading dock where you board your rocket for a journey through the stars (okay, maybe just in a circle above Tomorrowland). It's simple fairground fun with a space-age twist.

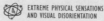

STITCH'S GREAT ESCAPE

Essential Information: 3 feet, 2 inches; Fastpass

Even in the future a city has need for a corrections unit, and you've been recruited as a prison guard at **Tomorrowland's Galactic Federation Prisoner Teleportation Center**, where they "teleport in the naughty."

The setting is exactly the same as it was when the former attraction, **Extra-TERRORestrial Alien Encounter**, showed here. However, the general consensus was that the former concept was "un-Disneylike" and far too frightening for children (and many adults). So it was **Stitch** to the rescue! The storyline changed, Stitch took the place of the alien, and Skippy's fate is far tamer than it was in the original production.

Move into the briefing room where **Sergeant C4703BK2704-90210** greets you, explaining that most prisoners the center deals with are Level 1, so your job should be easy.

HIDDEN MAGIC

The sergeant's nickname, 90210, is a famous Beverly Hills, California, zip code.

A transmission comes through, warning that the bad guy teleporting in is a Level 3 and you're going to have to deal with him in the **High Security Chamber** (where you strap into special seats with shoulder restraints). As the containment tube raises you find out the alien being transported is Stitch, and he's not interested in being detained.

Cannons fire at Stitch, Stitch spits at cannons, and the chamber plunges into near darkness as he breaks loose and begins running around. Your group of recruits experiences his antics in darkness as the guards shout to each other, trying to track him down. Stitch ultimately escapes by teleporting straight to a certain theme park in central Florida.

 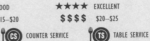

Some seats in the front row on either side of the entry aisle get spit on by Stitch, which—along with the darkness and loud noises—may unnerve young children.

BUZZ LIGHTYEAR'S SPACE RANGER SPIN

Essential Information: Fastpass

The 1995 blockbuster movie *Toy Story* involves a subplot featuring **Buzz Lightyear's** ongoing battle against the **Evil Emperor Zurg**, and here, that story is explored further, but in the form of a fairground shoot-em-up turned video game. As part of the story of Tomorrowland, you're at the **Headquarters for Star Command**, a futuristic peacekeeping force.

ROOKIE MISTAKES

You don't have to keep pulling the trigger to shoot at the targets in Space Ranger Spin. Simply hold the trigger in and the blaster will shoot continuously. And remember, just like a real fairground shooting gallery, the smaller targets and those farther away will score bigger points!

Enter the **Star Command** of Andy's imagination, where **Buzz Lightyear**, head Space Ranger, warns of yet another threat to galactic harmony. Zurg has stolen a crystolic fusion power unit, and Buzz needs a whole batch of Junior Space Rangers (you!) to help bring the evil emperor and his robot minions to justice.

Head to the flight deck, board your space cruiser, and get ready to shoot the robot hordes down with laser cannon ion pulses. You have time for a little bit of practice before heading into battle, then you're off to a wacky alien world, where your success rate will determine whether or not you advance to a position higher than **Junior Space Ranger**.

You've defeated Zurg, but as glorious as your triumphant return is, there's a tiny hint suggesting your next mission could begin soon. Remember **Stitch**

 MISS-ABLE
WILL ONLY WORRY YOUNG CHILDREN
VISUAL DISORIENTATION

 IF YOU HAVE TIME
MAY SCARE MANY YOUNG CHILDREN; FEW ADULTS
MILD PHYSICAL MOVEMENT

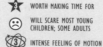 WORTH MAKING TIME FOR
WILL SCARE MOST YOUNG CHILDREN; SOME ADULTS
INTENSE FEELING OF MOTION

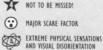 NOT TO BE MISSED!
MAJOR SCARE FACTOR
EXTREME PHYSICAL SENSATIONS AND VISUAL DISORIENTATION

making his great escape to central Florida? Take a look at the lower left corner of the mural just across from the ride photo area. Looks like trouble is on the way!

MONSTERS, INC. LAUGH FLOOR

Human visitors file through a portal to **Monstropolis** and into the stand-up comedy club hosted by **Mike Wazowski**, the green one-eyed monster from Disney-Pixar's movie, *Monsters, Inc.* Your goal is to fill up the energy tube with laughter, which has been proven to be ten times more powerful than screams. Various monster comedians are on hand to garner the "gigglewatts," and humans can also text their own jokes into the show. But **Roz**, the deep-voiced manager, isn't convinced. She'll be watching Mike and she'll be watching you. Beware, you might be "That Guy!"

Dining in Tomorrowland

COSMIC RAY'S STARLIGHT CAFÉ

When you step through the doors, you enter a lounge where the entertainment is provided by a futuristic lounge lizard by the name of **Sonny Eclipse**, from Yoo Nork on the planet Zork. Restaurant owner **Cosmic Ray** discovered Sonny performing his Bossa Supernova at cosmic weddings and space mall openings around the galaxy and offered him a full-time gig in Tomorrowland. Sonny performs a repeating twenty-five-minute set of music and comedy backed by his (invisible) **Space Angels**, marking this out as one of the real "hidden" attractions of the park.

For dining at Ray's take your pick from three "bays"—burgers, chicken, and sandwiches. A great toppings bar allows you to dress up your meal any way you want it.

★ POOR   ★★ FAIR   ★★★ GOOD   ★★★★ EXCELLENT   ★★★★★ GOURMET
$ UNDER $10 $$ $10–15 $$$ $15–$20 $$$$ $20–$25 $$$$$ $25+
 BREAKFAST   LUNCH   DINNER    COUNTER SERVICE   TABLE SERVICE   TABLE SERVICE (TWO CREDITS)

Sonny Eclipse was literally created in the dark. The intergalactic crooner's voice is provided by the smooth tones of blues singer-songwriter **Kal David**, who played with the likes of Etta James, Bonnie Raitt, Johnny Rivers, Ringo Starr, and B. B. King, and has his own blues club in Palm Springs with wife Lauri Bono. Kal also performed the "Unhealthy Living Blues" song in **Goofy About Health** at the former **Wonders of Life** pavilion in Epcot. He worked with Disney Imagineer George Wilkins to create Sonny at George's own studio at home. There was just one problem—George didn't have a vocal recording booth. So Kal sang all the tracks for Sonny in George's laundry room . . . which didn't even have the convenience of a light!

TOMORROWLAND TERRACE

★ $ 🍴L 🍴D 🍴CS

It's hard to put much of a story to this counter-service option between Tomorrowland and Main Street, U.S.A., as it has changed so many times over the years (it is currently on its fourth menu in seven years). Sadly, the Terrace ditched its health-conscious Noodle Station approach in 2010 for another burger-and-chicken outlet. Thankfully, there is also the choice of pasta and salads.

THE WISHES DESSERT PARTY AT TOMORROWLAND TERRACE

Essential Information: Book on 407-939-3463

$$$$** (ADULTS) AND **$$ (3- TO 9-YEAR-OLDS)

While **Tomorrowland Terrace** isn't a stellar choice for most of the day, it does boast a great Magic Kingdom "extra," the **Wishes Dessert Party**. Each evening it offers a viewing of the spectacular nightly fireworks from its dining terrace with a delicious self-serve dessert selection.

SNACKS AND QUICK SERVICE OPTIONS

LUNCHING PAD ★ $ AUNTIE GRAVITY'S GALACTIC GOODIES $

There are two other quick counter-service options with outdoor seating in Tomorrowland. At the base of Astro Orbiter is the well-named **Lunching Pad** (hot dogs, pretzels, drinks) and **Auntie Gravity's Galactic Goodies** for ice-cream, smoothies, and drinks. Note that Auntie Gravity's is not available on the Disney Dining Plan.

Shopping in Tomorrowland

MAGICAL MERCHANDISE

Space Mountain's Shop, featuring apparel and space-themed souvenirs, is housed in the Tomorrowland Light and Power Company. Notice the power lines above you, the towers along the side of the building, and the satellite receivers out front. You'll also find the **Tomorrowland Video Arcade** here. **Mickey's Star Traders** carries Stitch gear, apparel and house wares. **Merchant of Venus** (a takeoff on "The Merchant of Venice") teleports in Stitch-themed apparel and other Stitch stuff, including, apparently, Stitch himself, who is now stuck in the ceiling.

Parades, Tours, and Events

To book, call 407-WDW-TOUR or book online at *www.disneyworld.com*.

CELEBRATE A DREAM COME TRUE PARADE

Every good hometown parade starts with a marching band, and Magic Kingdom's is no exception. The **Grand Marshal** family riding in a fancy car comes next (that could be your group! Arrive at the park early, wear something conspicuously Disney, look eager, and hope for the best), then it's time to celebrate with all the Disney characters decked out in their party-wear, interacting with guests as the festivities make their way along Main Street.

★ POOR   ★★ FAIR   ★★★ GOOD   ★★★★ EXCELLENT   ★★★★★ GOURMET
$ UNDER $10 $$ $10–15 $$$ $15–$20 $$$$ $20–$25 $$$$$ $25+
 BREAKFAST    LUNCH   DINNER   COUNTER SERVICE   TABLE SERVICE   TABLE SERVICE (TWO CREDITS)

The lead float allows your hosts, **Mickey and Minnie**, to encourage you to celebrate "dreams come true," followed by floats with characters from *Pinocchio*, *Aladdin*, *Dumbo*, *Mary Poppins*, *Peter Pan*, *Alice in Wonderland*, *Cinderella*, *Beauty and the Beast*, *The Little Mermaid*, and *The Princess and the Frog*. The parade runs daily at 3 P.M.

MAIN STREET ELECTRICAL PARADE

When the sun goes down, the lights come on! And what a spectacular parade of lights it is. Tinker Bell's float is at the head of the glittering cavalcade, which includes floats with Goofy, Mickey and Minnie, and Alice and the Cheshire Cat. Cinderella waves from her sparkling pumpkin coach while Prince Charming holds the glass slipper under a canopy of lights, with lords and ladies dancing around them. Pinocchio and his pals are up to no good, Pete and his dragon Elliott are on hand, and Big Ben shines like a beacon, leading the way for Peter Pan and Captain Hook, with poor Mr. Smee relegated to a rowboat behind them. Snow White and the Seven Dwarfs show off the day's riches and it all ends with a patriotic display.

No one does a parade better, and this one has it all: glittering lights, bouncy music, and an aura of nostalgia that can only come from one of the longest running and most beloved pageants Disney has ever created. Check your park Times Guide when you visit, as parade times vary.

THE MAGIC, THE MEMORIES AND YOU!

This is a projection show on the castle, but words can hardly describe the immense creativity of this utterly compelling show, which runs for approximately 20 minutes before the **Wishes Nighttime Spectacular** starts. Five hundred pictures of the day's guests appear, but the real jaw-dropper is the way the castle seems to transform before your eyes. We won't give any of it away. You must see it for yourself!

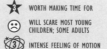
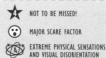

WISHES NIGHTTIME SPECTACULAR

Only Disney could weave a story into a fireworks show and have the color and style of the bursts create mental images of the characters they are talking about. As the show starts, your host **Jiminy Cricket** reminds you that wishes can come true, leading to a host of Disney characters who "appear" in song and through the colors of the fireworks, telling us their fondest wishes.

REALITY CHECK

Do you have children who are wary of fireworks? Watch **Wishes** from the beach at the Polynesian Resort and you can enjoy the Magic Kingdom's nightly pyrotechnics from a comfortable distance.

First it's Hercules in bold reds and whites; Cinderella is represented by diamond engagement rings; Belle and the Beast are grand banner-style and heart-shaped bursts; Genie from Aladdin appears as a sparkling blue cluster, granting wishes through multifingered flares; and the brooms from Fantasia march along in a series of single red shots.

Suddenly the story turns dark. The Disney villains have arrived! The evil Queen from Snow White shows up as crackling, chaotic, white explosions and smoky, green fog, but her dastardly intentions are swept away by the Blue Fairy, who casts a white fan across the sky. Believing in the power of our wishes again leads to glittering cascades, enormous waterfalls that fill the sky, and a colorful grand finale that leave you nearly breathless!

ROOKIE MISTAKES

Don't miss Tinker Bell's flight at the beginning of **Wishes**. After Jiminy Cricket tells you wishes can come true, Tink makes her nightly flight from a turret on the castle to Tomorrowland, and the effect is quite magical.

★ POOR   ★★ FAIR   ★★★ GOOD   ★★★★ EXCELLENT   ★★★★★ GOURMET

$ UNDER $10 $$ $10–15 $$$ $15–$20 $$$$ $20–$25 $$$$$ $25+

 BREAKFAST   LUNCH   DINNER   COUNTER SERVICE   TABLE SERVICE   TABLE SERVICE (TWO CREDITS)

The Resort-Only monorail out of Magic Kingdom stops at the Transportation and Ticket Center at the end of the day. Use it if the regular monorail has a long wait. And don't forget to check the line for the ferry, which is often quicker if you're not among the first out of the park at night.

WISHES FIREWORKS CRUISE

Essential Information: Reserve on 407-WDW-PLAY

View the nightly **Wishes** fireworks from a guided pontoon boat out on the waters of **Seven Seas Lagoon**. The **Basic Cruise** includes a boat and driver, water, soda, and light snack for up to eight people, but no piped-in music from the show. The **Premium Cruise** adds music and can hold up to ten people. They are not cheap options, but they offer a unique opportunity repeat visitors may want to try.

KEYS TO THE KINGDOM

Essential Information: Daily; lunch included; no under 16s; meet at City Hall

One of Disney's most popular **backstage tours**, this five-hour adventure delves deep into the creation of Magic Kingdom and a myriad of small details that bring the whole experience to life. Plus, you get to visit the underground **Utilidors** (the Disneyfied term for a utility corridor) which is seriously cool!

DISNEY'S FAMILY MAGIC

Essential Information: Daily, recommended for ages 4–10 but no restrictions; meet at City Hall

Spend an enjoyable two hours on a scavenger hunt, figuring out clues that will put a stop to a certain Disney villain's evil plot. Meet and interact with characters during this special family-friendly experience.

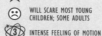
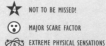

★ MISS-ABLE   ★ IF YOU HAVE TIME   ★ WORTH MAKING TIME FOR   ★ NOT TO BE MISSED!

☺ WILL ONLY WORRY   ☺ MAY SCARE MANY YOUNG   ☹ WILL SCARE MOST YOUNG   ☺ MAJOR SCARE FACTOR
  YOUNG CHILDREN   CHILDREN; FEW ADULTS   CHILDREN; SOME ADULTS

↻ VISUAL DISORIENTATION   🌀₂ MILD PHYSICAL MOVEMENT   🌀₃ INTENSE FEELING OF MOTION   🌀₄ EXTREME PHYSICAL SENSATIONS
                                                                                          AND VISUAL DISORIENTATION

THE MAGIC BEHIND OUR STEAM TRAINS

Essential Information: Mon., Tues., Thurs., Sat.; no under 10s; meet at Guest Relations

This is a thoroughly engrossing tour that even nonrailroad buffs will enjoy. Spend three hours alongside the engineers as they prepare the steam trains for the day, visit the backstage roundhouse, then take a ride around Magic Kingdom before the park is even open. Yes, it's early, but those trains have work to do!

REALITY CHECK Also see Backstage Magic, Holiday D-Lights, and Yuletide Fantasy, which start in Epcot before visiting Magic Kingdom.

PIRATE AND PALS FIREWORKS VOYAGE

Essential Information: Mon., Tues., Thurs., Sat., meet at Disney's Contemporary Resort

Join **Patch the pirate** on a swashbuckling **Seven Seas Lagoon** adventure. Captain Hook and Mr. Smee are on hand as you sail off into the moonlight (bring your camera!), where Patch leads you in sing-alongs and Disney trivia contests. Then, your pirate party has a fantastic view of **Wishes** from the comfort of your ship. As you head back to dry land you'll hear the story of **Peter Pan** . . . with a certain resident of Neverland awaiting your return!

Holidays at Magic Kingdom

Walt Disney World is magical all year round, but it takes on an added flair during holiday periods, with special decorations and seasonal events. And while all of the Disney theme parks dress up for Christmas, Magic Kingdom is especially stunning when Cinderella Castle is decked out in its glittering finery.

MICKEY'S NOT SO SCARY HALLOWEEN PARTY

Essential Information: Prices vary by night; ages 3–9. Call 407-W-DISNEY.

Mickey throws a fanciful dress-up party on select nights from mid-September to early November. As the title suggests, Mickey's party is heavy on the fun, light on the fright, making it terrific family fare, including a special Boo To You Halloween Parade, trick or treating, dance parties, costumed characters, and the spectacular Happy Hallo-Wishes fireworks show. Reserve your tickets early!

MICKEY'S VERY MERRY CHRISTMAS PARTY

Essential Information: Prices vary by night; ages 3–9. Call 407-W-DISNEY.

Mickey invites you to join him in celebration on select nights from early November through mid-December. This delightful experience includes **Mickey's Once Upon a Christmastime Parade**, special **Celebrate the Season shows**, costumed characters, cookies, hot cocoa, **snow on Main Street**, and **Holiday Wishes**. This specially ticketed event sells out quickly.

ROOKIE MISTAKES Mickey's Halloween and Christmas parties start at 7 P.M., but you can enter the park at 4 P.M. using your special party ticket. You will be given a wristband allowing you to remain in the park after the nonparty guests depart.

NIGHT OF JOY

Essential Information: See *www.disneyworld.com* for this year's schedule and to book online.

This festival of Christian music takes place from 7:30 P.M.–1 A.M. on two select nights in early September and features headliner Christian rock, pop, and gospel groups. Some attractions are open.

  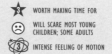 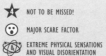

★	MISS-ABLE	★2	IF YOU HAVE TIME	★3	WORTH MAKING TIME FOR	★4	NOT TO BE MISSED!
☺	WILL ONLY WORRY YOUNG CHILDREN	☺	MAY SCARE MANY YOUNG CHILDREN; FEW ADULTS	☹	WILL SCARE MOST YOUNG CHILDREN; SOME ADULTS	☹	MAJOR SCARE FACTOR
⟳	VISUAL DISORIENTATION	⟳2	MILD PHYSICAL MOVEMENT	③	INTENSE FEELING OF MOTION	④	EXTREME PHYSICAL SENSATIONS AND VISUAL DISORIENTATION

Write Your Own Story

Write Your Own Story

Write Your Own Story

Write Your Own Story

Write Your Own Story

159

Write Your Own Story

MAGIC KINGDOM

MAIN STREET, U.S.A.

1. City Hall
2. Town Square Theater
3. Fire House 71
4. Main Street Railroad Station
5. Tony's Town Square Restaurant
6. Casey's Corner
7. Crystal Palace

ADVENTURELAND

8. Swiss Family Treehouse
9. Magic Carpets of Aladdin
10. The Enchanted Tiki Room
11. Jungle Cruise
12. Pirates of the Caribbean
13. Tortuga Tavern

FRONTIERLAND

14. Splash Mountain
15. Big Thunder Mountain Railroad
16. Tom Sawyer Island
17. Country Bear Jamboree
18. Pecos Bill Tall Tale Inn and Café

LIBERTY SQUARE

19. The Hall of Presidents
20. Liberty Square Riverboat
21. Haunted Mansion
22. Liberty Tree Tavern

FANTASYLAND

23. "it's a small world"
24. Prince Charming Regal Carrousel
25. Dream Along with Mickey
26. Under the Sea—Journey of the Little Mermaid
27. Mad Tea Party
28. The Many Adventures of Winnie the Pooh
29. Mickey's PhilharMagic
30. Peter Pan's Flight
31. Princess Fairytale Hall
32. Maurice's Cottage
33. Seven Dwarfs Mine Train
34. Cinderella's Royal Table
35. Be Our Guest Restaurant
36. Gaston's Tavern
37. Dumbo the Flying Elephant
38. Barnstormer hosted by The Great Goofini

TOMORROWLAND

39. Space Mountain
40. Tomorrowland Speedway
41. Tomorrowland Transit Authority
42. Walt Disney's Carousel of Progress
43. Astro Orbiter
44. Stitch's Great Escape
45. Buzz Lightyear's Space Ranger Spin
46. Monsters, Inc. Laugh Floor
47. Cosmic Ray's Starlight Café

SPECIAL EVENTS

48. Parade Route

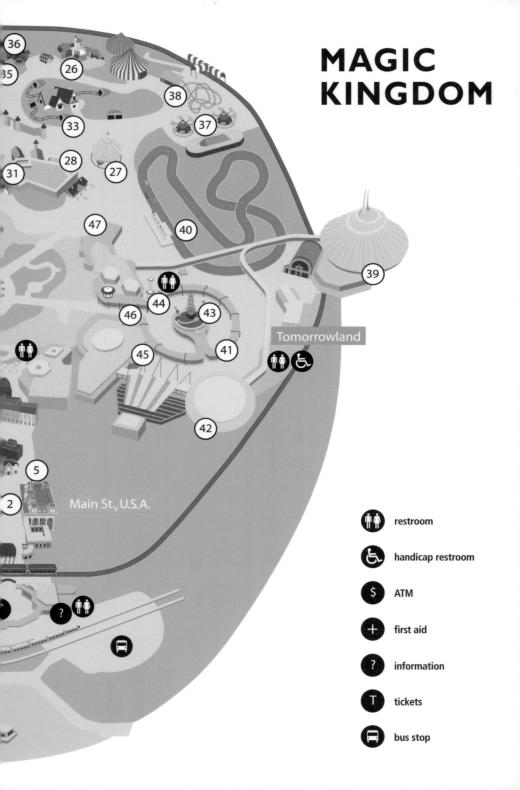

MAGIC KINGDOM

Tomorrowland

Main St., U.S.A.

restroom

handicap restroom

$ ATM

+ first aid

? information

T tickets

bus stop

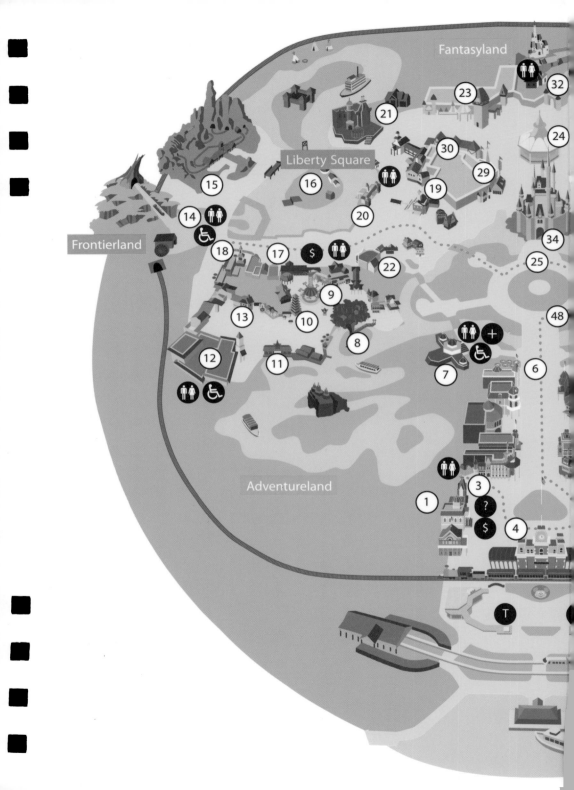

Chapter 4

A World of Discovery:
Epcot

THE STORY OF THE MAGIC KINGDOM was born from Walt Disney's desire to create a better place for parents and children to enjoy together, but Epcot was born from his passion for making the whole world a better place, based on conservation, technology, and cooperation. Epcot was originally supposed to be the Experimental Prototype Community of Tomorrow, a working community with a sense of progress, ecological awareness, and forward-thinking at its very heart. Although Epcot did not become a working city, the stories told by the attractions retain the ideals Walt set out to achieve.

Epcot is shaped like a figure eight; Future World is at the front, World Showcase is at the back, and Showcase Plaza acts as a transition point between the two. Future World's main focus is creativity and technology while the World Showcase allows you to take a journey through eleven countries, highlighting the iconic elements of each country, with a surprise or two thrown in for good measure.

Practical Information

Guest Relations is to the far right of the turnstiles. Find wheelchairs and stroller rentals on the left before you reach Spaceship Earth, lockers to the right. The Baby Care Center and First Aid Center are located near the Odyssey Center between Test Track and Mexico.

Future World

It isn't only the attractions that tell a story here in Epcot, it's the design of the park itself. In the case of Future World, which is all about thinking in new and better ways, you are symbolically inside a **giant brain**!

The right side of Future World represents the **right lobe**, and the attractions here concentrate on **creative thinking**. The atmosphere is soft, rounded, and flowing. The left side, or **left lobe,** does the factual, structured reasoning, and the attractions are more **scientific and technological**, while the design elements feature straight lines. **Innoventions Plaza** is the meeting of the two halves.

And now, let's discover those attractions!

Look at the circles in the pavement where the **pin trading center** is located. They represent the flowing nature of the right brain while the awnings overhead represent the linear reasoning of the left brain. With a little right-brain thinking, the red pavement could be mistaken for blood, since we're standing inside the brain, but the left-brain would be correct in telling us it's just the same Kodak Red you see in the Magic Kingdom, meant to enhance your pictures.

SPACESHIP EARTH

The mural to your right as you enter this Epcot icon tells the story in one quick picture: From the beginning of our existence the quest to communicate has compelled humans to find new ways to express their inner world to the world around them. Once inside, the story unfolds through lifelike audio-animatronics and realistic settings, snapshots of milestone moments in the journey toward a global neighborhood.

As you ascend the first hill, your picture is taken for a fun interactive element toward the end of your ride, so ham it up! Then, begin the timeline of human expression when communication was in its infancy; when prehistoric humans survived and thrived with a newfound ability to make their intentions known to one another, and to record the world around them on cave walls. The **Egyptians** perfected a mobile means of relaying information through the picture-words of hieroglyphics applied to papyrus, but it was the **Phoenicians** who really picked up the ball and ran with it, creating a written language we still use today.

Greek scholars took the spoken word to a new art form, through theater, debate, and fanciful storytelling, while the **Roman Empire** shattered former boundaries of communication and went out into the world with their own message. Though the **Dark Ages** brought near-silence to creative expression, the **Renaissance** was just around the corner, as it is during your journey

 MISS-ABLE

WILL ONLY WORRY YOUNG CHILDREN

VISUAL DISORIENTATION

 IF YOU HAVE TIME

MAY SCARE MANY YOUNG CHILDREN; FEW ADULTS

MILD PHYSICAL MOVEMENT

 WORTH MAKING TIME FOR

WILL SCARE MOST YOUNG CHILDREN; SOME ADULTS

INTENSE FEELING OF MOTION

 NOT TO BE MISSED!

MAJOR SCARE FACTOR

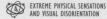 EXTREME PHYSICAL SENSATIONS AND VISUAL DISORIENTATION

toward the top of Spaceship Earth. Once again, the world opened up to a magnificent burst of information that would lead us to the printing press, stirring artworks, and finally, the opportunity to share our thoughts with the entire world—and beyond—in a split second via the **World Wide Web.**

It is fair to say Spaceship Earth's message has changed over time, from the poetic narration of **Larry Dobkin**, the grandfatherly lesson as told by former news anchorman **Walter Cronkite**, and the inspiring tones of **Jeremy Irons**, to today's rather simplified version, relayed by actress **Judi Dench**. It is a story of coming full circle, from a few guttural noises that allowed cavemen to hunt as a team to 140-character snippets on the Internet that tell the world our current mood. The question is no longer one of having the tools to communicate effectively; it is a question of whether what we put out into the world is meaningful, or just so much noise.

PROJECT TOMORROW

At the end of your ride on **Spaceship Earth**, Project Tomorrow offers several hands-on exhibits exploring creative communication solutions. Create a digital human body with the **3-D Body Builder**; keep your "smart car" out of trouble with the **Super Driver video simulator**; **Power Builder** challenges you to figure out smart energy solutions; and **Inner Vision** explores the future of medicine in a touchscreen matching game.

REALITY CHECK | Don't forget to look for your image on the giant globe as you enter Project Tomorrow. Remember that face you made when your picture was taken? Now everyone has the chance to see you at your goofiest!

 MISS-ABLE   IF YOU HAVE TIME   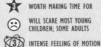 WORTH MAKING TIME FOR   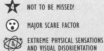 NOT TO BE MISSED!

☺ WILL ONLY WORRY YOUNG CHILDREN   ☺ MAY SCARE MANY YOUNG CHILDREN; FEW ADULTS   ☹ WILL SCARE MOST YOUNG CHILDREN; SOME ADULTS   ☺ MAJOR SCARE FACTOR

⟲₁ VISUAL DISORIENTATION   ⟲₂ MILD PHYSICAL MOVEMENT   ⟲₃ INTENSE FEELING OF MOTION   ⚛ EXTREME PHYSICAL SENSATIONS AND VISUAL DISORIENTATION

INNOVENTIONS EAST AND INNOVENTIONS WEST

THE SUM OF ALL THRILLS (WITH INVERSION)   STORM STRUCK / WHERE'S THE FIRE

These twin complexes showcase the cutting-edge technology of the real-world companies that sponsor each exhibit. In some ways it's like a trade show, and it could be argued the "educational" tag that plagued Epcot when it opened lives on in Innoventions, but this hands-on, experiential lesson is way more fun than any textbook. Think of it as a technological playground—where you might just learn something!

At **Innoventions East** find **The Sum of All Thrills**, where budding engineers use their math and physics skills to design their own roller coaster and then take it for a spin! It's as tame or as dynamic as you make it, with a vast range of motion available using Kuka Robotic Arm technology (height restrictions of 4 feet without inversion; 4 feet, 6 inches with inversions). **Test the Limits Lab** encourages you to do your worst against household products, just as engineers would in a safety testing facility. Trash has never been more fun than it is at **Don't Waste It!**, a "recycling adventure" that rewards creative thinking about turning garbage into useful energy. **Environmentality Corner** focuses on conservation, and for those who always wanted to experience a tornado without any of the danger, **StormStruck** brings the house down around you, then shows how to weather the storm safely.

Innoventions West proves financial planning can be hilarious at **The Great Piggy Bank Adventure**, where guests compete in a series of interactive games trying to fill their piggy bank before the evil wolf deflates their currency's value. **Smarter Planet** shows how technology is used in energy reduction and conservation efforts, **Segway Central** is your chance to try out the outrageously fun Segway personal transportation system (go on; it's easy!), **Videogame Playground** has the latest games your kids are probably begging to play, and if you enjoyed watching a house come down in StormStruck you're going to love watching it go up in flames in **Where's the Fire**, unless your team is quick enough to identify common household trouble spots before they become blazing infernos (don't worry; it's more fun than frightful).

ROOKIE MISTAKES Don't rush to exit the park at the end of the day. Take your time as you walk through **Innoventions Plaza**, and be sure to look down. The pavement on either side as you head toward **Spaceship Earth** and a small pavement area in front of the entry to **Innoventions West** hold a delightful surprise on your way out.

CLUB COOL

Is it a shop? Is it an attraction? Is it a quick-service dining spot? We don't know! But we can tell you the story here is about **Coke**. Grab a little cup, sample a Coke product from a foreign country, and that's the story. Sort of.

In its former incarnation this was **Ice Station Cool**, themed as polar expedition **Refreshus Maximus**, which came across an igloo housing a frozen caveman nicknamed "Thirst Man" for the fact he was reaching for a bottle of Coke when he expired. It was arctic, it was sticky, and it was great fun to stand in an igloo sipping weird flavors while you took a break from the heat. Now it's just sticky.

But the real story might be more accurately told through Disney's long-standing relationship with Coca-Cola, dating back to Coke's sponsorship of Walt Disney's first television program, *One Hour in Wonderland*. For the most part, the "partnership" has been strong ever since. Drop into Club Cool as you stroll through Innoventions Plaza and raise a cup of the Beverly to Coca-Cola for its support of Walt's early ventures into family television entertainment.

THE SEAS WITH NEMO & FRIENDS

 (UNDER 6)

Fables written for the youngest children are generally very simple, and that is certainly the case here. Just like a picture story with few words, the Seas with Nemo & Friends relies on gentle, beautiful graphics with only the hint of a plot. Nemo, the curious little clown fish from Pixar's blockbuster movie *Finding Nemo*, is missing. Again.

 MISS-ABLE   IF YOU HAVE TIME   WORTH MAKING TIME FOR   NOT TO BE MISSED!

 WILL ONLY WORRY YOUNG CHILDREN   MAY SCARE MANY YOUNG CHILDREN; FEW ADULTS   WILL SCARE MOST YOUNG CHILDREN; SOME ADULTS   MAJOR SCARE FACTOR

 VISUAL DISORIENTATION   MILD PHYSICAL MOVEMENT   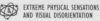 INTENSE FEELING OF MOTION   EXTREME PHYSICAL SENSATIONS AND VISUAL DISORIENTATION

Wind your way across the beach and along a boardwalk, taking note of signage indicating there are **No Reef Funds**, and **Daily Diving Departures** are provided by **Nautical Exploration & Marine Observation** (N.E.M.O.). Plunge into the ocean, where it's cool and dim, the overhead dock's pylons are covered in rust, and there appears to be someone fishing just above you. But you're looking for Nemo, which can only be done by boarding a **clamobile**.

Enter an undersea world filled with bright corals and tropical fish. **Mr. Ray** and his young charges are looking for Nemo in one part of the reef while **Marlin** and **Dory** scour another section. Young children adore the occasional tantalizing glimpses of the wandering adventurer, and while there are a few dark encounters with jellyfish and the menacing shark, Bruce, there is an overall lightheartedness, especially when **Crush** and his little dude **Squirt** take you along for a righteous surf through the East Australian Current.

It all ends happily when Nemo is finally found swimming in the big blue world of the pavilion's actual aquarium. The impressive technology that allows Nemo and his friends to mingle among the aquarium's sea life makes this attraction worth seeing even if you don't have preschoolers begging you for a ride.

SEA BASE

 (UNDER 7)

The story of **The Seas** doesn't end when you exit your clamobile, but it does change slightly. You are now in what remains of **Sea Base Alpha**, from the former attraction housed here. Now it's just called Sea Base, but the idea is the same. You're in a research base at the bottom of the sea, comprised of a series of pods dedicated to different projects. The first-floor pods hold the **nursery, small observation tanks**, and the interactive **Bruce's Sub House** (with photo ops!); the second-floor pods contain the **aquarium** and **manatee research centers**. In the center is the **diver lock-out chamber**, the point of entry when the story here included a journey to the base.

A real highlight for young children is **Turtle Talk with Crush**, where youngsters have the chance to talk directly to that cool surfer-dude Crush from

Finding Nemo. Crush wants to know more about the human world, and wants humans to know more about his undersea world, so he makes several appearances daily via an "underwater camera" and microphone. Children who would like the chance to be part of this humorous interactive show should sit on the carpet at the front of the theater.

THE LAND

How does a pavilion focused on agriculture fit into **right-brain thinking**? The focus here isn't on farming itself, it's on creative ways of coping with the demands of a burgeoning population, with a nod toward the fanciful as the crops begin to grow. Remember, Walt Disney's vision for EPCOT Center was to make life better in urban communities and around the world, facing challenges in new and inventive ways.

HIDDEN MAGIC | Look at your Epcot map. See the shape of the Land pavilion? What does it remind you of? It's a volcano! Now notice the shape of the entire walkway, from its beginning all the way up to the doors. Next, look at the shape of the Universe of Energy pavilion. Notice how the "cooler" end is wide and the "hot" end is sharp? At the front of the Energy pavilion you're standing "in" the volcano, the epicenter of earth's energy, and the pavilion's "V" shape fits into the Land pavilion's walkway cut-out.

LIVING WITH THE LAND

The interplay between humans and their environment is captured in inspirational quotes from children as you walk through the line toward the boarding area, where canopied boats await to take you on a journey that tells the story of human impact on the land. From the rainforest teeming with life to the vast prairies and arid deserts, each ecosystem reminds you of its importance in the balance of life.

 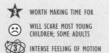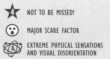

HIDDEN MAGIC

As you pass the farmhouse in Living with the Land, notice the house number on the mailbox. It's 82, the opening year of Epcot. The story of the agricultural mistakes humans have made in the past when meeting the demands of a growing population, and the resulting innovative solutions, are highlighted as you journey along the river. These segue into the real-life greenhouses and aqua-culture tanks that show how various ecological challenges are met with creative thinking.

As yawn-inducing as it may sound, the greenhouses are actually quite fascinating, even for kids, with some wonderfully whimsical sights such as Mickey-shaped tomatoes and pumpkins, enormous melons, and succulent cocoa pods. The fish farming tanks are pretty cool, too! You may just come away from it inspired to create your own garden or mini hydroponics system. Or at least inspired to have a meal at Epcot, where you could be dining on produce grown along your tour route.

The attraction is a brilliant example of the very thing Walt Disney envisioned for Epcot: creative, practical, ecologically sound solutions to worldwide challenges.

CIRCLE OF LIFE—AN ENVIRONMENTAL FABLE

 (UNDER 7)

Cute baby alert! The opening scenes of this movie-based attraction, set to the award-winning song "Circle of Life" from the hit film *The Lion King*, are meant to tug at the heartstrings, reminding us how beautiful our planet is, and how fragile. From the first wobbly moments of a wildebeest's life to great, crashing waterfalls and breaching whales, it is difficult not to be moved by the immensity of the nature that surrounds us—and depends on us.

Live-action clips combine with animation when Timon and Pumbaa reveal to Simba their grand scheme of building **Hakuna Matata Lakeside Village**. They have dammed the stream running through their savanna to create a lake, reveling in their motto of "more, more, more," until Simba tells them

★ POOR	★★ FAIR	★★★ GOOD	★★★★ EXCELLENT	★★★★★ GOURMET
$ UNDER $10	$$ $10–15	$$$ $15–$20	$$$$ $20–$25	$$$$$ $25+

 BREAKFAST   LUNCH DINNER COUNTER SERVICE TABLE SERVICE   TABLE SERVICE (TWO CREDITS)

a tale of what happened when humans forgot about living in harmony with nature. He shows his friends the grim side of "the good life" through scenes of pollution, deforestation, and thoughtlessness toward the environment, and he also shows them how humans have realized the importance of cleaning up the mess and recycling the waste.

Simba's story inspires Timon and Pumbaa to dismantle their dam and their plans for enormous wealth, choosing to work toward the betterment of the planet instead. Through their newfound understanding, you'll be guided to finding your place in the circle of life too, and while it can feel slightly preachy at times, the message encourages change, starting in your own backyard.

You won't find the typical Disney lightheartedness here, but the importance Walt Disney placed on **environmental awareness**, and was eager for Epcot to emphasize, comes through loud and clear.

SOARIN'

Essential Information: 3 feet, 4 inches; Fastpass

This is one **airport** you won't mind spending time in! You're preparing for a flight to California, where you'll spend a day **hang-gliding** over some of the state's most iconic landscapes. Happily, you won't have to deal with security, baggage claims, or traffic. Sadly, you don't get frequent flyer miles.

Your hang-gliding adventure begins high in the sky as you soar through puffy white clouds, dipping down for a view of the **Golden Gate Bridge**. Bank to the right over **San Francisco Bay** and you find yourself in a pine-scented forest, gliding over rafters and fishermen reveling in the natural beauty of **Redwood Creek**. As you catch an upward current your glider joins a festival of hot air balloons, floating lazily over the vineyards of **Napa Valley**.

Then it's out to sea again, soaring along the Pacific coast at **Monterey**, where white-capped waves crash against the craggy shoreline. A slight veer to the left brings you to the snowy mountainsides of **Lake Tahoe** (watch for the

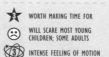
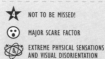

skier whose stunt ends in a spectacular crash!). One crash leads to another, this one being the crashing waters of **Yosemite Falls in Yosemite National Park**. As you turn gracefully away from the falls, you are joined by another hang-glider, playfully rising and diving on the air current.

From the natural wonders of Yosemite, drift over **PGA West in Palm Springs**, where the group of players in front of you are apparently Disney fans (watch for the Mickey head on the golf ball as it comes toward you). Then, enjoy the scent of oranges as you fly over the citrus orchards of **Camarillo** (lift those feet as you whiz above the treetops!).

HIDDEN MAGIC

Cast Members at the original Soarin' in California wear aviation suits, while at Epcot they are flight attendants. Why? Because in Disneyland they're already in California, while in Epcot you still have to fly there.

Next, it's over the mountains again, and you're in the **Anza-Borrego Desert State Park**, following a group of trail riders, and while your journey is set to the sounds of the wind (and an unforgettable musical score), the **U.S. Air Force Thunderbirds** that streak past are loud enough to send a small shockwave through your glider.

You don't have time to land on the aircraft carrier docked in **San Diego**, though you will get an excellent view of the deck, as you're off to **Malibu** for a bit of hang-surfing (smell that ocean breeze!) and then, as the sun sets, glide along the highways of **Los Angeles**, heading for the most famous **Main Street** in the world. **Disneyland** is just ahead, and you're in time for the Christmas parade—and the fireworks!

Just as the attraction itself is unlike any other, your three-tiered ride vehicle is unique, with canopied, swinging bench-style chairs that rise upward, enveloping you in California's beautiful scenery projected onto a wraparound screen. Although wait times can be outrageously long, this one is a sure-fire hit with all ages, and not to be missed!

ROOKIE MISTAKES

While it's possible the line might be shorter at night during off season, don't leave Soarin' until the end of the day assuming everyone will have seen it by then. Evening lines can still top two hours in peak season.

IMAGINATION!

★2 ☺ (UNDER 6)

You have been invited to an open house at **Imagination Institute**, where you'll find inventions created by great innovators from various Disney movies, including Wayne Szalinski from *Honey I Shrunk the Kids* and Philip Brainard from *Flubber*. As you wander the hallway leading to the **Sensory Labs**, notice Professor Brainard and Dean Higgins's offices have been Flubber-ized (stuff is floating everywhere!).

Dr. Nigel Channing, chairman of the Imagination Institute, encourages guests to discover their five senses. But **Figment**, that mischievous purple dragon that used to be the star at Imagination when he and his friend Dreamfinder hung out here, wants to tag along with your tour. Dr. Channing forbids it, and with good reason as you'll discover during your journey through the smell lab (with a choice between popcorn, jasmine, cherry, or skunk, guess which smell you're going to get?).

HIDDEN MAGIC

Look for the office door with Dean Finder's name on it. It's a reference to Dreamfinder, the "collector of dreams" who imagined "one little spark" that led to the creation of Figment. Before a 1999 redesign of the attraction, **Journey into Imagination** was housed here, featuring these two beloved characters. Sadly, only Figment returned, with just the slightest nod to Dreamfinder by promoting him to the position of dean.

As you make your way into the **Sound Lab**, Figment decides the tour would be much better if visitors use their imagination instead of their actual

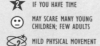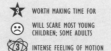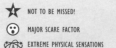

senses. Predictably, it all goes awry, causing Dr. Channing to cancel the **Touch and Taste** portions of the tour. Instead you divert into Figment's topsy-turvy world before being set free for some hands-on exploration at the **Institute's ImageWorks**. But the final scene will touch the hearts of longtime Disney fans; it's a whimsical sample of the cartoon-like scenes in the original Journey into Imagination attraction, with Figment and Dreamfinder.

IMAGEWORKS

ImageWorks invites you to set your imagination free with light, sound, and even the chance to morph a photo of your face into an imaginary animal and e-mail it as a postcard to a friend.

CAPTAIN EO

Also in the **Imagination pavilion**, this 3-D throwback to 1986 has returned to Epcot after the closing of Honey I Shrunk the Audience, and while the graphics are no longer state-of-the-art, it's the sort of "good versus evil" trip back in time that does tend to stir the imagination.

The renegade Captain EO (**Michael Jackson**) and his crew of misfits are determined to bring freedom to the universe, and today's mission is to deliver a gift to their target planet's Supreme Leader (**Anjelica Huston**).

But the captain and his friends have failed in the past, and Command will end their careers if they make a mess of things again. Of course, this is exactly what happens when they enter a battle as they attempt to locate Command's landing beacon, and one of the crew makes a snack of the planet's map. Luckily, their bumbling incompetence draws the attention of an armor-clad army, who take them directly to the villainous (and rather frightening) Leader.

Captain EO's gift is a song and dance routine aimed at "changing the world" and showing the wicked leader that beauty lies within. The Leader

remains unimpressed and orders her troops to cause him and his friends great bodily harm by turning them into trash cans. Instead, Captain EO pulls out his very best dance moves (moonwalking included), magically changing the menacing army into big-haired, shiny-suited backup singers and dancers.

With the Supreme Leader's minions now firmly on Captain EO's team, she has no choice but to succumb to the ways of goodness, giving up her evil ways and transforming into a vision of queenly beauty. Mission accomplished, Captain EO and his friends blast off for their next intergalactic freedom-fighting adventure.

It's nearly impossible not to appreciate Disney's contribution to 3-D moviemaking and Jackson's unique style of synchronized dancing. *Star Wars* producer **George Lucas's** influence is obvious in many scenes, and if you watch closely during the pre-show backstage peek at the creation of the attraction, quick-eyed viewers might catch a glimpse of an impossibly young Imagineer, **Joe Rohde**, creator of **Disney's Animal Kingdom**.

UNIVERSE OF ENERGY

That wacky **Ellen DeGeneres**! When she dreams, she dreams big, and we get a glimpse into her naptime nightmare when Ellen falls asleep after watching her former college roommate win on *Jeopardy!* Ellen doesn't fare as well as a contestant when all the categories in her dream are about energy.

But it's **Bill Nye the Science Guy** to the rescue. Bill offers Ellen the chance to experience the sort of firsthand learning that makes him so popular with school kids, and we're all off on a journey back in time—220 million years, to be exact!

Ride vehicles transport you to the **age of the dinosaurs**, when the world was misty and dim and everything smelled vaguely of potting soil. Your first encounter is with a herd of **brachiosaurus**, one of which appears to have a cold.

 MISS-ABLE   IF YOU HAVE TIME   WORTH MAKING TIME FOR   NOT TO BE MISSED!

 WILL ONLY WORRY YOUNG CHILDREN MAY SCARE MANY YOUNG CHILDREN; FEW ADULTS WILL SCARE MOST YOUNG CHILDREN; SOME ADULTS MAJOR SCARE FACTOR

 VISUAL DISORIENTATION   MILD PHYSICAL MOVEMENT   INTENSE FEELING OF MOTION 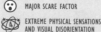 EXTREME PHYSICAL SENSATIONS AND VISUAL DISORIENTATION

Next you watch a **stegosaurus** as it fights off a **T. Rex** while something that looks a lot like Jar Jar Binks looks on, and one lucky time traveler gets spit on as Ellen fends off a snaggletoothed sea serpent.

As you leave the land of the dinosaurs behind, radio station KNRG is broadcasting all the latest climate updates and fashion reports. Moving further ahead in time, watch as man discovers fire, heralding the dawn of technology. Ellen and Bill Nye explore various energy possibilities, and then Ellen returns to the show to take on the *Final Jeopardy!* question: "This is the one source of power that will never run out."

HIDDEN MAGIC

You just know KNRG 750BC must mean something. The K stands for kinetic and NRG is what the attraction is about (say it quickly!).

Universe of Energy doesn't just tell us about energy, it also uses it in some interesting ways. Your ride vehicle rotates on giant moving platforms, and moves forward with the aid of rechargeable batteries, partially powered by the photovoltaic cells on the roof of the pavilion. You get a "big bang" for your buck here, including 45 minutes in air-conditioned comfort.

MISSION: SPACE

Essential Information: 3 feet, 8 inches; Fastpass

★ ☺ GREEN VERSION  ORANGE VERSION

The year is 2036, and you have been recruited by the **International Space Training Commission** for a special mission to **Mars**. Today's assignment involves a rehearsal in one of the ISTC's simulators. You know your duty (at least, you will when you choose one); as the navigator, pilot, commander, or engineer, you have tasks to perform, and the success of your mission depends on teamwork, bravery . . . and a lot of help from "computer override!"

★ POOR   ★★ FAIR   ★★★ GOOD   ★★★★ EXCELLENT   ★★★★★ GOURMET
$ UNDER $10 $$ $10–15 $$$ $15–$20 $$$$ $20–$25 $$$$$ $25+
Ⓑ BREAKFAST   Ⓛ LUNCH   Ⓓ DINNER   ⒸⓈ COUNTER SERVICE   ⓉⓈ TABLE SERVICE   ⓉⓈ2 TABLE SERVICE (TWO CREDITS)

Pioneers in space travel are immortalized by quotes along the center's outer walls, and by markers as you pass the moon mock-up in **Planetary Plaza**. The gold spheres represent the twenty-nine moon landings; those with a white center were unmanned missions, blue centers were manned missions, and the single red center is the **Apollo 11** mission, when one small step for a man represented one giant leap for mankind. But you get a hint of your task when you see the shuttle zooming toward the red planet.

HIDDEN MAGIC | Why is Jupiter so close to Earth when in reality Mars is closer? Because tests done prior to the attraction's formal opening showed guests were inclined to go to the right, toward the Fastpass entry, instead of going left to the main entry. Jupiter was a visual "stopper" that fixed the problem (see photo insert). You can see Jupiter's Great Red Spot if you go up the ramp to the right of the planet (it's on the back).

Enter the training center's exhibition hall, filled with great moments in space flight, passing its centerpiece gravity wheel (whose logo hints at the **Horizons** attraction formerly housed here). When you reach the **Ready Room** you are divided into teams of four, then **Gary Sinise** (who played the part of Co-Commander Jim McConnell in the movie *Mission To Mars*) gives your preflight briefing.

Your next stop is an antechamber for a final check, then you enter the simulator center and board your **X-2 Deep Space Shuttle** in assigned order. Each person has two tasks. Go ahead and push the buttons, flick switches, and play with stuff before takeoff. Some of the gadgets make sounds.

Then, it's down to serious business when **Mission Control** makes contact. The sense of realism as your rocket launches into space is immense. Slingshot around the moon and the sensation intensifies. As you prepare to enter hyper-sleep you have a view of the Earth that is nothing short of awe-inspiring, but when you wake up months later your skills are immediately called into play. You've entered an **asteroid field**, and evasive maneuvers are your only hope! Your skills save the day, but it's not over yet. Autopilot is lost just as you plum-

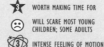
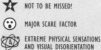

★ MISS-ABLE
😊 WILL ONLY WORRY YOUNG CHILDREN
↻ VISUAL DISORIENTATION

★ IF YOU HAVE TIME
😐 MAY SCARE MANY YOUNG CHILDREN; FEW ADULTS
MILD PHYSICAL MOVEMENT

★ WORTH MAKING TIME FOR
☹ WILL SCARE MOST YOUNG CHILDREN; SOME ADULTS
INTENSE FEELING OF MOTION

★ NOT TO BE MISSED!
😵 MAJOR SCARE FACTOR
EXTREME PHYSICAL SENSATIONS AND VISUAL DISORIENTATION

met into a deep crevice, where fancy flying and a less-than-stellar landing bring your mission to a successful close.

This attraction isn't far from the real thing, especially if you ride the **Orange version**, where the centrifuge packs a whopping 2.4G force. Keep your head straight and your eyes looking forward, and remember, it only lasts five minutes (although it feels much longer). The **Green version** is much less intense, and is more appropriate for those who suffer motion discomfort. There is a short sequence of gentle tipping, but any impact from the visuals can be overcome by closing your eyes.

ROOKIE MISTAKES

That whole "keep your head straight and your eyes forward" advice really does matter when you ride the Orange version of Mission: Space. Ignore it at your peril!

ISTC'S ADVANCED TRAINING LAB

If you're more about terra firma than terra-fied, check out the less intense offerings at **ISTC's Advanced Training Lab**. Here you'll find **Expedition Mars** (a joystick-style computer game); **Postcards from Space** (star in your own space-themed mini-movie, then e-mail it to a friend); and **Mission: Space Race**, where two teams race to get their rockets from Mars back to Earth.

TEST TRACK

Essential Information: 3 feet, 4 inches; Fastpass

People rarely think of it when they purchase a shiny new automobile, but the amount of testing that went into it to make it safe, dependable, and environmentally friendly is enormous. The place all that testing is done to ensure the

manufacturer lives up to its claims are the company's **Proving Grounds**, and you're heading into that part of the story today!

HIDDEN MAGIC Notice the Proving Grounds posters on the wall in the pre-show area where you get your test schedule for today. One of them is an aerial shot of the Milford Proving Grounds in Michigan, the oldest proving grounds in the world, opened by General Motors in 1924.

Enter the facility and you're surrounded by dummies. No, not that kid in front of you who keeps sitting on the railing when the Cast Members tell him not to; we're talking about **crash test dummies**! Car parts and chassis in various stages of disassembly are everywhere. This is the work environment of the mechanics who engineer every detail with quality and reliability in mind. Even the music is in rhythm with the tools of the trade.

Beyond the testing center lies the actual proving grounds, and this is where you're headed (if you make it through the crash barrier!). Since it's your first day as a special performance driver, Bill up in the tower runs through your test schedule. First you'll perform an **accelerated hill climb**, then rumble over **German and Belgian blocks** before testing the **anti-lock brake system**. Then you're on to **environmental testing**, to ensure the car's integrity against heat, cold, and corrosion.

Finally you'll rev it up on the handling runs to see how your vehicle does with **hairpin turns** and **high-speed loops**. As an added bonus you get to see the last thing those crash test dummies see, so fasten your seat belt, pluck up your courage, and hold on tight!

In reality, it's a thrilling ride but not really a thrill ride. The force of the banked turn is powerful, but in fact, your car never even reaches 70 mph. It just feels a whole lot faster!

REALITY CHECK Single Rider can save a great deal of time, but they mean it when they say you'll be split up. Avoid an embarrassing episode and don't try to talk them into letting you ride with someone else in your group (even if it's a child).

 MISS-ABLE   IF YOU HAVE TIME   WORTH MAKING TIME FOR   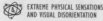 NOT TO BE MISSED!

 WILL ONLY WORRY YOUNG CHILDREN   MAY SCARE MANY YOUNG CHILDREN; FEW ADULTS   WILL SCARE MOST YOUNG CHILDREN; SOME ADULTS   MAJOR SCARE FACTOR

 VISUAL DISORIENTATION   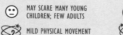 MILD PHYSICAL MOVEMENT   INTENSE FEELING OF MOTION   EXTREME PHYSICAL SENSATIONS AND VISUAL DISORIENTATION

Dining in Future World

DINING IN INNOVENTIONS PLAZA

FOUNTAINVIEW CAFÉ

$

This cafe is all about ice cream. Edy's ice cream, to be exact, with a great view of the Fountain of Nations.

HIDDEN MAGIC Even the fountain has a story! When Epcot opened, representatives from around the world each poured a gallon of water into the fountain as a sign of peace and friendship. We'll just ignore the laws of evaporation and be happy that rivers and bodies of water from all over the world mingle together here in Epcot.

THE ELECTRIC UMBRELLA

$

This restaurant is the counter-service choice, with standard burgers, chili, and a vegetarian wrap.

DINING AT THE SEAS WITH NEMO & FRIENDS

THE CORAL REEF

★★★ $$$$

Perhaps the most restful restaurant in Epcot, the Coral Reef curves gracefully around one side of the pavilion's aquarium, offering excellent views of the sea life to all diners. Extending the idea that you're in Sea Base, apparently marine biologists certainly dine at the height of elegance. However, the name of the restaurant hints at another story, as does the atmosphere, with its cool blues and greens, gentle lines reminiscent of waves, and sand-colored walls. You're actually in a reef, but thankfully, you won't have to hold your breath

 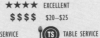

for the duration of your meal. The menu is heavy on seafood, as would be expected, but chicken, steak, and pork are also available. Service and food can be uneven, but when it's good, it's very good.

DINING IN THE LAND

SUNSHINE SEASONS

★★★ $

This restaurant offers a variety of choice, much of it healthier than your average counter service. Fresh, seasonal foods are highlighted at five counters (the bakery, sandwiches, Asian noodles, soup and salad, and the grill), and there are grab-and-go coolers with lighter snacks, drinks, beer, and wine.

GARDEN GRILL

★★★ $$$$$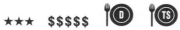

Garden Grill brings the freshness of the farm to the table, with a view overlooking Living with the Land as this circular restaurant slowly rotates while you dine. Farmer Mickey, Pluto, Chip, and Dale are on hand and dinner is served family style, beginning at 4 P.M. The set Family Style Platter includes breads, salads, fish, turkey, beef, potatoes, dressing, and dessert, with kid-friendly entrees available.

Shopping in Future World

MAGICAL MERCHANDISE

All of the attractions have **gift shops** featuring signature items, but you'll also find Disney merchandise at the vast **Mouse Gear**, artwork at **The Art of Disney**, and Epcot merchandise at **Gateway Gifts**. And now, let's discover those attractions!

 MISS-ABLE   IF YOU HAVE TIME   WORTH MAKING TIME FOR   NOT TO BE MISSED!

 WILL ONLY WORRY YOUNG CHILDREN   MAY SCARE MANY YOUNG CHILDREN; FEW ADULTS   WILL SCARE MOST YOUNG CHILDREN; SOME ADULTS   MAJOR SCARE FACTOR

VISUAL DISORIENTATION   MILD PHYSICAL MOVEMENT   INTENSE FEELING OF MOTION   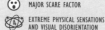 EXTREME PHYSICAL SENSATIONS AND VISUAL DISORIENTATION

World Showcase

The story behind the World Showcase is simple: This section of Epcot demonstrates the ability of people, cultures, and concepts to sit side-by-side in harmony, each made better by the inclusion of the others. World Showcase draws you into the story, inviting you to explore, and it does so with a flair that only Disney Imagineering could achieve.

ROOKIE MISTAKES It's nearly impossible to keep children out of the water play areas and splash fountains in the parks. Bring a towel, swimsuit, change of clothes, or water shoes so they're not squelching around all day or soaking the liner of their stroller.

Mexico

The sight of a third-century **Mesoamerican temple** rising out of an ancient **Mexican jungle** is spectacular indeed. The pyramid's stairway leads to a traditional-style altar used by high priests, where serpent sculptures symbolizing the **Aztec god Quetzalcoatl** keep watch over the goings-on below. Three cultures are represented, with the architecture being **Mayan**, the bright murals and sculptures of **Aztec** influence, and the design elements bring to mind **Toltec** art.

There is an air of excitement inside the pyramid as you find yourself in a small **Mexican village**, where everyone is preparing for a special event. Colorful banners with images of the popular musical group **The Three Caballeros** are strewn across the **Plaza de Los Amigos** in anticipation of the concert they are putting on tonight. Carts laden with souvenirs are everywhere, and diners at the local inn take advantage of the cool evening air to gather at tables along el Río del Tiempo, "the River of Time," enjoying a festive meal. You'll learn how to say goodbye in Spanish here, but if you'd like to say hello to the Cast Members, say "hola" (pronounced "O-lah").

★ POOR	★★ FAIR	★★★ GOOD	★★★★ EXCELLENT	★★★★★ GOURMET
$ UNDER $10	$$ $10–15	$$$ $15–$20	$$$$ $20–$25	$$$$$ $25+
(B) BREAKFAST	(L) LUNCH	(D) DINNER	(CS) COUNTER SERVICE	(TS) TABLE SERVICE — (TS2) TABLE SERVICE (TWO CREDITS)

GRAN FIESTA TOUR STARRING THE THREE CABALLEROS

 (UNDER 6)

José Carioca, Panchito, and Donald Duck, better known as **The Three Caballeros**, are making a grand festival tour, and tonight they're playing in **Mexico City**. But Donald decides he wants to see the sights. As your boat makes its way along the **River of Time** heading for the concert, you pass a mysterious pyramid hidden in the jungle before encountering José and Panchito, who enlist the help of a flying *serape* (Spanish for blanket) in trying to track Donald down. But Donald is always one step ahead, touring Mexico's greatest cities.

First the duo looks for Donald at the church tower in **Toluca**, then they're on to **Palacio de Bellas Artes** and the **National Museum of Anthropology** (with its goggle-eyed stone head) in **Mexico City**. Plying the waters of the canals of **Xochimlico** in a traditional Aztec boat gets them no closer, so they move on to the **Teotihuacán pyramid** and the **Angel of Independence statue** before stumbling upon a traditional **Day of the Dead celebration**. Donald is here, but in piñata form.

They keep searching, this time on and above the waters in **Acapulco**, where the famous cliff divers are performing for the tourists. As the sun sets over **Cancun** it's not looking good for Jose and Panchito, but when they arrive back in Mexico City the festival is in full swing, with mariachi bands and traditional dancers, and—finally—Donald is found! They arrive just in time for the show, and you're treated to a concert as fireworks burst overhead in the best fiesta style!

DINING IN MEXICO

LA HACIENDA DE SAN ANGEL

★★★★ $$$$$

The stand-out choice here for authentic Mexican, redolent with flavors that positively burst with joy, is **La Hacienda de San Angel** (you're a welcome guest in a traditional hacienda in Mexico's Yucatan region). You won't find Tex-Mex

 MISS-ABLE   IF YOU HAVE TIME   WORTH MAKING TIME FOR   NOT TO BE MISSED!

 WILL ONLY WORRY YOUNG CHILDREN   MAY SCARE MANY YOUNG CHILDREN; FEW ADULTS   WILL SCARE MOST YOUNG CHILDREN; SOME ADULTS   MAJOR SCARE FACTOR

 VISUAL DISORIENTATION   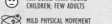 MILD PHYSICAL MOVEMENT   INTENSE FEELING OF MOTION   EXTREME PHYSICAL SENSATIONS AND VISUAL DISORIENTATION

here; this is the real deal. Tortillas are patted into shape daily by hands that know how, only the freshest ingredients and most traditional techniques are used in creating each dish, and we challenge you to find a more astonishingly delightful drink than the restaurant's signature **Rosita Margarita**. We could wax poetic about the **Chiles toreados y choizitos** appetizer, but we won't. You simply have to try it for yourself.

LA CANTINA DE SAN ANGEL

★★ $$

This counter-service location has tacos, empanadas, nachos, and kids' choices, plus churros and wonderfully fruity paletas (popsicles) in startlingly refreshing flavors.

SAN ANGEL INN

★★★ $$$$$

Inside the pavilion is San Angel Inn, the outdoor dining spot along the River of Time. It's cool, dim, and blissfully relaxing, with large portions of familiar Americanized Mexican fare. The food is tasty, but the real draw here is the atmosphere.

LA CAVA DEL TEQUILA

$ TO $$

If you're just in the mood for a light bite and something to take the edge off, **La Cava del Tequila** positively celebrates **tequila**, with more than 70 varieties available. Try the flight of tequila to sample a few, and don't forget a side of **Queso Blanco**.

REALITY CHECK Want to give one of Epcot's great restaurants a try, but don't want to break the bank? Make your main meal reservation before 4 P.M. The lunch menu switches to the dinner menu after 4 P.M., but most items will be the same, in slightly smaller portions and at a lower price.

SHOPPING IN MEXICO

MAGICAL MERCHANDISE

La Plaza de Los Amigos is a festival of carts and local vendors selling clothing, piñatas, foods, and gifts, while **La Princesa de Cristal** sells crystal and glass.

Norway

Visit the villages and cities of Norway, found in the imposing medieval edifice of **Oslo's Akershus castle**, the **fjords at Bergen in Maelstrom**, the coastal architecture of **Alesund** as seen in **The Fjording**, and the pretty, rustic style of traditional sod-roofed buildings of the **Setesdal Valley** at **Kringla Bakeri og Kafe**.

MAELSTROM

Essential Information: Fastpass

The mural along the wall in the boarding area could be considered a billboard if you're in a skeptical mood, but it does represent Norway's proud seafaring heritage, from the age of Vikings to the luxury Royal Viking cruise liners (you thought it was Norwegian Cruise Line, didn't you?). As mysterious as Norway is, its myths and folklore are even more intriguing, especially when it comes to its fabled trolls. If you're not a believer when you set off on your journey, you will be by the time you get back.

 MISS-ABLE
 WILL ONLY WORRY YOUNG CHILDREN
 VISUAL DISORIENTATION

 IF YOU HAVE TIME
 MAY SCARE MANY YOUNG CHILDREN; FEW ADULTS
 MILD PHYSICAL MOVEMENT

 WORTH MAKING TIME FOR
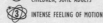 WILL SCARE MOST YOUNG CHILDREN; SOME ADULTS
INTENSE FEELING OF MOTION

 NOT TO BE MISSED!
 MAJOR SCARE FACTOR
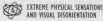 EXTREME PHYSICAL SENSATIONS AND VISUAL DISORIENTATION

Waits for Maelstrom can be long, so this is a great chance to annoy friends and family by asking them to find the reference to Mickey Mouse hidden in the giant wall mural. But first, you need to know where it is. It's the set of mouse ears worn by a Viking in the ship to the far left. Look directly under the sail's middle red stripe. Neat, right?

The first hint that mischief is afoot is the glimpse you get of a **Viking ship** heading toward catastrophe, before you even enter the attraction. When your own ship begins its ascent up the first hill toward the **eye of Odin**, you know there's going to be trouble! But then, any attraction whose name comes from a whirling vortex of water that sucks everything in its path to a watery doom must be rife with peril!

A very short drop takes you to a small coastal fishing village, where tales of trolls abound. Sure enough, when you invade their territory you're spotted by a three-headed creature who casts you down a waterfall—backward! It's a short drop, but sufficient to land you in Norway's frozen region of polar bears, who are none too happy to see you either.

Thankfully you reach the safe haven of a lovely fjord, but your relief is short-lived. Those pesky trolls come in tree form too, and this wild-eyed specimen is determined to fling you into the **North Sea**! Another drop and you're at the foot of an oil rig, but while the weather is vicious, the sea is uncharacteristically calm (river-like, almost!) as you glide gently out of the storm and into the welcoming harbor of a charming Norwegian hamlet.

The ride is brief but the memory of it is strangely long-lasting, and the attraction does have a bit of a cult following among Epcot fans. Many people walk straight through the theater at the end of the ride, skipping the travelogue that shows every two minutes, but it's worth watching if you need some more time in air-conditioned comfort. Then, drop into the **Stave Church**, where a small exhibit has changing displays telling more of the Norwegian story. Greet the Cast Members here with a hearty "Hei" (hi).

DINING IN NORWAY

KRINGLA BAKERI OG KAFÉ

★★ $ 🍴L 🍴D 🍴CS

This is the quick service choice, featuring snacks, open-faced sandwiches, salads, and baked goods. Try the Rice Cream dessert. Yummy!

AKERSHUS ROYAL BANQUET HALL

★★★ $$$$$ 🍴B 🍴L 🍴D

Calling all princesses! Akershus Royal Banquet Hall is the gathering place of royalty, where Disney princesses greet their loyal subjects as they dine amid the splendors of **Akershus Castle**. A set **Royal Feast buffet** is served, featuring fruit, eggs, bacon, sausage, and potatoes at breakfast; salmon burger, venison sausage, chicken, sandwiches, and pasta at lunch; and fish, chicken, beef, pork, and pasta at dinner. It's popular. Book early.

SHOPPING IN NORWAY

PUFFINS ROOST

This store is the place for wonderful woolens, glass, toys, and those all-important troll dolls.

China

Welcome to **Beijing** during the **Tang Dynasty**. Symbolism is everywhere, from the evil **Prince Min** being guarded by helpful animals on each corner of the rooftops, to the predominant color red, believed to bring luck, happiness, and prosperity, as well as to ward off evil spirits.

Enter through **Zaho Yang Men (Gate of the Golden Sun)**, taking note of the immense tranquility here. The pond appears completely natural, an important element in Chinese design, and the gentle stroll toward the **Temple of Heaven** invites you to move slowly, absorbing the beauty around you.

 MISS-ABLE
 WILL ONLY WORRY YOUNG CHILDREN
VISUAL DISORIENTATION

 IF YOU HAVE TIME
 MAY SCARE MANY YOUNG CHILDREN; FEW ADULTS
MILD PHYSICAL MOVEMENT

 WORTH MAKING TIME FOR
 WILL SCARE MOST YOUNG CHILDREN; SOME ADULTS
 INTENSE FEELING OF MOTION

 NOT TO BE MISSED!
 MAJOR SCARE FACTOR
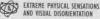 EXTREME PHYSICAL SENSATIONS AND VISUAL DISORIENTATION

All of China uses a simplified version of Mandarin, which is less descriptive than traditional Mandarin. For example, the second traditional character on the gate means "door" whereas in simplified Mandarin it would mean something akin to "hole" or "opening." Traditional Mandarin is more nuanced, so the symbolism of the description "Going Toward Sun Gate" is that you are literally going toward the new day's sun, immersing in its power. Beautiful, isn't it?

The Temple itself is a calendar of sorts. As you stand in the center, look around and up. The four large columns represent the four seasons while the twelve smaller columns are the months. There are twelve columns further up, one for each year in the cycle of the Chinese calendar. Every architectural detail has meaning, but the detail that defines the building's use is the five-toed dragon. Those five toes (rather than the more common four toes) indicate this is a temple specifically for the Emperor and Empress, who come here to pray for a fruitful harvest. As you stand in the central circle, notice how your own voice bounces straight back into your ears. The building is acoustically perfect.

Enter **the marketplace outside** and you immediately notice things go from serene to a hectic, bustling pace. The street here is narrow, adding to the feeling of being in a city packed with people. Greet Cast Members here with "Nín hǎo" (nin how).

Epcot is filled with excellent street entertainment. Make time in your day to see a few performances, especially those in Canada, China, Japan, Italy, and France.

REFLECTIONS OF CHINA

Sure, it's a fancy **Circle-Vision travelogue**, but it's so well done you'll never notice you're watching an advertisement. Set to a background of sweetly haunting music, **The Great Wall** stretches around you as **eighth century poet Li Bai** guides you across the country, and across history, beginning with the modern face of China in Shanghai, where towering skyscrapers blend seamlessly with centuries-old traditions.

Journey to the craggy mountains of the **Sea of Clouds**, soar over the sweeping **Yangtze River**, marvel at the ancient water-city of **Suzhou**, and explore diverse cultures and cuisines in inner **Mongolia**, **Hong Kong**, **the Forbidden City**, and **Tiananmen Square**, and finally, the "dragon's teeth" landscape of **Guilin**.

From the terra cotta warriors guarding the **tombs of the Emperors** to the giant **Buddha of Li Shan**, China is reflected in such a way that it is nearly impossible not to be swept away by it.

You must stand through the entire thirteen-minute movie, but there are railings to lean on and the scenery is utterly captivating, so the time passes quickly.

DINING IN CHINA

LOTUS BLOSSOM CAFÉ

★★ $

This café is the "street vendor" selling Americanized egg rolls, orange chicken, beef rice bowls, vegetable stir-fry, and sesame chicken salad.

NINE DRAGONS

★★★ $$$$

This full-service restaurant will probably call to mind the Chinese takeout back home more than anything you'd really find in China, but there are some interesting combinations and the atmosphere is pleasant, with a good view of **World Showcase**. Entrees include sweet and sour pork, a noodle sampler, vegetable and tofu stir-fry, and Canton pepper beef. Or try the set Family Dinner, with a selection of entrees and sides.

MISS-ABLE

WILL ONLY WORRY
YOUNG CHILDREN

VISUAL DISORIENTATION

IF YOU HAVE TIME

MAY SCARE MANY YOUNG
CHILDREN; FEW ADULTS

MILD PHYSICAL MOVEMENT

WORTH MAKING TIME FOR

WILL SCARE MOST YOUNG
CHILDREN; SOME ADULTS

INTENSE FEELING OF MOTION

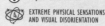
NOT TO BE MISSED!

MAJOR SCARE FACTOR

EXTREME PHYSICAL SENSATIONS
AND VISUAL DISORIENTATION

If you want the healthier option of carrots or apple slices rather than fries, remember to tell the counter-service cashier who takes your order. They are supposed to ask each guest but many just assume people want fries.

SHOPPING IN CHINA

YONG FENS SHANDGIAN

In the market for fine imported goods from the "land of the sleeping dragon"? If the massive Yong Feng Shandgian shop doesn't have it, you probably don't need it. Jewelry, silk clothing, Oriental rugs, tea pots, cloisonné, and so much more.

The Outpost

So what's the deal with the **Outpost**? It looks like an afterthought, it's strangely situated, and—besides offering African-style souvenirs and the chance to beat on some drums—it's really just an elaborate soda station. But wait; there's more to it than that, even if only through its potential.

Originally Epcot intended to include a full-blown **Equatorial Africa pavilion**, complete with giant trees from which to view animals of the savanna, a show entitled "Heartbeat of Africa," and a cultural experience called "Africa Rediscovered" hosted by Alex Haley, author of the best-selling novel *Roots*. Alas, it was not meant to be (at least, not so far), but a place marker arrived in 1983 as the Outpost. Essentially, you're on safari and have come upon a supply outpost (primarily featuring **Coca-Cola products**, but that's not really the story here). Local artisans and musicians may drop by to entertain weary travelers with their skills; rest and refreshment is available, and it really does feel like the oasis it's meant to be. It's a short story, but a good one.

HIDDEN MAGIC
You may remember the kopje at Disney's Animal Kingdom Lodge. The Outpost here is protected by this natural enclosure too. That's what the rock work over by the lagoon represents. It's a safe haven, where the wild animals are kept at bay by nature's own design (or, that of the Imagineers).

 ★ POOR $ UNDER $10   ★★ FAIR $$ $10–15   ★★★ GOOD $$$ $15–$20   ★★★★ EXCELLENT $$$$ $20–$25   ★★★★★ GOURMET $$$$$ $25+

B BREAKFAST L LUNCH D DINNER CS COUNTER SERVICE TS TABLE SERVICE TS2 TABLE SERVICE (TWO CREDITS)

DINING IN THE OUTPOST

AFRICA REFRESHMENT COOLPOST

Essential Information: Not DDP

$

Make a quick-service stop at the Africa Refreshment Coolpost, where you can get that most African of meals, a hot dog.

Germany

Here you'll find the romanticized version of **sixteenth-century Germany**—folklore come to life—from the gingerbread trim common in **Bavaria** to the heroic statue of **Saint George** slaying the dragon, thus securing his place as the sentimentally symbolic protector of Germany.

The look of the pavilion brings the medieval town of **Rothenburg** to mind, but the overall idea is an amalgam of historical Bavaria. To the left, **Karamell Küche** boasts the charming decorative elements you'll find all over Bavaria. **Das Kaufhaus** on your right is based on **Freiburg's Historisches Kaufhaus** (merchant's hall) in the Black Forest, built in 1520. But here in Epcot there was only room for three of the four Hapsburg princes that grace the upper storey of Freiburg's building. At the back of the pavilion stands a medieval castle recalling characteristics of **Eltz Castle** and **Stahlek Fortress**.

The eye-catching red building just to the left of the entry to the **Biergarten** restaurant is based on the medieval **Haus Römer (city hall)** in Frankfurt's Römerberg plaza, and the massive central clock tower features a traditional glockenspiel.

HIDDEN MAGIC   You'll find the Germany pavilion's obvious tie to Magic Kingdom in Cinderella Castle, which is based on the castle Neuschwanstein. However, if you listen closely to the music to the left of "It's a Small World" and across from Peter Pan's Flight, you'll notice the same music is played here in Germany.

 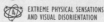

There is no ride or movie here, but the shopping is good and the scenery is even better. As beautiful as this area is during the day, the Germany pavilion's best hours are after dark. Greet the Cast Members here by saying "Guten tag" (goo-ten tahg).

DINING IN GERMANY

BIERGARTEN

★★★ $$$$$

It's always **Oktoberfest** at twilight in Germany's Biergarten! You've arrived at a **Bavarian beer garden** during the celebrations, when good food (a vast hot and cold buffet), plentiful drink, and uniquely German entertainment are in full swing. Just as they are in traditional biergartens, tables are communal, meaning you may be dining with other revelers. But that's the point; it's a time of coming together in the cool of evening to hoist a stein, eat some wienerschnitzel, and maybe even dance until your feet hurt.

SOMMERFEST

$

If you don't have time for an evening of ompah-pahing, pick up a bratwurst, soft pretzel, or other snack at Sommerfest.

SHOPPING IN GERMANY

MAGICAL MERCHANDISE

Der Teddy Bar carries your new best cuddly friend, **Volkskunst** has your next favorite beer stein or cuckoo clock, **Die Weihnachts Ecke** is all about Christmas ornaments, and **Kunstarbeit In Kristal** carries crystal, including Swarovski.

 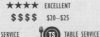

Italy

Bella Venizia! With its towering campanile, graceful lines, and an air of romance that only comes from a city that can't be bothered to drive when a gondola works just as well (and the roads, frankly, are waterways), the Italy pavilion calls to mind the timelessness of that great European city, **Venice**.

But Italy is far more than the **City of Water**, as seen in the pink and white marble **Doge's Palace**. It is picturesque **Sicily**, whose scenery can be found in the paintings on the donkey cart out front. It is **Rome**, playfully depicted by Neptune and his dolphins in the Renaissance-inspired fountain. And it is **Naples**, whose richness of cuisine comes to life at Via Napoli. But this is also Italy during a time when the country was divided and hopes for reunion burned strong in the hearts of its citizens, as seen in the mural inside **Tutto Italia,** titled **Unity of Italy.**

Italy demands a slow, scenic wander. To your left is the **Doge's Palace**, connected by the **Bridge of Sighs** to what would have been a prison in the original building. The campanile mimics the one found in **St. Mark's Square in Venice**, as does the pavement, and from high atop two towers, a winged lion, protector of Venice, and St. Theodore watch over Italy's namesake pavilion. Greet Cast Members here by saying "ciao" (chow).

HIDDEN MAGIC

Look for the sculpted face with its mouth open on the back of the Doge's Palace as you walk into the pavilion (see photo insert). It represents the method used to report transgressors to officials, when the citizenry was encouraged to drop a note into the mouth ratting out their neighbors if they did anything wrong. Bummer!

DINING IN ITALY

VIA NAPOLI

★★★★ $$$$

 MISS-ABLE

 IF YOU HAVE TIME

 WORTH MAKING TIME FOR

 NOT TO BE MISSED!

 WILL ONLY WORRY YOUNG CHILDREN

 MAY SCARE MANY YOUNG CHILDREN; FEW ADULTS

 WILL SCARE MOST YOUNG CHILDREN; SOME ADULTS

 MAJOR SCARE FACTOR

 VISUAL DISORIENTATION

 MILD PHYSICAL MOVEMENT

 INTENSE FEELING OF MOTION

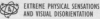 EXTREME PHYSICAL SENSATIONS AND VISUAL DISORIENTATION

As enthusiastic as we are about Mexico's La Hacienda, we're equally enamored with Italy's Via Napoli, and for the same reason: It's authentic. Order a wood-fired pizza here and you get a thin, crisp crust covered in fresh ingredients and just the right amount of cheese. The Parmegianas are positively silky, the spaghetti is like your grandmother should have made, and if you wash it all down with a fruity Aqua Fresca you'll feel like you're drinking summertime.

> **HIDDEN MAGIC** | Those three wood-burning ovens in Via Napoli recreate the goddess of Mount Etna, the demigod Hercules in the form of Mount Vesuvius, and Stromboli, home to Aeolus, the keeper of the winds. Etna, Vesuvius, and Stromboli are, appropriately, all volcanoes.

TUTTO ITALIA

★★★ $$$$$

Tutto Italia means "all of Italy" and the menu reflects regional cuisines, from the pesto culture of Genoa to the unmistakable olive oil hallmark of Sicilian fare. Most menu items will be familiar, perhaps with a slight twist that makes them just a bit special, and the bold flavors of the Mediterranean go over well on a hot Florida day.

SHOPPING IN ITALY

MAGICAL MERCHANDISE

There is no torture chamber inside this version of the Doge's Palace, unless you find the perfect piece of Murano crystal in **Il Bel Cristallo** and have no way to get it home.

The American Adventure

Playing host to the **World Showcase**, the American Adventure tells the story of the grandeur and majesty of this proud country—a sentiment held

---

★ POOR   ★★ FAIR   ★★★ GOOD   ★★★★ EXCELLENT   ★★★★★ GOURMET

$ UNDER $10 $$ $10–15 $$$ $15–$20 $$$$ $20–$25 $$$$$ $25+

 B BREAKFAST   L LUNCH   D DINNER    CS COUNTER SERVICE   TS TABLE SERVICE   TS2 TABLE SERVICE (TWO CREDITS)

strongly by Walt Disney—as she welcomes and embraces the global community that surrounds her.

The building itself represents **Philadelphia** and **Boston** during **colonial times**, not seeking to replicate any one place, but rather to blend them. Its Georgian-style architecture is reminiscent of **Independence Hall** in Philadelphia, home to the **Liberty Bell**, site of great debates over declaring independence from England, and the reading of the final Declaration of Independence. The single second-story window above the restaurant and gift shop call to mind **Boston's Old State House**, the governmental seat in 1776, where Colonel Thomas Crafts read the newly penned **Declaration of Independence** to Boston's citizens from a small balcony. The columned entryways are similar to those at Thomas Jefferson's home, **Monticello**, and inside the pavilion, the exquisite rotunda calls to mind **Monticello's Dome Room** (have a pre-2004 nickel? Thomas Jefferson is on the front, and on the back you'll see Monticello).

Inspiration abounds inside the pavilion, through historical paintings by Disney Imagineers (and NASA artist Robert McCall), quotes from influential people of the twentieth century, and the American Heritage Gallery, filled with artifacts belonging to some of the nation's most famous citizens.

AMERICAN ADVENTURE

This multimedia attraction's story is clear: It's the adventure that began on the *Mayflower* and led to a whole new country. The show opens as your hosts, **Benjamin Franklin** and **Mark Twain** (in animatronics form), chat about the founding of America. The story of the *Mayflower* and the first tentative steps into a new land, the **Boston Tea Party**, and the **Declaration of Independence** are told through paintings, similar to the ones you see in the pavilion's rotunda. **Ben Franklin** and **Thomas Jefferson** reveal the challenges faced by a fledgling nation considering separation from Britain.

Paintings were the means used to capture scenes of the **Revolutionary War**, and they are used here, too. We, the People, won our freedom to act as a

 MISS-ABLE   IF YOU HAVE TIME   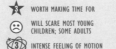 WORTH MAKING TIME FOR   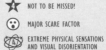 NOT TO BE MISSED!

😊 WILL ONLY WORRY YOUNG CHILDREN   😊 MAY SCARE MANY YOUNG CHILDREN; FEW ADULTS   😕 WILL SCARE MOST YOUNG CHILDREN; SOME ADULTS   😲 MAJOR SCARE FACTOR

VISUAL DISORIENTATION   MILD PHYSICAL MOVEMENT   INTENSE FEELING OF MOTION   EXTREME PHYSICAL SENSATIONS AND VISUAL DISORIENTATION

country in our own right, expanding beyond the colonial states into the "new world." But not all people living in this land of plenty were free. **Frederick Douglass** tells the story from the perspective of a slave, during the time when **Harriet Beecher Stowe's** controversial book, *Uncle Tom's Cabin*, stirred passions on both sides.

Brother speaks out against brother as the story turns to daguerreotypes, and then photography, to express the split between slave and nonslave states. At the end of the **Civil War**, prosperity took hold and immigrants poured into the country. But while some were welcomed for the hard work they provided, one race was pushed aside, to useless, unfertile ground: the Native American. **Chief Joseph**, whose words you see on the wall in the pavilion's rotunda, laments the betrayals his people experienced, and vows he "will fight no more, forever."

Women take up the quest for equality, as **Susan B. Anthony** demands rights for all of the nation's daughters. Progress is everywhere, and the country rides a tide of hope and prosperity. The story is told now through moving pictures. Nature's rights take center stage, and the **National Parks** are born.

The outbreak of **World War I** through present times unfolds in live-action film, as technology advances and America's role in the world expands. And then, **The Great Depression**. The courageous words of **President Roosevelt** and the wit of **Will Rogers** inspire a nation coping with the horrors of **World War II**. Women find their place is in the workplace, and at the close of the war we are a nation completely changed, poised to "spread its golden wings," facing each new challenges with courage, the spark of creativity, and unfailing optimism.

It is a show almost guaranteed to bring a patriotic tear to the eye. And when it's over we're pretty sure you know how to greet the Cast Members!

ROOKIE MISTAKES
Summertime concerts at the American Garden Theater are free with your admission. Seating for the most popular bands will fill up quickly, so be sure to arrive at least thirty minutes early if a big-name group is performing.

★ POOR   ★★ FAIR   ★★★ GOOD   ★★★★ EXCELLENT   ★★★★★ GOURMET
$ UNDER $10 $$ $10–15 $$$ $15–$20 $$$$ $20–$25 $$$$$ $25+
 BREAKFAST   LUNCH   DINNER   COUNTER SERVICE   TABLE SERVICE   TABLE SERVICE (TWO CREDITS)

DINING IN AMERICA

LIBERTY INN

★ $

If you haven't had enough burgers or chicken nuggets during your vacation, you won't want to miss Liberty Inn. The most creative thing on the menu is a pulled pork sandwich, but if the kids are craving a plain old PB&J, you can get one here. Uninspired, but it's familiar and sometimes that counts for a lot.

SHOPPING IN AMERICA

HERITAGE MANOR GIFTS

This U.S.A.–themed store has appropriately U.S.A.–themed T-shirts and gifts.

Japan

Serenity. Graceful simplicity. Flowing lines. These features combine with a powerful belief in symbolism and a healthy dash of superstition to make the Japan pavilion one of the most interesting in World Showcase. Everything here has meaning, some of it obvious, some of it obscure.

Two structures stand out most when telling Japan's story; the **torii gate** standing in the low waters of the lagoon and the **pagoda** at the front of the pavilion. Symbolic of the gateway between the physical and spiritual world, it also bestows good luck upon those who pass by. The torii here is based on the sixth century **Itsukushima Shrine in Hiroshima Bay**, its three distinct parts indicative of a belief in the sacredness of the number three.

Japan's goju-no-tu, or five-storied pagoda, represents the five elements from which Buddists believe all things emanate: Earth, Wind, Fire, Water, and Sky. At the top is a sorin, its discs symbolic of six religious elements important in Japanese culture.

A recreation of **Shishinden Hall** at the **Kyoto Imperial Palace** stands opposite to the pagoda, and this is where Japan's oldest department store, built in 1672,

 MISS-ABLE

 WILL ONLY WORRY YOUNG CHILDREN

VISUAL DISORIENTATION

 IF YOU HAVE TIME

 MAY SCARE MANY YOUNG CHILDREN; FEW ADULTS

 MILD PHYSICAL MOVEMENT

 WORTH MAKING TIME FOR

 WILL SCARE MOST YOUNG CHILDREN; SOME ADULTS

 INTENSE FEELING OF MOTION

 NOT TO BE MISSED!

 MAJOR SCARE FACTOR

EXTREME PHYSICAL SENSATIONS AND VISUAL DISORIENTATION

brings "service with serenity" to central Florida. The Mitsukoshi branch here is best visited from back to front, where a timeline of art is played out, from pottery and textiles to modern-day items, including popular anime characters children love.

HIDDEN MAGIC

Anime makes for fun cartoons, but the characters are actually modern recreations of ancient Japanese legends, myths, and artworks. Kit Sune, the fox, was the guardian of sacred shrines and temples; Saru, the trickster monkey, came from Kabuki drama; Tanuki, part dog, part raccoon, excelled in shape-shifting; legends abound about Moon Rabbit; cat spirit Bakeneko impersonates humans, and dog spirit Inugami reflects a belief we also share regarding this beloved companion's intense sense of loyalty. How many of these mythical characters do you recognize from our own pop culture?

The style of the fortress at the back of the pavilion brings to mind the traditional Japanese architecture seen in castles throughout the country, including **Nagoya-jo**, built by Takugawa Ieyasu, a famous shogun, and **Himeji-jo**, nicknamed Shirasagijo, or "dancing egret" due to its shape and stark white coloring. But the shachihoko, or golden orca, on the roof hints at its ties to Nagoya, as they are symbols of that city. The mythical shachihoko also play two "good luck" roles: first, they are placed on the rooftops to ward off destruction due to fire by splashing water on the blaze (that's what the blue color symbolizes); and second, they are believed to entice storks to nest on the roof, which is a sign of good luck for that home. Greet the Cast Members with a sincere "konnichiwa" (ko-nee-tse-wa).

DINING IN JAPAN

TOKYO DINING

★★★★ $$$$

This restaurant is the more casual of the two full-service options in Japan, and it's a great choice for sushi while you look out over World Showcase. Tempura, bento boxes, katsu, and grilled selections are available for a fulfilling, if not completely authentic, meal.

TEPPAN EDO

★★★★ $$$$

Mothers of the chefs at Teppan Edo apparently never told them not to play with their food. Along with perfectly cooked dishes prepared on a central grill (a teppan) around which diners sit, your meal becomes an experience as the chefs wield their knives (and your food!) in the most entertaining style. Steak, seafood, pork, chicken, or vegetarian selections are featured at this American interpretation of traditional hibachi-style dining.

YAKITORI HOUSE

★★ $

Cross a small bridge behind the pagoda and you reach the cozy Yakitori House, based on the tea house at Katsura Imperial Villa in Kyoto. Enjoy quick-service sushi or Japanese noodles.

SHOPPING IN JAPAN

MITSUKOSHI

Formerly a kimono shop, Mitsukoshi is Japan's oldest department store, dating back more than 335 years. Mitsukoshi Department Store here in Epcot

★ MISS-ABLE	★ IF YOU HAVE TIME	★ WORTH MAKING TIME FOR	★ NOT TO BE MISSED!
😊 WILL ONLY WORRY YOUNG CHILDREN	😐 MAY SCARE MANY YOUNG CHILDREN; FEW ADULTS	😟 WILL SCARE MOST YOUNG CHILDREN; SOME ADULTS	😨 MAJOR SCARE FACTOR
🌀 VISUAL DISORIENTATION	MILD PHYSICAL MOVEMENT	INTENSE FEELING OF MOTION	EXTREME PHYSICAL SENSATIONS AND VISUAL DISORIENTATION

sells just about everything, from pottery and chopsticks to Hello Kitty and Pokemon toys.

Morocco

Travel from **Casablanca** to **Fez** to **Marrakech** in just a matter of minutes! The atmosphere here is immensely appealing, in part because it is the most visually authentic of all the World Showcase pavilions. The design work here was crafted by artisans from Morocco to ensure it remained true to beliefs strongly held by that country's citizens. The design also blends in with the surounding scenery. If you stand in Mexico and look towards Morocco, you'll see the Tower of Terror in the background, blending in seamlessly (see photo insert).

Worship is a primary focus of daily life in Morocco, as hinted at by the prominent position of the twelfth-century replica of **Koutoubia Minaret**, part of the largest mosque in Marrakech. The front of the pavilion represents **Ville Nouvelle** (the "new city"); pass through a reproduction of **Bab Boujeloud**, the gateway in Fez that leads to the Medina ("old city"). Here you'll find the castle around which the city was built, just as cities are in Morocco.

Once through the gate you have entered the **bazaar**, with its winding streets, homes above family businesses, and quiet courtyards affording space for privacy and reflection. **Fez House**, on your right, is a wonderful example of storytelling, Disney-style. If you slow down and listen, you'll hear the family living upstairs as they go about the task of preparing for a special visitor.

Just beyond is **Casa Carpets**, with the shop open to the family's living space in the area above, as would be common in Fez. In the streets outside the shops you may hear children playing or singing as they head to school. On your left is the **Chellah Minaret** found in Rabat during better times (the archway you passed under is also similar to one at the ruins in Rabat); just beyond **Restaurant Marrakech** is the **Nejjarine Fountain** in Fez, a refreshing oasis for weary Moroccans and a beautiful example of the geometric art the country is known for. If you stand in the street near the fountain you might hear a shopkeeper having a conversation with a potential buyer. Greet Cast Members here with the casual greeting, "marhaba" (mar-hubba).

HIDDEN MAGIC

Look for the board on the wall to the right of the last door in Tangier Traders, just before you reach Tangierine Café. In the center of the board is Arabic writing that reads "God is the Greatest." Since 2002, Cast Members have signed the board using their Arabic names, connecting their homeland with its namesake here in Epcot. The board is replaced as it fills up, but see if you can find the earliest Cast Member on the board when you visit.

DINING IN MOROCCO

TANGIERINE CAFÉ

★★★★ $$

Tangierine Café serves some of the healthiest quick-service food in Epcot, and some of the most appealing. Wonderfully fresh shawarma platters, wraps, kefta, and vegetarian combos offer a real Eastern Mediterranean taste treat. And while it is tempting to think the café's name refers to the zesty little citrus fruit native to China, it actually just means "café of Tangier."

HIDDEN MAGIC

The writing over the door at Tangierine Café must surely be the restaurant's name. But no. It's Arabic for "Tourist Information."

RESTAURANT MARRAKECH

★★★ $$$$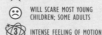

If you've come here for the belly dancing, Restaurant Marrakech has it, along with rather hit-or-miss Moroccan dishes, including the massive Sultan's Feast, just right for sharing. Try Shish Kebab, roast lamb, couscous, or fish. Want to be completely authentic? Use your right hand to scoop up your food. We dare you!

SHOPPING IN MOROCCO

MAGICAL MERCHANDISE

Shopping is abundant, as you would expect, seeing as how you're in a marketplace. There is less distinction in the wares here as you more or less amble from one area into another, with rugs, pottery, clothing, and brass being the primary goods.

France

Paris, the City of Lights! You're visiting at the height of her beauty—**La Belle Époque**—and she pulls you in with her glittering fountains, captivating scents, and the inescapable lure of the **Eiffel Tower**, always just a few blocks away.

The architecture on the left is typically Parisian; on the right the lines and colors are reminiscent of **Nice** in southern France. Wind your way along the boulevard toward **Boulangerie Patisserie** and the village of **Mormant**, just outside Paris, comes to mind. **Palais du Cinema** is based on **Château de Fontainebleau** in Paris.

It wouldn't be France if it didn't have a certain "je ne sais quoi"; there is something familiar about the food, the wine, the art, and the architecture, but at the same time, it's elusive, distinct, undeniably French. Say "bonjour" (bonh-joor) as your greeting.

IMPRESSIONS DE FRANCE

This attraction is really a glorified travelogue, just as the movie in China is, but in this instance it would be fair to replace "glorified" with "glorious." The vistas are truly stunning, blending a playful sense of adventure with an introspective eye toward all things artistic.

You only have a few days (eighteen minutes, actually) to see the best France has to offer. Begin with the serene settings of **Normandy**, **La Rochelle**, and **the Loire Valley**; then join a fox hunt; harvest grapes for wine; visit the

★ POOR	★★ FAIR	★★★ GOOD	★★★★ EXCELLENT	★★★★★ GOURMET
$ UNDER $10	$$ $10–15	$$$ $15–$20	$$$$ $20–$25	$$$$$ $25+
Ⓑ BREAKFAST	Ⓛ LUNCH	Ⓓ DINNER	Ⓒ COUNTER SERVICE	Ⓣ TABLE SERVICE	TS2 TABLE SERVICE (TWO CREDITS)

castles and caves of **Versailles**, **Cognac**, and **Dordogne**; check out the Bugatti races in **Cannes**; ride a bike; take to the skies; ski **the Alps**; go fishing; visit **Mont-Saint-Michel** at low tide, and attend a wedding. As night falls, travel along the **Champs-Elysées** toward your boat ride on the **Seine**, then visit magnificent **Notre Dame de Paris**. Your whirlwind tour draws toward a close with the splendor of Paris as seen from the Eiffel Tower, as day turns to night.

It is all set to the music of well-known classical French composers, and just as the French have a knack for tapping into the finer emotions, so too does Impressions de France give a tug at the place inside where your longing for adventure lives.

DINING IN FRANCE

BOULANGERIE PATISSERIE

Oh, the sinfully delicious pastries you find at bakeries in France! You have stumbled upon the village bakery of Boulangerie Patisserie, filled with tempting little cakes, cookies, and other niceties. Being good? You'll find croissants, quiche, and sandwiches here too. The desserts make a divine finale while watching IllumiNations.

CHEFS DE FRANCE

★★★★ $$$$

This restaurant represents all of those wonderfully atmospheric cafés you find in Paris, where the pace is slow, the food is exceptional, and the service is just a tiny bit supérieure. La perfection! The well-rounded menu of seafood, meats, poultry, and vegetarian selections live up to France's well-deserved reputation for cuisine gastronomique. In best French tradition, a three course prix fixe menu is also available.

 MISS-ABLE   IF YOU HAVE TIME   WORTH MAKING TIME FOR   NOT TO BE MISSED!

WILL ONLY WORRY YOUNG CHILDREN   MAY SCARE MANY YOUNG CHILDREN; FEW ADULTS   WILL SCARE MOST YOUNG CHILDREN; SOME ADULTS   MAJOR SCARE FACTOR

 VISUAL DISORIENTATION   MILD PHYSICAL MOVEMENT   INTENSE FEELING OF MOTION   EXTREME PHYSICAL SENSATIONS AND VISUAL DISORIENTATION

BISTRO DE PARIS

★★★★★ $$$$$

Bistro de Paris, located above Chefs de France, puts the exclamation point on the term "fine French dining." This is the premier dining spot, not just in Epcot but in any Disney park. Seafood, duck, veal, lamb, beef, and pork are prepared to perfection, in traditional French style. Order à la carte or from the prix fixe menu, with or without wine pairings.

SHOPPING IN FRANCE

MAGICAL MERCHANDISE

France is known for its fine perfumes, and **Plume et Palette** is the place to procure them. **La Mason du Vin** carries France's other popular exports: fine wine and exceptional chocolates. And if you really need a beret, a tiny Eiffel Tower, or other touristy items, head into the helpfully named **Souvenirs de France**.

> **REALITY CHECK**
>
> As you leave France, you cross the scenic (and often-painted) river Seine along the Pont des Arts, which links the Louvre and the Institute of France. And yet, somehow, you end up in the United Kingdom. Let's just pretend the Seine merges with the English Channel in the center of Paris, shall we?

United Kingdom

The United Kingdom in the World Showcase is a timeline of British history compressed into one charming pavilion, starting in the 1500s at the front (that cute little thatched cottage), to the Victorian era at the **Rose & Crown Pub**, to post-war **London** with its hedge-maze gardens. At the back of the pavilion is a lovely retreat complete with a bandstand similar in style to one in **London's Hyde Park**. The building on the left as you face the bandstand represents the 1910 Edwardian style. Walk around to the front of that same building and it becomes London of the 1950s. Even the old-style roundabout has found its way here, this time with a picturesque sundial.

The most outstanding feature may be the palace across from the Rose & Crown, a near-recreation of the **Tudor-era Hampton Court**, once the grand home of **Cardinal Wolsey** until that unfortunate man displeased grouchy King Henry VIII. Wolsey got off easy, having lost only his homes and all of his possessions. Two of Henry's six wives lost their heads!

HIDDEN MAGIC What's up with that wonky-looking house with the overhang? During medieval times, Britons were taxed only on the ground floor footage of their homes, so they built upper floors with more space.

The Rose & Crown is an adventure in British dining, and while the cuisine is fairly representative of the comfort foods from that fair isle, the building is even more appetizing. Visiting a pub in England is like opening a gift; you never know what you'll get when you walk through the door, but you know it's going to be good. The Rose & Crown plays on this unique characteristic: Various architectural styles are evident in recognition that no two pubs are the same. There is even an outdoor seating area similar to those that look out over a canal or a river, perfect for a cool summer evening. Go ahead and just say "Hello!" If you want to be really friendly, say "Cheers!"

DINING IN THE UNITED KINGDOM

YORKSHIRE COUNTY FISH SHOP

★★ $$

If it's quick service, it's got to be fish and chips. Yorkshire County batters it up and dishes it out at the Yorkshire County Fish Shop, and while the fare isn't even close to the chippies in England, it's enough to give you a rough idea of how addictive this fried feast of fishy goodness can be. Eat your fish and your chips with vinegar. Really. Just try it.

 MISS-ABLE
WILL ONLY WORRY YOUNG CHILDREN
VISUAL DISORIENTATION

 IF YOU HAVE TIME
MAY SCARE MANY YOUNG CHILDREN; FEW ADULTS
MILD PHYSICAL MOVEMENT

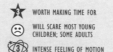 WORTH MAKING TIME FOR
WILL SCARE MOST YOUNG CHILDREN; SOME ADULTS
INTENSE FEELING OF MOTION

 NOT TO BE MISSED!
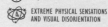 MAJOR SCARE FACTOR
EXTREME PHYSICAL SENSATIONS AND VISUAL DISORIENTATION

ROSE & CROWN

★★ $$$$

You've just dropped 'round to the pub, and the Rose & Crown is your "local" (the British version of "where everybody knows your name"). The atmosphere is smart but casual, the food is what Mum would have made if she'd had the time, and it's all very convivial. Traditional dishes include bangers and mash, shepherd's pie, and Sunday roast.

SHOPPING IN THE UNITED KINGDOM

MAGICAL MERCHANDISE

Tudor Lane boasts the thatch-roofed **Tea Caddy**, based on the home of Anne Hathaway (Shakespeare's wife) in Stratford-upon-Avon and specializing in the fine art of tea. Next to that is the **Queens Table**, then **Lords and Ladies**. Along the right side of the street is the Ireland-inspired **Sportsman's Shop** for all your Guinness needs. Just beyond is a nod to Scotland in the **Crown and Crests**, then **Toy Soldier**, which has become a meet-and-greet for Tigger and Pooh, and Mary Poppins.

ROOKIE MISTAKES

Many shops have a Daily Quiz about the country they're in. Look for the small board with today's question (usually by a cash register) and don't be afraid to pipe up!

Canada

With ten Canadian provinces and three territories to visit, you'd need months to see them all. Or, you can tour the Canada pavilion and hit the highlights in just an hour or so, including time for a concert and a cold Molson beer.

Start in an aboriginal **First Nation village** in the Northwest Territories, where trappers and traders exist comfortably alongside Native Americans, whose totem poles are stories in their own right. The rustic totem here references Raven, a mischief-maker whose tales are popular with many of Canada's native people. To the far right, **Victoria Gardens** is based on the famous Butchart Gardens in British Columbia.

Hotel du Canada encompasses the stunning Chateau Frontenac in Quebec, luxurious Chateau Laurier in Ottawa, and the grandeur of Banff Springs Hotel in Alberta, three Canadian hotels owned by the Fairmont group. And the small village just beyond is representative of coastal villages in Nova Scotia, New Brunswick, and Prince Edward Island.

It's tempting to think the falls toward the back are those in Niagara, but they're really **Salmon Falls in Ottawa**. After all, these are the **Canadian Rockies** you're looking at. Again, it's just a friendly "Hello" to our near neighbors to the north!

O CANADA!

Don't have time for even an hour-long wander across Canada? See it all in just fourteen minutes in this Circle-Vision 360 movie (bearing in mind there are railings to lean on, but no seats).

Comedian Martin Short is your host for this humorous tour of his native country, seeking to dispel the notion that Canada is nothing but snow, all day every day. Start at **Canada's Niagara Falls**; travel to the **Bay of Fundy in New Brunswick**, where the remarkable tides are the main feature; explore glorious **Butchart Gardens on Vancouver Island**, then revel in magnificent **Cathedral Grove**, with its ancient Douglas fir trees. Wildlife, winter sports, warm-weather sports . . . Canada has a passion for anything outdoors.

Visit **Calgary** during the famous Calgary Stampede, moving on to **Toronto** during the International Film Festival, the walled city of **Quebec**, and the eminently French city of **Montreal**, where Martin even gives us a glimpse into the famous Cirque du Soleil. And no visit to Canada would be complete without the **Royal Canadian Mounted Police**.

 MISS-ABLE IF YOU HAVE TIME WORTH MAKING TIME FOR NOT TO BE MISSED!

 WILL ONLY WORRY YOUNG CHILDREN — MAY SCARE MANY YOUNG CHILDREN; FEW ADULTS — WILL SCARE MOST YOUNG CHILDREN; SOME ADULTS — MAJOR SCARE FACTOR

VISUAL DISORIENTATION — MILD PHYSICAL MOVEMENT — INTENSE FEELING OF MOTION — 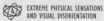 EXTREME PHYSICAL SENSATIONS AND VISUAL DISORIENTATION

Like its sister movies in China and France, Canada's attraction appeals to your wanderlust, inviting you to head north when your vacation here in the south is over.

DINING IN CANADA

LE CELLIER

★★★★ $$$$

Quirky as it sounds, you're in the wine cellar of Hotel du Canada when you visit Le Cellier steakhouse. As you might expect, the menu is heavy on beef, but chicken, bison, salmon, pork, and quiche can be found here, too. The specialty of the house is a luxuriously creamy Canadian cheddar cheese soup, and due to a rather curious following the restaurant has gathered over the years, it is now a Signature Dining location on the Disney Dining Plan.

SHOPPING IN CANADA

MAGICAL MERCHANDISE

Deep in the forests of the Northwest Territory, you've stumbled upon rustic **Northwest Mercantile** and adjoining **Trading Post,** with their woodsy vignettes and all those bottles of pure maple syrup. Find art glass, perfume, hockey wear, and clothing.

Parades, Tours, and Special Events!

ILLUMINATIONS: REFLECTIONS OF EARTH

 (LOUD FIREWORKS)

Epcot is filled with stories, but **IllumiNations: Reflections of Earth** may tell the greatest story of them all. In preparation for the show, nineteen torches are lit around **World Showcase Lagoon**, representing the nineteen millennia of modern history (notice that each has a number on it, from 1-19). So where is the torch representing the twentieth century? It's inside the globe.

As the show begins, **fireworks** explode across the sky, representing the chaos of the creation of the Earth. Once formed, a **giant globe** slowly makes its way to the center of the lagoon, and through LED screen technology, the story of evolution unfolds.

Plants are the first thing to make their appearance on the globe, then animals arrive. The first evidence of humans comes in the form of cave paintings, then you see actual people forming ever-growing communities. Exploration comes next, as curiosity and technology allow people to move beyond their homelands and marvel at the splendors opening up before them.

This appreciation of different races and cultures is symbolized in the lighting of the majority of the World Showcase pavilions as the globe continues to move through time. A montage of art, creativity, and influential people speaks to an evolution of society, which is summed up beautifully in a final burst of celebration.

The music, moving from chaos to joy, and finally to contented hopefulness, is so evocative that it positively tugs at the heartstrings. IllumiNations debuted for the Millennium Celebration in 2000, but remains a timeless experience. There are enhanced shows for Independence Day, Christmas, and New Year's Eve.

 MISS-ABLE   IF YOU HAVE TIME   WORTH MAKING TIME FOR   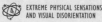 NOT TO BE MISSED!

 WILL ONLY WORRY YOUNG CHILDREN   MAY SCARE MANY YOUNG CHILDREN; FEW ADULTS   WILL SCARE MOST YOUNG CHILDREN; SOME ADULTS   MAJOR SCARE FACTOR

 VISUAL DISORIENTATION   MILD PHYSICAL MOVEMENT   INTENSE FEELING OF MOTION   EXTREME PHYSICAL SENSATIONS AND VISUAL DISORIENTATION

ROOKIE MISTAKES

You didn't take a picture of your parking row number and now you're one of those sad people wandering around clicking the panic button on your keychain. If you don't have any luck, head back to the tram and tell a Cast Member that you need assistance. They can call someone who will help you find the right area if you know (roughly) what time you arrived that day.

BEHIND THE SEEDS

Essential Information: Daily; meet at the reservations desk in the Land

This is a one-hour tour offered daily where you go into the greenhouses at **Living with the Land** for a Q&A session.

DOLPHINS IN DEPTH

Essential Information: Mon.-Fri.; no under 13s, 13–17 with adult only; meet at Epcot's Guest Relations

Go backstage at the Seas with Nemo & Friends, then enter the water to interact with dolphins during this fascinating three-hour tour.

DIVEQUEST

Essential Information: Daily; no under 10s, 10–14 with adult only; SCUBA certification required; meet at Epcot's Guest Relations

Pay a visit behind the scenes at the Seas with Nemo & Friends pavilion, then enjoy forty minutes diving in the aquarium. Three hours total.

 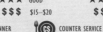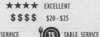

EPCOT SEAS AQUA TOUR

Essential Information: Daily; no under 8s, 8–16 with adult, 17 with waiver; meet at the Seas with Nemo & Friends

Head behind the scenes at the Seas with Nemo & Friends, then enjoy 30 minutes swimming in the aquarium. Two-and-a-half hours total.

SEGWAY TOUR

Essential Information: Daily; no under 16s; 250 pounds max; meet at Innoventions

This tour offers a unique two-hour tour around World Showcase on a Segway! Instruction provided, then you're off for a tour of each country.

UNDISCOVERED FUTURE WORLD

Essential Information: Mon., Wed., Fri.; no under 16s, ID required; meet at Epcot's Guest Relations

This tour allows you to go behind the scenes and learn the backstory about how the park incorporates Walt Disney's vision for Epcot. A must-do for die-hard Disney fans. Four hours.

FLOWER AND GARDEN FESTIVAL

Epcot transforms into a topiary wonderland from early March through mid-May. Enjoy seminars, themed weekends, special events, and **Flower Power concerts**. Free with admission.

FOOD AND WINE FESTIVAL

From late September through early November, this immensely popular event brings the tastes of countries around the world to World Showcase, in nearly

 MISS-ABLE   WILL ONLY WORRY YOUNG CHILDREN   VISUAL DISORIENTATION

 IF YOU HAVE TIME   MAY SCARE MANY YOUNG CHILDREN; FEW ADULTS   MILD PHYSICAL MOVEMENT

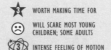 WORTH MAKING TIME FOR   WILL SCARE MOST YOUNG CHILDREN; SOME ADULTS   INTENSE FEELING OF MOTION

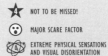 NOT TO BE MISSED!   MAJOR SCARE FACTOR   EXTREME PHYSICAL SENSATIONS AND VISUAL DISORIENTATION

thirty sampling kiosks (samples for a fee), seminars, marketplaces, and ideas for entertaining. You can also experience **Eat to the Beat concerts** daily. Festival is free with admission. Special dining experiences and exclusive seminars can be enjoyed for an additional fee.

YULETIDE FANTASY (SEASONAL)

Essential Information: Mon.–Sat.; no under 16s; meet at Epcot's Guest Relations

Take a three-hour, thirty-minute tour backstage at Epcot and Magic Kingdom to see the backstory of how Walt Disney World transforms its parks into a Christmas wonderland.

HOLIDAY D-LIGHTS (SEASONAL)

Essential Information: Select nights Nov. and Dec.; no under 16s; meet at Epcot's Guest Relations

One of the most stunningly beautiful holiday additions to the theme parks is the draping of sparkling lights that cover **Cinderella Castle** from November through December. Enjoy this five-hour tour which includes Epcot's inspirational **Candlelight Processional**, a stroll through the **Osborne Family Spectacle of Dancing Lights at Hollywood Studios**, and viewing of the ice-crystal effect of Cinderella Castle, all the while hearing how a magical season becomes even more spectacular from the people who make it happen. Light buffet included.

HOLIDAYS AT EPCOT

The World Showcase is the center of festive fun starting in late November. Each pavilion has its own storyteller, who brings to life the holiday traditions of the country he or she represents.

CANDLELIGHT PROCESSIONAL

Essential Information: call 407-WDW-DINE

This inspirational Christmas event shows three times nightly at the **American Gardens Theater**, and is a premier holiday attraction you won't want to miss. The story of Christ's birth is told through narration and in song, with a choir, orchestra, and special celebrity guest. **The Candlelight Dinner Package** ensures seating at this popular event.

REALITY CHECK There are several routes out of Epcot and it's easy to go wrong when you're tired. Be sure to pay attention to signs as soon as you leave the parking lot or you might find yourself on I-4 or Highway 192 when you don't mean to be.

 MISS-ABLE

 IF YOU HAVE TIME

 WORTH MAKING TIME FOR

 NOT TO BE MISSED!

WILL ONLY WORRY YOUNG CHILDREN

MAY SCARE MANY YOUNG CHILDREN; FEW ADULTS

WILL SCARE MOST YOUNG CHILDREN; SOME ADULTS

MAJOR SCARE FACTOR

 VISUAL DISORIENTATION

MILD PHYSICAL MOVEMENT

 INTENSE FEELING OF MOTION

 EXTREME PHYSICAL SENSATIONS AND VISUAL DISORIENTATION

Write Your Own Story

Write Your Own Story

Write Your Own Story

Write Your Own Story

Write Your Own Story

Write Your Own Story

Write Your Own Story

Write Your Own Story

Write Your Own Story

Write Your Own Story

Write Your Own Story

Write Your Own Story

EPCOT

FUTURE WORLD

1. Spaceship Earth
2. Innoventions West
3. Innoventions East
4. Club Cool
5. The Seas with Nemo & Friends
6. Turtle Talk with Crush
7. The Land
8. Living with the Land
9. Circle of Life
10. Soarin'
11. Imagination!
12. ImageWorks
13. Captain EO
14. Universe of Energy
15. Mission: SPACE
16. ISTC's Advanced Training Lab
17. Test Track
18. Fountainview Café
19. The Electric Umbrella
20. Sunshine Seasons Food Court
21. Garden Grill
22. Mouse Gear

WORLD SHOWCASE

MEXICO

23. Gran Fiesta Tour Starring The Three Caballeros
24. La Hacienda de San Angel
25. La Cantina de San Angel
26. San Angel Inn

NORWAY

27. Maelstrom
28. Stave Church
29. Kringla Bakeri og Kafé
30. Akershus Royal Banquet Hall

CHINA

31. Reflections of China
32. Lotus Blossom Café
33. Nine Dragons

THE OUTPOST

GERMANY

34. Biergarten
35. Sommerfest

ITALY

36. Via Napoli
37. Tutto Italia

THE AMERICAN ADVENTURE

38. American Gardens Theater
39. Liberty Inn

JAPAN

40. Mitsukoshi
41. Tokyo Dining
42. Teppan Edo
43. Yakitori House

MOROCCO

44. Restaurant Marrakech
45. Tangierine Café

FRANCE

46. Impressions de France
47. Boulangerie Patisserie
48. Chefs de France
49. Bistro de Paris

UNITED KINGDOM

50. Rose & Crown
51. Yorkshire County Fish Shop

CANADA

52. O Canada!
53. Le Cellier

SPECIAL EVENTS

54. IllumiNations: Reflections of Earth

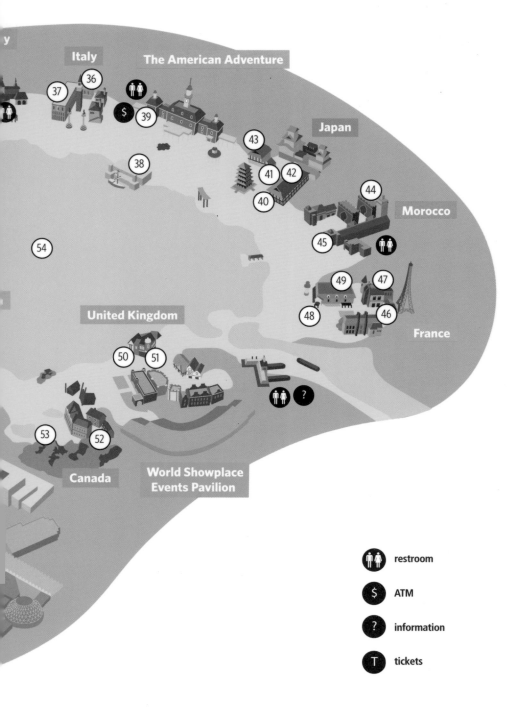

Italy

The American Adventure

37 36

$ 39

43

Japan

38

41 42

44

40

Morocco

45

54

49 47

United Kingdom

48 46

France

50 51

53 52

Canada

World Showplace
Events Pavilion

restroom

$ ATM

? information

T tickets

EPCOT

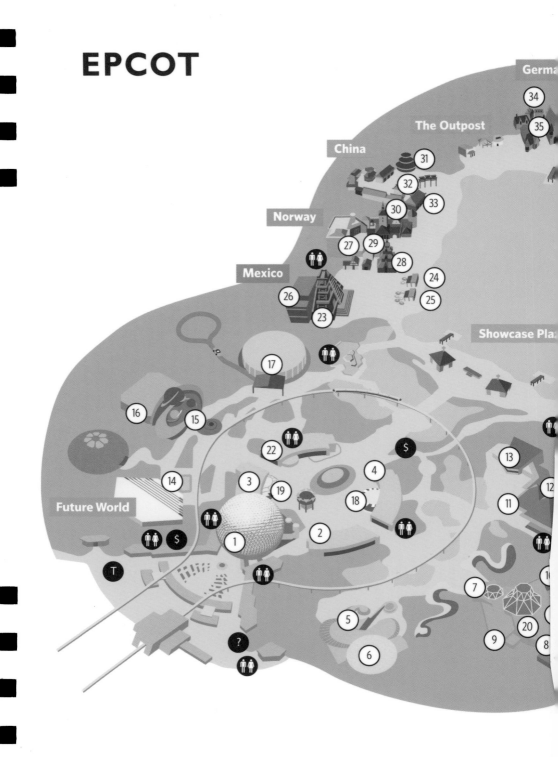

Movie Magic:
Disney's Hollywood Studios

THE STORIES ARE DIFFERENT HERE. Hollywood Studios is more about how the story is told rather than what the story is, and the art of moviemaking stands front-and-center. As you tour the park, tricks of the movie trade are revealed, and there are countless references to real locations in California—and to 1928—that all-important year when Mickey Mouse made his debut as Steamboat Willie.

Hollywood Studios, a "working movie studio," began its life in 1989 as Disney-MGM Studios, but the name was changed in 2008, in part because licensing with Metro Goldwyn Mayer ended, but also because the formerly movie-based park had evolved to include television and music, offering a fuller entertainment experience.

It's all about "how do they do that?" And now, let's find out!

Practical Information

Guest Relations is to the far left of the turnstiles as soon as you walk into the park. You'll find locker, wheelchair, and stroller rentals next to **Oscar's gas station**. The **Baby Care Center** and **First Aid Center** are located at the back of the Guest Relations building. There is a **Guest Information Board** at the junction of **Hollywood Boulevard and Sunset Boulevard** with all the current wait times for attractions.

Hollywood Boulevard

This is the park's "main street," the functional side of Hollywood in the 1920s and '30s, where industry professionals advertise their services in the **upper story windows**, offering everything from casting directors to stunt dogs. And if your celebrity status is so great that you've taken on a stalker, or if your leading man or lady has suddenly gone missing, **Eddie Valiant**, private detective from the hit movie *Who Framed Roger Rabbit*, is there to take your case.

 MISS-ABLE

 IF YOU HAVE TIME

 WORTH MAKING TIME FOR

 NOT TO BE MISSED!

☺ WILL ONLY WORRY YOUNG CHILDREN

☺ MAY SCARE MANY YOUNG CHILDREN; FEW ADULTS

☹ WILL SCARE MOST YOUNG CHILDREN; SOME ADULTS

😨 MAJOR SCARE FACTOR

 VISUAL DISORIENTATION

 MILD PHYSICAL MOVEMENT

 INTENSE FEELING OF MOTION

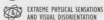 EXTREME PHYSICAL SENSATIONS AND VISUAL DISORIENTATION

THE GREAT MOVIE RIDE

  (ALIEN SCENE ONLY)

Housed inside **The Chinese Theater**, which is based on Grauman's Chinese Theatre in Hollywood, **The Great Movie Ride** is a beautiful culmination of what happens when individual elements come together to create a magnificent moviegoing experience.

As you "ride the movies" you appropriately start with **Busby Berkley's** bubbly *Footlight Parade*, Gene Kelly in *Singin' in the Rain*, and the charming *Mary Poppins*. You're right there as live theater makes its inevitable move to film, and you can see how Busby Berkley's innovative choreography generated an insatiable appetite for musicals in the 1930s that would continue into the 1950s.

But the lure of the gangster genre was strong too. And no one did it better than James Cagney, reviving his role here in *The Public Enemy*. The 1950s and early '60s brought about a wave of Westerns, making John Wayne—seen here in *The Man Who Shot Liberty Valance*—into an American icon. Younger moviegoers will recognize Clint Eastwood, who starred in a series of spaghetti Westerns long before Dirty Harry ever shot up the silver screen.

As the story continues, Westerns give way to science fiction with the advent of the space age, eventually spawning such sci-fi thrillers as *Alien*, a modern blend of monster and horror flicks. The tension is thick as you pass through the spaceship *Nostromo*; you're not going to get out of here without a close encounter! Adventure films, significant since the 1930s, are represented by the immensely popular *Raiders of the Lost Ark*. But in the 1940s heroes like Johnny Weissmuller in the *Tarzan* series brought courage and justice to eager audiences. And then there's romance . . . could there be a more iconic scene than the parting of Rick Blaine and Ilsa Lund in *Casablanca*? Love and loss; we never tire of it. Mickey Mouse transitions into family movies in his famous role as the Sorcerer's Apprentice in the 1940 animated movie *Fantasia*, and your tour enters a spectacular Munchkinland scene from *The Wizard of Oz*. The grand finale is a blitz of classic black and white films, bursting into color with *Showboat*, then through a series of comedy, action, horror, classics, romance, and into

the astonishing age of virtual-reality moviemaking with *Star Wars*. But there's one last element to every great movie, and you supply it: Cue a wild round of applause!

Dining on Hollywood Boulevard

THE HOLLYWOOD BROWN DERBY

★★★★ $$$$$ 

This restaurant, the park's fine dining venue, is a near replica of the 1946 version of the Hollywood Brown Derby in Los Angeles, with the exception of tables (the original only had booths). The walls are lined with caricatures of Hollywood's biggest and brightest stars and the guest book has signatures from stars who have dined here. It even serves Cobb salad and grapefruit cake, items developed for the original restaurant. The Brown Derby's classic American menu has been given a contemporary twist. Desserts are a notable feature along with a crab cake appetizer and the signature Cobb salad for two.

Shopping on Hollywood Boulevard

MAGICAL MERCHANDISE

Crossroads of the World is the place to pick up an autograph book and fat pen. Find camera needs, film, and gifts here too. **Sid Cahuenga's One of a Kind** is one of the most interesting shops in Disney's Hollywood Studios if you enjoy movie star memorabilia. Predictably, **Celebrity 5 & 10** carries Hollywood Studios merchandise; **The Darkroom** (styled after a camera store of the same name in Los Angeles) has all your camera needs; try **Keystone Clothiers** for adult apparel; **Mickey's of Hollywood** is filled with character merchandise; and the **Sorcerer's Hat Shop** can't be missed in terms of how easy it is to find (it's giant!). This is where you'll find those all-important trading pins.

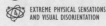

Echo Lake

Grab the biggest Q-tip you can find; you're inside Mickey's ear! Okay, that's not really what Echo Lake is about, but when the park was initially built, the **Echo Lake area**, the central courtyard where the **Sorcerer's Hat** now stands, and the area where **Hollywood Boulevard and Sunset Boulevard intersect** formed the three-circle icon representing Mickey Mouse. Echo Lake represents Mickey's right ear.

Many Disney locations are based on real places in California, and Echo Lake is one of them. Here in the Studios, it is a showcase for the unique building style known as **California Crazy**, evidenced by **Dinosaur Gertie** and **Min and Bill's Dockside Diner**. This is also an upscale area occupied by the movers and shakers from nearby Hollywood, and, inexplicably, an **archeological dig site**.

AMERICAN IDOL EXPERIENCE

This attraction's inclusion in tiny Echo Lake, away from the glare of the spotlights, hints that Hollywood hopefuls must pay their dues before they're welcomed into the grand and glittering echelons achieved by those who have gone on to superstardom.

American Idol Experience is the starting point along the golden path to fame and fortune. Contestants are selected from each day's park guests, who go through two auditions, singing their hearts out for the chance to win a **Dream Ticket** that earns them an audition for the television show. If selected, it's on to hair, makeup, and rehearsal before taking to the stage, with a live audience judging their performance. And you get to be part of that audience. Disney's version of the popular American television show is terrific amateur entertainment, but it also stirs up that butterflies-in-the-tummy feeling as each performer gives it their all. It's a unique insight into the first small step toward celebrity status. If you want to see the day's winner, aim for the final show. Guests age 14 and up who want to be in the show should arrive at the park early for an audition call time ticket.

★ POOR   ★★ FAIR   ★★★ GOOD   ★★★★ EXCELLENT   ★★★★★ GOURMET
$ UNDER $10 $$ $10–15 $$$ $15–$20 $$$$ $20–$25 $$$$$ $25+
 BREAKFAST   LUNCH   DINNER   COUNTER SERVICE   TABLE SERVICE   TABLE SERVICE (TWO CREDITS)

SOUNDS DANGEROUS WITH DREW CAREY

  (UNDER 5)

Sound plays a starring role in the movies, and this attraction is all about how audio creates images in our minds, adding to the power of any theatrical experience. At this attraction, ABC is testing an idea for a new television show, **Undercover Live**, and you get to preview it. Actor **Drew Carey** stars as **Detective Foster**, working undercover as a security officer in an effort to bust a smuggling ring. Equipped with a spy camera and a microphone he infiltrates a snow globe company, but the picture shorts out and the theater is plunged into darkness. Foster's microphone still works so the show keeps rolling. When Foster pays a visit to the circus the case is solved, the bad guy is apprehended, and (inexplicably) the video feed returns.

With the importance of audio cues in mind, you exit to an interactive exhibit, with **individual sound booths** and **various hands-on opportunities**. Make horse hoof sounds using half of a coconut, add audio to Disney shorts, and insert sound effects into *Star Wars* clips.

INDIANA JONES EPIC STUNT SPECTACULAR!

Essential Information: Fastpass

The Studios are shooting several scenes from the *Raiders of the Lost Ark* movie, and you have a behind-the-scenes view. Not only that, but every movie needs extras so this is your chance to become a minor star, or at least give a small glimmer (wave wildly when asked if you would like to volunteer).

The stage is set as an **ancient Incan temple**. Indy makes a dramatic entrance, acting out the golden idol scene from *Raiders* before giving the audience insight into how seemingly dangerous stunts from the movie are performed. The scene changes to **Cairo**, where Indy and Marion are watching street entertainers in the marketplace. But these acrobats are not who they seem to be. Nazi mayhem ensues, a knife-wielding ninja appears, and Indy uses his quick wit to

 MISS-ABLE   IF YOU HAVE TIME   WORTH MAKING TIME FOR   NOT TO BE MISSED!

 WILL ONLY WORRY YOUNG CHILDREN   MAY SCARE MANY YOUNG CHILDREN; FEW ADULTS   WILL SCARE MOST YOUNG CHILDREN; SOME ADULTS   MAJOR SCARE FACTOR

 VISUAL DISORIENTATION   MILD PHYSICAL MOVEMENT   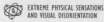 INTENSE FEELING OF MOTION   EXTREME PHYSICAL SENSATIONS AND VISUAL DISORIENTATION

take care of the situation. Marion is kidnapped, then rescued from an exploding truck and . . . cut! As the next set is put into place you learn about the dangers of working with explosives and how fight scenes are choreographed, then Marion shows one lucky volunteer the finer points of "taking a punch."

HIDDEN MAGIC Although it is implied, and we're aware of who the bad guys are from the movie, there are no direct references to Nazis here. When the attraction debuted there were swastikas on the German Flying Wing airplane. Now, your eye is fooled into seeing a swastika, but the icons you see are really a combination of background on the Nazi flag, minus the swastika, with the Luftwaffe insignia (Balkan Cross) in the center. This little trick of the eye tells a crucial part of the story without having an actual swastika in the park.

Once the scene has been reset, the action moves to **North Africa** where Indy and Marion are spying on an enemy airfield. Just as in the movie, when they attempt to steal a plane, they are thwarted by a great hulking baddie. Shots are fired, explosions go off all around, but, in a triumphant escape as the set erupts in flames, our heroes are safe!

STAR TOURS

Essential Information: 3 feet, 4 inches; Fastpass

As filmmaking evolved, movement was added to still pictures, then sound, then animation made its big screen debut with our good friend **Gertie the Dinosaur**. Color enhanced the experience, but computer-generated imagery took the art to a whole new level. Add motion to CGI and you have the most realistic experience possible, even though the reality of what you're seeing is impossible.

Enter the space port at Star Tours, where exploring the galaxy is commonplace. You've signed up for a little sightseeing tour chosen from a selection of more than fifty adventures. But when you board your **Star Speeder 1000**, you discover **C-3PO** is forced into captain duty. This could be bad.

One possible tour begins with **Darth Vader** stopping your Speeder, insisting there is a rebel spy on board. Flustered, C-3PO accidentally launches your space liner (backward!), making a quick jump to light speed to avoid intergalactic traffic. Malfunctions happen, and unfortunately your speeder decides to act up as you zoom over the frozen landscape of **Hoth**, straight into a battle between the forces of good and evil. You barely escape a snowy fate, when **Admiral Ackbar** transmits a message insisting you deliver the undercover agent to a special rendezvous point. Jump to light speed again, straight into another battle, taking a dive (literally) into **Jar Jar Binks's** underwater bubble-dome domain in search of a safe haven. But it can't be that easy, can it? Of course not! Prepare for some fancy flying and near-misses as you attempt to deliver the secret agent without being blown up, swallowed, or impaled!

STAR WARS: JEDI TRAINING ACADEMY

 (UNDER 12)

There has been a disturbance in **the Force** and the **Empire** is growing stronger, creating a need for a new crop of **Jedi** to help protect the universe. The latest batch of **padawans** (apprentices) who are taking this **training class** at the Jedi Training Academy need to learn how to use a lightsaber. They're first welcomed by their Jedi Master and then handed over to a Jedi Knight for instruction. As the lessons progress, **stormtroopers** show up, with **Darth Vader** close behind. Now it's time to prove you're a Force to be reckoned with! This one is for kids only, but it's so delightful you'll want to stop and watch even if you don't have little Jedis in tow.

PIXAR PALS COUNTDOWN TO FUN! PARADE

Movie studios don't have parades, but it wouldn't be Disney without one. Characters from Pixar favorites *The Incredibles*, *A Bug's Life*, *Ratatouille*, *Monsters, Inc.*, *Up*, and *Toy Story* star in this high-energy procession that makes its way through the Studios each afternoon, starting in the **Star Tours** area and ending near **Sid Cahuenga's**. Stake out a spot near the courtyard of busts for a terrific view.

 MISS-ABLE   IF YOU HAVE TIME   WORTH MAKING TIME FOR   NOT TO BE MISSED!

 WILL ONLY WORRY YOUNG CHILDREN   MAY SCARE MANY YOUNG CHILDREN; FEW ADULTS   WILL SCARE MOST YOUNG CHILDREN; SOME ADULTS   MAJOR SCARE FACTOR

VISUAL DISORIENTATION   MILD PHYSICAL MOVEMENT   INTENSE FEELING OF MOTION   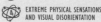 EXTREME PHYSICAL SENSATIONS AND VISUAL DISORIENTATION

Dining in Echo Lake

50S PRIME TIME CAFÉ

★★★ $$$$

The story of the **50s Prime Time Café** takes you to **hometown America**, back when televisions had feet and ears. Designed to look like a typical 1950s home, "the kids" (that's you) relax in **retro-style living rooms** until they are called to dinner. Your aunt, uncle, or cousin will be serving you while mom whips it all up in the kitchen. The menu reads like a family recipe file, and you're sure to find the **comfort foods** you grew up with. You can even watch **classic television shows** from the 1950s while you eat.

HOLLYWOOD & VINE

★★★ $$$$$

Named for the famous intersection in Los Angeles, you're dining in the "cafeteria to the stars." These days the stars are **Leo and June** from *Little Einsteins* and **Handy Manny**, who host the Disney Junior Play 'n Dine character buffet each day.

Take your pick from a character buffet breakfast or lunch or the dinner buffet (without characters), which offers salads and seafood, fresh-carved meats, fresh fish, and children's selections (ideal for picky eaters).

MIN AND BILL'S DOCKSIDE DINER

★★ $

This diner pays tribute to the 1930s movie *Min and Bill* about an innkeeper, Min, and her fisherman boyfriend Bill (that's them on the sign, from a picture used on an original theater poster). With all those crates waiting to be unloaded on the dock in front of Bill's fishing boat, it's strictly quick-service drinks and sandwiches.

★ POOR	★★ FAIR	★★★ GOOD	★★★★ EXCELLENT	★★★★★ GOURMET
$ UNDER $10	$$ $10–15	$$$ $15–$20	$$$$ $20–$25	$$$$$ $25+

 BREAKFAST   LUNCH   DINNER    COUNTER SERVICE   TABLE SERVICE   TABLE SERVICE (TWO CREDITS)

DINOSAUR GERTIE'S ICE CREAM OF EXTINCTION

$

The treats are frozen, but the story is a warm one. **Gertie**, immortalized here in concrete, was the first projected cartoon and the creation of vaudevillian actor **Windsor McCay**, who interacted with Gertie as part of his show. His work inspired Walt Disney to use a multiplane camera in filming *Snow White and the Seven Dwarfs*.

BACKLOT EXPRESS

★★ $

All those movie props have to be stored somewhere, and for convenience sake, you can grab a burger, hot dog, salad, or sandwich in this counter-service warehouse, amid famous and not-so-famous movie props (check out the internal framework of the Toontown taxi from *Who Framed Roger Rabbit*).

OASIS CANTEEN

$

There is a major archeological movie being filmed nearby, and those hungry actors are going to need refreshment. One of their movie sets has been commandeered as a quick-service canteen, serving up funnel cakes, ice cream, and drinks.

Shopping in Echo Lake

MAGICAL MERCHANDISE

Find *Star Wars* character merchandise at **Tatooine Traders**. **Adventure Outpost** carries all the things you'll need for your next great archeological dig (including hats, T-shirts, and rubber snakes).

HIDDEN MAGIC Take a walk down the small alley to the right of **Adventure Outpost**. There are some fun movie props, and if you look at the roof of the Outpost you'll see a sniper has set up his nest there.

 MISS-ABLE    IF YOU HAVE TIME   WORTH MAKING TIME FOR   NOT TO BE MISSED!

WILL ONLY WORRY YOUNG CHILDREN   MAY SCARE MANY YOUNG CHILDREN; FEW ADULTS   WILL SCARE MOST YOUNG CHILDREN; SOME ADULTS   MAJOR SCARE FACTOR

VISUAL DISORIENTATION   MILD PHYSICAL MOVEMENT   INTENSE FEELING OF MOTION   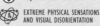 EXTREME PHYSICAL SENSATIONS AND VISUAL DISORIENTATION

Streets of America

When the park first opened, Streets of America was called New York Street and was part of the tram portion of the **Studio Backlot Tour**. **Lights, Motors, Action! Extreme Stunt Show** now sits on what was Residential Street, lined with the façades of homes shown on popular television shows. After the 2003 redesign, a San Francisco backdrop was added and the area became a walking street, but none of its charm was lost, in part due to the wonderful ambient sounds that make you forget you're in the middle of a giant theme park.

So what is the connection with entertainment? Movie sets! You are walking through a movie set designed as a convincing location without the cost and inconvenience of having to go to the real location. Indeed, various productions have been shot here, including a former Studios attraction, The Lottery, starring Bette Midler. Although this is New York Street, with a few tweaks of the removable façades you really could be in any big city.

HIDDEN MAGIC | As you pass through the archway from New York Street to the Muppet's plaza, notice that the road surface changes to brick. Another of those transition points that uses a tactile signal (underfoot) to indicate you're somewhere new.

MUPPET*VISION 3-D

Essential Information: Fastpass

In this attraction, the Muppets are preparing for a big movie production, and everyone wants to be in it, including lovable **Bean Bunny**. While Kermit and the gang are rehearsing in the theater, various acts show off their talents (or lack thereof) backstage.

Kermit opens the show, offering to give you a tour around the top secret 3-D lab, where **Professor Bunsen Honeydew** and **Beaker** are perfecting Muppet*Vision 3-D. But their creation, **Waldo, the Spirit of 3-D**, turns out to be rather mischievous. It all goes wrong when Beaker tries to deactivate Waldo and instead sets him free.

How many 3-D glasses can you find during the show? To get you started, look at the top of the Muppet*Vision 3-D machine when you enter the secret lab, then watch for glasses on the bird statue right after Kermit starts the tour again after you leave the lab.

Meanwhile, Bean Bunny has grand plans to enhance **Miss Piggy's** rendition of "Dream a Little Dream of Me," and ends up making a mess of things. Chastised and humiliated, he decides to run away, sending everyone into a tizzy as they search for him and convince him to stay by giving him an important job in the final production. Bean lights off the fireworks in a rousing finale where, in true Muppet style, chaos ensues that literally brings the house down.

The "Dream a Little Dream of Me" sequence is a loose pop culture reference to the great 1960s singer "Mama" Cass Elliot. In a promotional campaign when she went solo with the song after years with the Mamas and the Papas, Elliot posed nude (but obstructed) in a field of daisies.

HONEY I SHRUNK THE KIDS MOVIE SET ADVENTURE

 (UNDER 10)

Some movie sets are so appealing they just beg you to come in and explore. The backyard set from the 1989 movie *Honey I Shrunk the Kids* is one of them. In the movie, **Dr. Wayne Szalinski** invents an **electromagnetic shrink ray**, and his two children and their friends accidentally shrink themselves. When you enter the play area you "shrink" down to their size and find yourself in the Szalinski's yard, where all sorts of interesting items are lying around in the grass. There are worm holes to clamber through, spiderwebs to climb, leaves to slide down, a leaky hose to cool off with, and even the Szalinski's dog, whose giant black nose sniffs at you!

 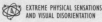

While some attractions are geared toward children, don't automatically assume there is nothing there for older kids and adults. Even places like Honey I Shrunk the Kids Movie Set Adventure and the Boneyard in Disney's Animal Kingdom have plenty to keep grownups amused.

LIGHTS, MOTORS, ACTION! EXTREME STUNT SHOW

In this real stunt show, Hollywood Studios is shooting an espionage sequence, set in a small town in France (a nod to the original attraction at Walt Disney Studios in Paris). Our hero needs to get out of town with a secret envelope, but the bad guys are not going to let that happen. With carefully choreographed chaos, various chase scenes are "filmed" and as each new scene is set, the director, his assistant, and the drivers explain secrets of how the perilous stunts you just saw are achieved, with minimal hazard, tremendous skill, and a little movie magic.

We won't give away any of the clever tricks; it's fun to be surprised as the show progresses. The good guy does get away in the end (of course), and as the show wraps up we see the finished product in movie form, complete with all the stunts performed during today's show.

STUDIO BACKLOT TOUR

During this 35-minute, four-part tour, you learn how special effects add that all-important thrill factor to the movies, and how set pieces are used to create a convincing location. Start at the **Special Effect Water Tank**, where *Harbor Attack*, a takeoff on a scene from the movie *Pearl Harbor*, is being shot. Audience volunteers (chosen ahead of time; wave wildly when asked!) play bit parts, enduring physical and mechanical effects including an avalanche of water and great walls of fire. Once assembled, the scenes they just acted out are shown as a completed segment of *Harbor Attack*.

HIDDEN MAGIC

The *234 Mickey Mouse* is the plane Walt used to scope out the Florida Project, which would become Walt Disney World.

Board a **tram** for your backlot tour, where working sections such as Creative Costuming, the Scenic Shop, and the Props Department are located. Enter the "boneyard" next, featuring large props such as the steam roller from *Who Framed Roger Rabbit* and our sentimental favorite, N234MM. When your tram reaches **Catastrophe Canyon**, you are allowed to enter the working set where filmmakers are shooting a disaster test sequence. A **sudden earthquake** occurs, your tram begins to move, and all the great moments in disaster films happen right before your eyes! After your near miss, you exit into the **American Film Institute**, with wardrobe and prop displays from popular movies.

Dining along Streets of America

MAMA MELROSE'S RISTORANTE ITALIANO

★★★ $$$

Welcome to traditional backlot dining—Italian style. Legend has it that **Mama Melrose** was an Italian actress who headed to Hollywood to find fame on the silver screen only to find that her cooking was a bigger hit than her acting. So she opened up her own restaurant, which quickly became popular with the actors at the studios, and now it is open to visitors, too. Seeing as Mama originally hailed from the Old Country but remains starstruck by the movie business, the décor is a wild mix of Italy and film memorabilia, with movie posters, signed photos, and bric-a-brac from her native land, making for a fun **Little-Italy-in-Hollywood ambience** that is accented by the hustle and bustle of the open kitchen.

"Keep it simple and keep it Italian" could well be Mama Melrose's culinary motto. Mama serves up large portions of traditional fare—antipasti, minestrone, flatbread pizza, chicken parmagiana, and pasta dishes—in hearty fashion.

★ MISS-ABLE

☺ WILL ONLY WORRY YOUNG CHILDREN

↻ VISUAL DISORIENTATION

★ IF YOU HAVE TIME

☺ MAY SCARE MANY YOUNG CHILDREN; FEW ADULTS

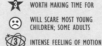 MILD PHYSICAL MOVEMENT

★ WORTH MAKING TIME FOR

☹ WILL SCARE MOST YOUNG CHILDREN; SOME ADULTS

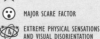 INTENSE FEELING OF MOTION

★ NOT TO BE MISSED!

☺ MAJOR SCARE FACTOR

EXTREME PHYSICAL SENSATIONS AND VISUAL DISORIENTATION

REALITY CHECK Want to enjoy the evening finale Fantasmic! show without having to get in line? Book the Fantasmic! Dining Package by making a lunch or dinner reservation for Mama Melrose's (or the Brown Derby or Hollywood & Vine) and, for a set-price, three-course meal, you receive designated seating for the big show.

PIZZA PLANET ARCADE

★ $

The story here is obvious! You've entered the scene in *Toy Story* in which Andy and his family go to Pizza Planet for dinner. There is even an arcade, just as there is in the movie. While the *Toy Story*–themed idea is good, the pizza is not.

STUDIO CATERING CO.

★★ $

This dining option is reminiscent of a covered, open-air backlot dining area where actors and crew members enjoy the fresh air between takes. Sandwiches, wraps, and salads are available and you can get alcoholic beverages just around the corner at **High Octane Refreshments**.

Shopping along Streets of America

PARKSIDE ANTIQUES

When you pass by Parkside Antiques you may be tempted to think Disney is trying to convince you that it has snowed in Florida. But remember, you're in the Studios; this is a movie set, decked out for filming a Christmas show. Find holiday decorations and gifts here.

MAGICAL MERCHANDISE

The Stage 1 Company Store has loads of visuals that will tickle the funny bone, as befits a shop that carries **Muppets** merchandise. Even the architectural

details evoke favorite Muppet characters. **The Writer's Shop** has books published by Disney, and just like most good bookstores in the "real world," you'll find a nice little coffee and pastry shop here, too. **Youse Guys Moichendise** is another indication you're in New York (just listen to that accent!). It mainly features sports stuff with a Disney theme.

Commissary Lane

Every production studio needs a commissary (lunchroom), not only to feed what amounts to a small city, but also as a place where giant bunnies can have lunch next to a Stormtrooper or a bloodthirsty alien. There are no attractions here since, well, it's where the **studio commissaries** are located (even Disney doesn't put a show in the backstage area).

SCI-FI DINE-IN THEATER

★★★ $$$ 

Great movies are being made—and what better way than in a convertible at a drive-in movie? This drive-in shows only **science fiction flicks** (as the name suggests), but there's another reference to all things alien here. Take a look at the license plates on the cars around you. They are all from California, New Mexico, and Arizona. Why? Because those are the three states with the most UFO sightings. How cool is that?

The setting is wonderfully convincing but the food sticks to diner standards like chili, burgers, and sandwiches for lunch and a slightly more adventurous selection, including steak, ribs, and shrimp pasta at dinner, plus great shakes and desserts.

ABC COMMISSARY

★★ $ 

 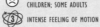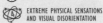

This commissary may not look like it is telling much of a story, but the idea is you're in the cafeteria for the American Broadcasting Company, whose history with Disney began in 1953 when the company helped finance the creation of Disneyland in California. In 1996, Walt Disney Company purchased ABC, and the commissary here is a nod to that long-standing relationship.

It's no-frills, just like a real studio commissary, and some would say the food carries on the theme by complying with cafeteria standards. It offers a light breakfast and a lunch/dinner menu with just five entrees—chicken curry, fish and chips, Asian salad, cheeseburgers, and chicken Cordon bleu—that are less than thrilling.

Pixar Place

You're at Pixar Studios! No, really, you are—or at least it looks like you could be. Disney's Pixar Place is a replica of Pixar Studios in Emeryville, California, from the big archway you passed under to the design of the brickwork all around you. And Pixar's animation studio has been recreated here to house the place where "toys come to work and play."

TOY STORY MIDWAY MANIA

Essential Information: Fastpass

The story here is arguably one of the most elusive, but it will be delightfully obvious once you know it. From the outside, you're looking at a replica of Pixar Animation Studios. When you pass the pale blue crayon just before you enter the building, you have symbolically shrunk down to the size of a toy. Step into the line and you're under Andy's bookshelf, then inside his toy box, where an array of classic toys have been jumbled together. Next, you sneak out of the toy box and hustle under the bed, then into a Midway Games Play Set box that's lying in the middle of Andy's room.

The box hints at what awaits you, and sure enough, the games "come to life." Woody, Buzz, and Jessie give you the chance for target practice before you begin, then you're off to the first carnival stall, **Hamm and Eggs**, where you can chuck eggs at farmyard targets. Next is **Dino Darts** for a bit of sheep-shaped balloon popping, and **Green Army Men Shoot Camp** where you break plates with baseballs. **Buzz Lightyear's Flying Tossers** is a classic ring-toss game with a three-eyed rubber alien twist. **Woody's Rootin' Tootin' Shootin' Gallery** is your final challenge, but you can kick up your score a bit during the **Woody's Roundup bonus round**. This is where the real "mania" comes in, so keep that shooter going! It's just like being at a carnival, minus the popcorn and surly ride attendants, and it's a given you'll want to ride again.

HIDDEN MAGIC When you reach the prize booth, notice that Buzz Lightyear's language setting has been switched to Spanish, just as it was in the movie *Toy Story 3*.

Dining in Pixar Place

HEY HOWDY HEY TAKE AWAY

$

At this kiosk, Andy is having a snack after his day at school (notice the box of **Cowboy Sugar Crunchies**, his **Woody's Roundup lunch box thermos**, and a **cookie jar**) and you're symbolically one of the toys on the table. Mosey on up to the chuck wagon and join him in having a treat (popcorn, ice cream, drinks).

Mickey Avenue

The phrase "blink and you'll miss it" applies here; Mickey Avenue is a tiny area. But good things sometimes come in tiny packages, and that would certainly be the truth in this instance. There is only one attraction here and it's a doozy!

MISS-ABLE
WILL ONLY WORRY YOUNG CHILDREN
VISUAL DISORIENTATION

IF YOU HAVE TIME
MAY SCARE MANY YOUNG CHILDREN; FEW ADULTS
MILD PHYSICAL MOVEMENT

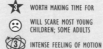
WORTH MAKING TIME FOR
WILL SCARE MOST YOUNG CHILDREN; SOME ADULTS
INTENSE FEELING OF MOTION

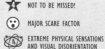
NOT TO BE MISSED!
MAJOR SCARE FACTOR
EXTREME PHYSICAL SENSATIONS AND VISUAL DISORIENTATION

WALT DISNEY: ONE MAN'S DREAM

  (IF YOU'RE A DIE-HARD DISNEY FAN!)

This fascinating walk-through exhibit, created to honor the **100th anniversary of Walt Disney's birth**, describes the journey of Walt's life, from his humble beginnings through his inspirations, his frustrations, and finally, the great achievements he realized on his own and through the persistent hard work of those who worked alongside him. Audio clips, video clips, photographs, original artifacts, models, and more tell Walt's story, but it doesn't end there. In a relatively short but surprisingly emotional movie, Walt tells his own story, in his own words. Brilliant stuff, and while it may be a minor diversion for many, it's must-see material for the real die-hard Disney fan.

HIDDEN MAGIC Look for the street sign indicating the corner of Mickey Avenue and Minnie Lane, just after One Man's Dream and before Pixar Place (see photo insert). The original sign is at Walt Disney Studios in Burbank, California. You can see it in the One Man's Dream film as Walt talks about building studios with money from Disney's 1937 animated movie, *Snow White and the Seven Dwarfs*.

★ POOR   ★★ FAIR   ★★★ GOOD   ★★★★ EXCELLENT   ★★★★★ GOURMET
$ UNDER $10 $$ $10–15 $$$ $15–$20 $$$$ $20–$25 $$$$$ $25+
 BREAKFAST   LUNCH   DINNER   COUNTER SERVICE   TABLE SERVICE   TABLE SERVICE (TWO CREDITS)

Animation Courtyard

If you had to name one thing, besides its theme parks, that the Disney brand is best known for, it has to be their animated movies. These stunning works of art tell well-loved, classic fairy tales; inspiring stories of courage and adventure; and gentle tales that become treasured family memories, generation after generation. Animation Courtyard represents the place where all of that happens.

VOYAGE OF THE LITTLE MERMAID

Essential Information: Fastpass

The Voyage of the Little Mermaid is the Disney version of Hans Christian Andersen's fable about a young mermaid who longs to be part of the human world, and dreams of marrying the handsome prince she has watched from afar. The tale is told through puppetry, live actors, and clips from the 1989 movie.

In contrast to Ariel's predicament, you're a human standing on the deck of a ship, then you become one of the merfolk when you enter the theater and go under the sea (notice **the carpet** looks like the sandy sea floor). At first you're inside a grotto looking out over the water at an approaching ship. As the boat comes by you dive down in its wake and swim with Ariel to her undersea world, where a "hot crustacean band" led by Sebastian remind her how great mer-life is through the song "Under the Sea." The scene changes as Ariel is scolded by her father, who has discovered she disobeyed his orders not to go up to the surface. Sitting amid her human treasures, Ariel sings "Part of Your World" as she remembers the glimpses she has had of Prince Eric during his shipboard birthday celebration, and strolling the beach with his dog Max.

Things take a dark turn as Flotsam and Jetsam plot to steal Ariel's voice. The evil sea witch Ursula convinces Ariel through the song "Poor Unfortunate Souls" that she has a shot at getting her man, then movie clips move the story forward until Ursula is defeated and King Triton relents, giving Ariel her legs and his blessing for her marriage to Prince Eric.

 MISS-ABLE   IF YOU HAVE TIME   WORTH MAKING TIME FOR   NOT TO BE MISSED!

 WILL ONLY WORRY YOUNG CHILDREN   MAY SCARE MANY YOUNG CHILDREN; FEW ADULTS   WILL SCARE MOST YOUNG CHILDREN; SOME ADULTS   MAJOR SCARE FACTOR

 VISUAL DISORIENTATION   MILD PHYSICAL MOVEMENT   INTENSE FEELING OF MOTION   EXTREME PHYSICAL SENSATIONS AND VISUAL DISORIENTATION

Avoid the front third of the theater for the best view, as the stage is rather high.

THE MAGIC OF DISNEY ANIMATION

Most attractions give insight into how real-life elements work together to create a memorable movie. This one is all about how animated characters come into being, from concept to completion. The real charm here is that the **Drawn To Animation** show host interacts directly with **Mushu**, the fiery little dragon from the movie *Mulan*. We, along with Mushu, get a humorous look at how he evolved, and we meet (in video form) the design team who made him what he is today. It's a fascinating look at the importance of getting a character "just right," from the rough idea to research, inspiration, and actualization.

Exit into exhibits and hands-on animation kiosks, **Digital Ink and Paint** (touch-to-color), **The Sounds Stage** (add your voice to animated movie clips), and **You're a Character** (find out which Disney movie character you are). There are also various character meet-and-greets here and you can even join the twenty-minute **Animation Academy** where guests produce their own drawing of an animated character (with surprisingly good results!).

DISNEY JUNIOR—LIVE ON STAGE!

  (UNDER 6)

Mickey Mouse invites you to come to his clubhouse, where he, Donald, Daisy, and Goofy are throwing a surprise party for **Minnie Mouse's birthday**. They each have a task to perform, but they need help. Mickey is inspired by stories, so he calls on his **Playhouse Disney** friends, Handy Manny, Rockit from *Little Einsteins*, and Jake from *Jake and the Never Land Pirates*, who tell the gang how they solved various problems using their own special talents. Handy Manny fixes a bubble machine with all the tools working as a team, Rockit goes super-fast and wins the race when his friends cheer him on, and Jake finds a treasure chest Captain Hook stole. Their tales encourage Donald as he creates a special

★ POOR   ★★ FAIR   ★★★ GOOD   ★★★★ EXCELLENT   ★★★★★ GOURMET

$ UNDER $10 $$ $10–15 $$$ $15–$20 $$$$ $20–$25 $$$$$ $25+

B BREAKFAST   **L** LUNCH   **D** DINNER   **CS** COUNTER SERVICE   **TS** TABLE SERVICE   **TS2** TABLE SERVICE (TWO CREDITS)

song for Minnie, Daisy as she hangs the birthday banner, and Goofy as he bakes the perfect cake. You get to join the party by yelling "Surprise!" It's a gentle message about good friends working together, there's lots of singing, dancing, and clapping, and preschoolers love it. Hint: Don't sit too close. The best view is from further back.

Shopping in Animation Courtyard

MAGICAL MERCHANDISE

One of our favorite shops is here, and if you're into Disney collectibles we think you'll like it too. Don't miss **Animation Gallery** for a vast selection of Disney art, including paintings, cels, and figurines. Nearby at **In Character**, Disney's costume shop provides the accessories youngsters need for Disney dress-up play.

Sunset Boulevard

This is **Hollywood, California**, in the 1930s and '40s. The story is full of glitz and glamour, but it also reminds you that the United States was in the midst of a world war. There are reminders of sacrifice, but there is a sense of hope and determination here, too. Hollywood seeks to make a difficult time easier by providing an escape, and the Sunset Boulevard theater district is the hot spot for all things entertainment.

BEAUTY AND THE BEAST—LIVE ON STAGE

This is your chance for a "night out" at the theater. The **Theater of the Stars**, inspired by the Hollywood Bowl in Los Angeles, is hosting *Beauty and the Beast*, telling the story from the blockbuster Disney movie in musical form. While most attractions at Hollywood Studios give insight into how great entertainment is made, here you can just sit back and be entertained.

MISS-ABLE
WILL ONLY WORRY YOUNG CHILDREN
VISUAL DISORIENTATION

IF YOU HAVE TIME
MAY SCARE MANY YOUNG CHILDREN; FEW ADULTS
MILD PHYSICAL MOVEMENT

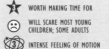
WORTH MAKING TIME FOR
WILL SCARE MOST YOUNG CHILDREN; SOME ADULTS
INTENSE FEELING OF MOTION

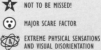
NOT TO BE MISSED!
MAJOR SCARE FACTOR
EXTREME PHYSICAL SENSATIONS AND VISUAL DISORIENTATION

The play opens as an arrogant, selfish prince is transformed into a beast by an enchantress disguised as an old woman, when he refuses her refuge in his castle. He will remain a Beast until he finds true love, but he only has until his twenty-first birthday, when the last petal falls from a magical rose. But who could love such a hideous Beast? The curtain rises to reveal Belle with her face in a book while a host of townspeople singing her namesake song lament her inability to fit into a provincial life. Gaston arrives with a solution; he intends to marry Belle. But she is having none of it.

HIDDEN MAGIC In the original version of "Beauty and the Beast" there is no character by the name of Gaston. Instead, it is the Beast who repeatedly asks Belle to marry him. Gaston is a takeoff on Gascony, France, which, some say, has more than its share of hot-tempered citizens. Gaston as a character is, in a way, the Prince's beastly alter-ego.

Belle wants the sort of adventure she reads about in her beloved books, and as the scene changes she finds herself in the Beast's castle, where the enchanted servants make her their guest. Their master, obsessed with his own unhappiness, does not take this well, but through one small gesture of kindness Belle understands there is something beyond his rough exterior. A mob led by Gaston is forming outside, intent on killing the Beast, but Belle's love for him is strong enough to transcend the Beast's wounded body and broken spirit. Transformed back into a handsome prince, this tale as old as time ends happily ever after.

There are no tricks here, just the delicate elegance of simple props and resonant voices combined to create the gentle timelessness of a story well told.

HIDDEN MAGIC Take a few moments to look at the handprints in front of the theater and see if you can find an unintended link to a major roller coaster in a rival Orlando park. They belong to Lou Ferrigno, who played the lead role in *The Incredible Hulk* television series, and the Hulk Coaster is a signature ride at Universal's Islands of Adventure park.

★ POOR	★★ FAIR	★★★ GOOD	★★★★ EXCELLENT	★★★★★ GOURMET
$ UNDER $10	$$ $10–15	$$$ $15–$20	$$$$ $20–$25	$$$$$ $25+

 B BREAKFAST   **L** LUNCH   **D** DINNER **CS** COUNTER SERVICE **TS** TABLE SERVICE   **TS2** TABLE SERVICE (TWO CREDITS)

ROCK 'N' ROLLER COASTER STARRING AEROSMITH

Essential Information: 4 feet; Fastpass

If you're an Aerosmith fan (and even if you're not), this is one story you wish would come true. In this story, you're visiting **G-Force Records** during a recording session, and as you watch the band from outside **Studio C** their manager interrupts to hustle them off to tonight's concert. They're late already, but Steven Tyler—always thinking of the fans—insists the manager scores a limo and some backstage passes so you can join them at the concert.

Head out to the back alley, where your super-stretch limo awaits. You've got to get across town quickly, so the moment the stoplight turns green you're off like a shot (0 to 60 in 2.8 seconds!), navigating a rather mysterious route (with inversions and barrel rolls) through the streets of Los Angeles while the Aerosmith concert blares from the radio. Within seconds you're a mile from the Civic Center. You streak through an "O" in the Hollywood sign, whiz past signs for Interstate 5, Highway 101, and Beverly Hills, and through a giant donut before taking the Rock and Roll exit. Concert Event Parking is just ahead, but you're aiming for the VIP lot. When your limo pulls up to the curb and lets you out, stumble up to the backstage door for a view of the band, who are already on stage (and don't forget to look at your ride photo!). Watch for a few minutes and Steven Tyler may turn your way and shout, "Rock 'n' Roller Coaster!"

THE TWILIGHT ZONE TOWER OF TERROR

Essential Information: 4 feet; Fastpass

The Tower is one of the most heavily themed of any Disney attraction, and you may end up wishing you could check in for a few days just to look around at all the fantastic detail. But for now, you're in an episode of *The Twilight Zone* television show, and something terrifying is about to happen.

 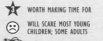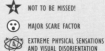

HIDDEN MAGIC

As you pass through the lobby, notice there is evidence that the hotel closed abruptly. Luggage, coats, and hats are abandoned, a mahjong game sits unfinished, and even the clock has stopped at 8:05 P.M., preserving the moment lightning struck for all time (see photo insert).

Proceed into the library where Rod Serling, host of the original *Twilight Zone* television show, tells of a family visiting the elite Hollywood Tower Hotel that fateful night, while a fierce thunderstorm raged outside. Tonight you're experiencing a tempest similar to the one that caused this family—and part of the hotel—to mysteriously disappear. And like them, you will be entering (say it with us . . .) the Twilight Zone!

Your next stop is the bowels of the hotel, a rank, dusty boiler room deep in the basement. Machinery here still functions, giving off the low rumble of a hungry beast, and while the maintenance man is long gone, he has left behind his tools. Does this mean there might be issues with the safety of these service elevators? You can bet on it! And although the hotel doesn't actually have one, your service elevator is heading for the thirteenth floor.

After the doors slam shut, you rise up one level and are looking down a long hallway at the storm howling outside the window. Ghostly figures of the family appear, then your elevator rises again, a door opens, and you travel down a second dark hallway. When you reach the end, Rod Serling's voice advises you are about to pass beyond the **Fifth Dimension**. This is your cue to hang on!

The nightmare is over for the ghostly apparitions that appear again, but you're not done yet. There is no telling how many times you'll rise and fall, but one thing is sure: This tower is chock-full of terror, and in a moment your elevator is going to be ringing with screams—or laughter!

HIDDEN MAGIC

You have survived the Fifth Dimension, but before you check out, watch the painted letter "B" on the inside of your elevator door. When the doors open, you have one final, eerie surprise.

HIDDEN MAGIC Are you remembering to look for the number 1928, referencing the year Mickey made his grand debut? If so, you'll find one in the residential area at the foot of the Hollywood Tower hotel. Sunset Hills Estates real estate development was established in that famous year, and you'll find a plaque on the fieldstone marker to the right of the hotel.

FANTASMIC!

Without one key element there wouldn't be a story and there wouldn't be any entertainment; that key element is imagination. **Hollywood Hills Amphitheater** was purposefully built to house the Fantasmic! show, which features Mickey Mouse as the **Sorcerer's Apprentice**, imagining more than a dozen classic Disney movies.

From a happy start filled with beloved characters, things turn dark. **Monstro** from the movie *Pinocchio* tries to invade Mickey's pleasant dreams, but Mickey's imagination is strong. Live action scenes featuring **Pocahontas** and the **Disney princesses** and their **princes** play out next, but the **evil queen** from *Snow White* has other plans for Mickey's musings as she conjures up the Disney villains, turning the dream into a nightmare.

Good always vanquishes evil in Mickey's world, and through his ingenuity, the help of a magical sword, and a sprinkling of pixie dust from **Tinker Bell**, his happy dreams are restored. A cavalcade of Disney characters bid you a good night from the deck of a paddlewheel boat, the perfect finale to a long day in Tinsel Town.

Dining on Sunset Boulevard

STARRING ROLLS CAFÉ

This is the one place in all of Hollywood where, if you pay your dues, you are guaranteed a "starring roll" (pastries, sandwiches, and coffee).

 MISS-ABLE   IF YOU HAVE TIME   WORTH MAKING TIME FOR   NOT TO BE MISSED!

 WILL ONLY WORRY YOUNG CHILDREN   MAY SCARE MANY YOUNG CHILDREN; FEW ADULTS   WILL SCARE MOST YOUNG CHILDREN; SOME ADULTS   MAJOR SCARE FACTOR

 VISUAL DISORIENTATION   MILD PHYSICAL MOVEMENT   INTENSE FEELING OF MOTION   EXTREME PHYSICAL SENSATIONS AND VISUAL DISORIENTATION

SUNSET RANCH MARKET

There are several quick-service dining spots in Sunset Ranch Market, which is based on the Los Angeles Farmers' Market located on the corner of Fairfax Avenue and Third Street. The Farmers' Market is a longstanding hot spot for celebrity sightings, and Walt Disney is said to have sketched out Disneyland while sitting at a table there.

ROSIE'S ALL AMERICAN CAFE

★ $

This café is a nod to **Rosie the Riveter**, the popular World War II "personality" who became the symbol of women's role in the war effort. Now, Rosie puts the flame to your burger rather than a B-24 Bomber. Rosie's may offer a clever motif but its food is decidedly ordinary—chicken nuggets, burgers, veggie burgers, soup, cakes, and drinks.

HIDDEN MAGIC

What's up with that scarecrow wearing a gas mask to the left of Catalina Eddies? Rosie has built a Victory Garden, as all good citizens did during the war (see photo insert). By growing their own produce, communities took some of the pressure off the nation to supply food when the war made huge demands on agricultural and transportation departments. They were literally "sowing the seeds of victory."

TOLUCA LEGS TURKEY CO.

★ $

Toluca Legs is a takeoff on **Toluca Lake, California**, where Walt Disney's nephew, Roy E. Disney, had a home. As an interesting side note, the icon for Toluca Lake is a swan. We're pretty sure smoked turkey legs taste better, and it's the only food served here.

CATALINA EDDIE'S

★ $

The story behind Catalina Eddie's may seem entirely obscure unless you know something about the ocean currents near the **island of Catalina**, off the coast of southern California. When the ocean currents become unstable, coastally trapped disturbances called **mesoscale eddies** form. These swirling rotations that appear in spring and summer are known as **Catalina eddies**. How cool is that? This kiosk serves pizza, salads, and sandwiches.

FAIRFAX FARE

★★ $$

Fairfax is the famous Los Angeles avenue that boasts Culver City to its south and Hollywood to its north. This location serves smoked meat, hot dogs, and salads.

Shopping on Sunset Boulevard

MAGICAL MERCHANDISE

Beverly Sunset Sweet Spells carry Disney movie merchandise, including villain themed goods at **Villains in Vogue**. **Legends of Hollywood** has character apparel and figurines; find Aerosmith and Rock 'n' Roller Coaster–themed items at **Rock Around the Shop**; jewelry and art can be found at **Sunset Club Couture**; and **Tower Hotel Gifts** has mementos from your stay at the Tower Hotel.

Tours and Special Events

STAR WARS WEEKENDS

The **Star Tours area** turns into a thrilling festival of *Star Wars* characters, events, and photo and autograph opportunities on weekends in late May and early June. Meet the actors and voice actors from the blockbuster movie series, with

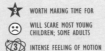

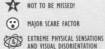

no added fee above park admission. Crowd levels on these weekends reflect the event's immense popularity.

INSPIRATION: THOUGH WALT'S EYES

Essential Information: Mon., Fri., Sun.; no under-16s; meet at Guest Services

This three-hour tour gives a wonderful insight into Walt Disney's influence on movie-making, and how simple concepts lead to the grand creations that make up the Walt Disney World parks. Start on Sunset Boulevard, then head backstage for a peek at **Events and Decorating Support** before visiting Magic Kingdom to see the famous **utilidors.**

MISCELLANEOUS TOURS AND SPECIAL EVENTS

Also see **Backstage Magic** and **Holiday D-Lights** which start in Epcot before visiting the Studios.

Holidays in Hollywood Studios

THE OSBORNE FAMILY SPECTACLE OF DANCING LIGHTS

Yes, even the holiday light display has a story behind it. In 1986, Arkansas family man **Jennings Osborne** wanted to surprise his young daughter Breezy by decorating the exterior of their home with a beautiful Christmas light display. Eight years later the display was so enormous their neighbors could no longer tolerate the amount of seasonal traffic it was generating, and they protested in a most un-Christmaslike way, including a pesky lawsuit that drew national attention, notably from some creative minds at Walt Disney World. The display was moved to the park's **Residential Street**, expanded to more than 5 million lights, enhanced with music, snow, and "dancing lights" segments, and now it truly is spectacular. Open dusk through park closing, November–January.

Write Your Own Story

Write Your Own Story

Write Your Own Story

DISNEY'S
HOLLYWOOD STUDIOS

HOLLYWOOD BOULEVARD
(1) The Great Movie Ride
(2) The Hollywood Brown Derby

ECHO LAKE
(3) American Idol Experience
(4) Sounds Dangerous with Drew Carey
(5) Indiana Jones Epic Stunt Spectacular!
(6) Star Tours
(7) Jedi Training Academy
(8) 50s Prime Time Cafe
(9) Hollywood & Vine
(10) Min and Bill's Dockside Diner
(11) Dinosaur Gertie's Ice Cream of Extinction
(12) Backlot Express
(13) Oasis Canteen

STREETS OF AMERICA
(14) Muppet*Vision 3-D
(15) Honey I Shrunk The Kids Movie Set Adventure
(16) Lights, Motors, Action! Extreme Stunt Show
(17) Studio Backlot Tour
(18) Mama Melrose's Ristorante Italiano
(19) Pizza Planet Arcade
(20) Studio Catering Co.

COMMISSARY LANE
(21) Sci-Fi Dine-In Theater
(22) ABC Commissary

PIXAR PLACE
(23) Toy Story Midway Mania
(24) Hey Howdy Hey Take Away

MICKEY AVENUE
(25) Walt Disney: One Man's Dream

ANIMATION COURTYARD
(26) Voyage of the Little Mermaid
(27) The Magic of Disney Animation
(28) Disney Junior—Live On Stage!

SUNSET BOULEVARD
(29) Beauty and the Beast—Live On Stage
(30) Rock 'n' Roller Coaster Starring Aerosmith
(31) The Twilight Zone Tower of Terror
(32) Fantasmic!
(33) Sunset Ranch Market
(34) Starring Rolls Café

DISNEY'S HOLLYWOOD STUDIOS

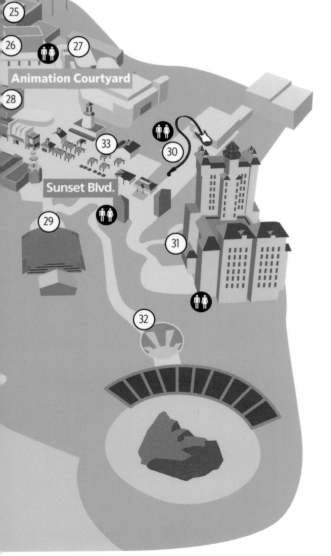

25

26

27

Animation Courtyard

28

33

30

Sunset Blvd.

29

31

32

restroom

$ ATM

+ first aid

? information

T tickets

bus stop

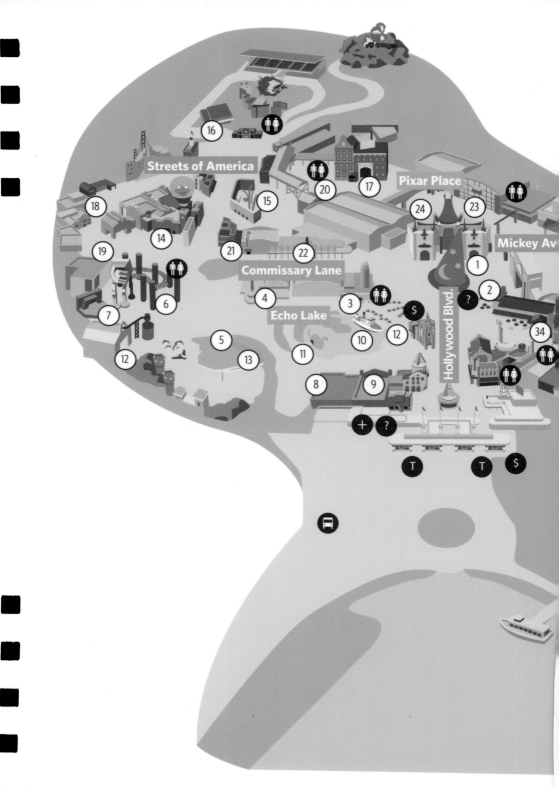

Chapter 6

Nature Tells Its Own Tale:
Disney's Animal Kingdom

OF ALL THE DISNEY PARKS, Animal Kingdom has the most cohesive story. It's not just a collection of unrelated or semi-related allegories; instead the story here has an overriding theme that encompasses the whole park. It is the story of humans living in harmony with nature, of nature's power and fragility, and of the consequences that result when humans break natural law. It also rejoices in the outcomes that occur when we choose to maintain balance.

As you walk through the park, look over the sides of the bridges and you'll see evidence of river traders and fishermen. Look in the landscaping and you'll find items important to the communities nearby. Pay attention to the ground on which you tread and you'll see animal prints that tell you who or what has passed this way. Everywhere you look small details enhance the story, convincing you these are real places, where real people live and work.

Even the foliage is presented in ways that are different from the other Disney parks. There, a featured plant is potted and put on show; here it's planted and intended to grow. And in keeping with Disney's penchant for using bridges as transition points, one of the most spectacular bridges, just before you reach Discovery Island, leads out of a time before humans and into a world when we must choose which path we will take: one of creating or one of destroying.

Practical Information

In the Animal Kingdom, **Guest Relations** is to the far left of the turnstiles. Find lockers to the left after the turnstiles, and wheelchair and stroller rentals to the right. The **Baby Care Center** and **First Aid Center** are located just beyond **Pizzafari** in **Discovery Island**.

The Oasis

Just as the name implies, this area is an oasis of calm, where nature and animals exist in peaceful companionship. You won't see typical animal enclosures here. Instead, the Oasis's inhabitants appear to be completely unhindered in their habitats (in truth, their barriers blend seamlessly into the landscape). There are no attractions here; you are simply meant to observe and reflect.

The story of the Oasis begins quietly, gently compelling you to slow your steps. This section of the park is lush and green and close; even the ground beneath your feet speaks out, sloping imperceptibly upward so that your pace is in harmony with the scenery around you. Here, you have entered the world during a time when animals ruled and nature was in perfect balance.

Discovery Island

Just as great cities are built around a central point, so too did Discovery Island evolve. The Tree of Life came first, and the village grew up around it. It is a place of contentment and joy, that celebrates the abundance of life that drew the villagers here. This delight in the animal kingdom is expressed in every facet of the villagers' lives including the artwork animals that you'll see throughout Discovery Island.

ROOKIE MISTAKES Don't stop for pictures of the Tree of Life first thing in the morning. If you return here mid-afternoon there will be far fewer people in the area, making picture taking much easier—and you won't end up with pictures of strangers in your photo album!

THE TREE OF LIFE

The Tree of Life doesn't just tell a story; in some ways it *is* the story. In keeping with many **creation myths**, a tree has sprung up, nurtured by the waters surrounding it. But the water doesn't just exist around the tree, it actually pours forth from it. Over time, images of **creatures** emerged within the very fabric of the tree's bark, ultimately becoming live animals, who now thrive in its shadow. Just as living animals were drawn to the waters and the shade it offered, so too were people drawn to the tree. It is a life-sustaining domain where all living things exist in harmony.

You would never know it from ground level, but as you wind your way through the roots of the tree you're heading toward an attraction that could only make its home underground. . . .

"IT'S TOUGH TO BE A BUG!"

Essential Information: Fastpass

What do bugs do when they want an evening out? Why, they go to the **Tree of Life Repertory Theater**, of course! And today you get to enter the bugs' world for a unique view of the critters that comprise eighty percent of the animal kingdom. **Flick**, the tenacious ant from the hit Pixar movie *A Bug's Life*, is your host, inviting you to become an honorary insect.

With your special 3-D **Bug Eyes**, you are able to see your fellow insects in all their glory, and they can finally share their 300-million-year-old story with you. It's a story of survival techniques, partially told by a super-scary, ultra-hairy **South American tarantula**, who specializes in throwing poisonous quills. And yes, you guessed it; he's going to be throwing some at you.

Next up is a **soldier termite**, whose unique defense is spraying acid. Bearing in mind this is a 4-D show, you know what's going to happen when he sees you! And when the **stink bug** comes out . . . well . . . let's just say she starred in the bug movie, Clair de Room. Get it?

Hopper, the angry grasshopper from the movie, makes a sudden appearance (cue the crying preschoolers!), and the attraction's title begins to make sense. Hopper decides humans should experience the same things they do to bugs, and you find yourself being swatted, sprayed, stung, and overrun by **black widow spiders**. It's tough being a human watching **It's Tough to Be a Bug**!

 MISS-ABLE   IF YOU HAVE TIME   WORTH MAKING TIME FOR   NOT TO BE MISSED!

 WILL ONLY WORRY YOUNG CHILDREN   MAY SCARE MANY YOUNG CHILDREN; FEW ADULTS   WILL SCARE MOST YOUNG CHILDREN; SOME ADULTS   MAJOR SCARE FACTOR

 VISUAL DISORIENTATION   MILD PHYSICAL MOVEMENT   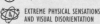 INTENSE FEELING OF MOTION   EXTREME PHYSICAL SENSATIONS AND VISUAL DISORIENTATION

Only through the intervention of a **lizard** living in the roots of the trees are you spared the worst the bug world has to offer. In a joyful grand finale, bugs remind us of all the good things they do for the Earth, not the least of which is making sure the planet can sustain human life. There is one more surprise before you go, but it's funny rather than frightening so we won't give it away.

REALITY CHECK

More than any other attraction, It's Tough to Be a Bug! is the one most parents think won't scare their preschooler, and the one where older kids who saw it when they were preschoolers tend to shy away from years later. Not all youngsters are unnerved by it, but it's dark, loud, and menacing. Those warning signs are there for a reason!

DISCOVERY ISLAND TRAILS

Technically these trails aren't an attraction, but they certainly are attractive and it's hard not to spend a great deal of time just wandering here. And why not? There are 325 animals gazing out at you from the bark of the Tree of Life, and it would be a shame not to notice each one of them. But there are living animals here too, drawn to the shelter the tree provides. Take time to enjoy these small animal habitats, which make wonderful backdrops for your photos.

ROOKIE MISTAKES

While you don't want to spend your whole vacation looking through a viewfinder rather than looking right at whatever catches your eye, the pictures you take will be priceless memories when you get home (it all tends to blur a bit, especially for first-timers). And don't be afraid to take some wacky pictures. Some of the best shots are when no one is posing.

Dining in Discovery Island

PIZZAFARI

★★ $

When it comes to categorizing animals, Pizzafari gets in on the act too. Each room has its own theme in this **pizza parlor**. Look for nocturnal animals, animals with built-in homes, hanging animals, camouflaged animals, and animals that are just downright fancy. This restaurant serves a breakfast platter, biscuits and gravy, pizza, sandwiches, and salad.

FLAME TREE BARBECUE

★★★ $

Themed as a **Balinese water garden**, Flame Tree Barbecue is all about the conflict between predator and prey (appropriate for an eating establishment). While you're munching on your barbecue, notice that you have symbolically become part of this timeless dance of survival. Here you'll find ribs, chicken, sandwiches, and salads.

Shopping in Discovery Island

MAGICAL MERCHANDISE

The shops in Discovery Island's village are colorful works of art, but they also express various animal attributes. **Beastly Bazaar** (Animal Kingdom–themed items) rejoices in animals found in and around water, **Island Mercantile** (house wares, clothes) focuses on migrating animals, herding animals are showcased at **Island Outfitters** (clothes, jewelry), and **Creature Comforts** (kids' clothes, toys) features patterned animals.

 MISS-ABLE   IF YOU HAVE TIME   WORTH MAKING TIME FOR   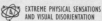 NOT TO BE MISSED!

 WILL ONLY WORRY YOUNG CHILDREN   MAY SCARE MANY YOUNG CHILDREN; FEW ADULTS   WILL SCARE MOST YOUNG CHILDREN; SOME ADULTS   MAJOR SCARE FACTOR

 VISUAL DISORIENTATION   MILD PHYSICAL MOVEMENT   INTENSE FEELING OF MOTION   EXTREME PHYSICAL SENSATIONS AND VISUAL DISORIENTATION

DinoLand U.S.A.

There are two overlapping storylines here. First, the area was once a sleepy, rather backward town, with a passel of residents, most of them related to each other. The town had a gas station and a fishing lodge with a restaurant, but not much else. That is, until someone made a discovery. A *big* discovery!

The unearthing of **fossils** was the catalyst for change. The fishing lodge turned its focus to bones, and once the **Dino Institute** was built the lodge evolved into a **dormitory** for the students studying there. A **Quonset hut** was built for storage and maintenance (though the students seem to think it's funny to make pictures on the walls with their hands and a can of Dynoil), and one of the fishing cabins became **The Hip Joint** student hangout, where all the songs on the jukebox have a dinosaur theme. Evidence of the students' prankster ways is everywhere.

But the professors don't think their chosen career is funny. No sir! They're all about serious, and their dedication to understanding long-gone reptiles literally knows no boundaries.

However, if you ask **Chester and Hester**, owners of the gas station turned gift shop, they tell a different story. According to them, that "someone" who discovered the dino bone was their dog. Chester and Hester (husband and wife? cousins? both? no one knows) have been collecting fossils since the 1950s, and they have boxes full of bones to prove it.

Regardless of how the first fossils were discovered, Chester and Hester are going to make the most of it, and have set up **Dino-Rama**, a roadside attraction built on what was once a parking lot (look for the parking space lines still evident on the pavement), hoping to make a killing on long-dead reptiles. All of the employees are their cousins, as they aim to spread the wealth around. And they're not afraid to compete with the stuffy researchers at the Institute, creating homespun versions of some of the institute's key features.

CHESTER AND HESTER'S DINO-RAMA

Can you say "ripoff"? No, we don't mean the games are a ripoff, we're talking about the source of inspiration that led to Chester and Hester building their entrepreneurial empire. The institute has a gift shop, and so do Chester and Hester. The institute has a **Time Rover**, the happy couple have **Primeval Whirl**, made from items they found around the house and the yard. The institute has **dinosaur topiaries**, our creative copycats have that **freakish sculpture** cobbled together with rocks and glass and all manner of found items (see photo insert). Even the sign advertising their amusement park is made from old license plates. Tacky? You bet. Creative? Without a doubt!

REALITY CHECK | If you have a problem, don't stew on it and write a letter when you get home, and expect more than a form-letter apology. Mention it to a Cast Member right away, or ask to speak to someone in charge. You are more likely to get a satisfactory resolution if you allow Disney to address the issue when it happens.

PRIMEVAL WHIRL

Essential Information: 4 feet, Fastpass

Dino Institute has nothing on Chester and Hester. The institute may have super-secret scientific Time Rovers, but Primeval Whirl has **kitschy plywood timepieces** with hands moving counterclockwise, and a great big spinny thing that proves you're speeding toward the age of the dinosaurs. Plus, they've put up a sign that comes right out and tells you you're traveling back in time, in case you weren't sure.

Instead of threatening to make you their lunch, the plywood dinosaurs here are friendly, warning you the **meteor** is coming. And you can see that it is. As asteroids whiz by, your car dodges, dips, and spins (and we do mean spins!) toward impact with the Big One. There is no onboard computer here, but Ches-

 MISS-ABLE   IF YOU HAVE TIME   WORTH MAKING TIME FOR   NOT TO BE MISSED!

 WILL ONLY WORRY YOUNG CHILDREN   MAY SCARE MANY YOUNG CHILDREN; FEW ADULTS   WILL SCARE MOST YOUNG CHILDREN; SOME ADULTS   MAJOR SCARE FACTOR

VISUAL DISORIENTATION   MILD PHYSICAL MOVEMENT   INTENSE FEELING OF MOTION   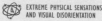 EXTREME PHYSICAL SENSATIONS AND VISUAL DISORIENTATION

ter and Hester have thoughtfully put up a pole that counts down how many seconds you have left. Then, just in the nick of time, the hands on the plywood clocks begin spinning forward and you're rescued from a flaming fate!

It's a wild mouse-style coaster with a whole lot of spin, and while your tour here is more into cartoon-land than the late Cretaceous, the screaming is certainly of the happier variety.

TRICERATOP SPIN

  (UNDER 6)

Chester and Hester must have paid a visit to Disneyland, because they have their own version of the **Dumbo ride**. Now, even the littlest paleontologists can take a trip back in time, with all the fun and none of the fear. Plus, you get to spend much of the ride looking at the backside of the flying baby **Triceratops** in front of you, and what six-year-old doesn't think that's a riot?

DINOSAUR

Essential Information: 3 feet, 4 inches; Fastpass

Scientists at the Dino Institute have perfected time travel and are giving tours to the early Cretaceous period so that everyone can enjoy the thrill of seeing live dinosaurs. **Dr. Marsh,** director of Dino Institute, welcomes your group, briefing you about the tour you're about to take. But when you enter the **Control Center** and **Dr. Grant Seeker** (groan) gives you your safety instructions, he reveals a rather more exciting plan. He's setting coordinates for the late Cretaceous, hoping your tour will find and bring back an **iguanodon** he has already tagged with a locating device.

Dr. Marsh gets wind of his ploy, admonishing Dr. Seeker and reminding him the late Cretaceous meteor impact is far too close for comfort. Living up to the motive implied by his name, this intrepid researcher won't be stopped that easily. You're going to the late Cretaceous, my friend, so as you head to the secret underground loading bay, get ready for the thrill of a lifetime!

HIDDEN MAGIC | Look at the right-hand wall before you depart the loading bay. Your Time Rover is powered by **Vortex Capacitor Sector WDI CTX AK 98**, a reference to Walt Disney Imagineering and Countdown to Extinction (the former name of the ride). AK 98 is a reference to the park and the year it opened. Hidden within the ride's former name is a cryptic warning: Countdown to Extinction didn't just mean the extinction of the dinosaurs; it meant your extinction, too!

As your Time Rover launches into the past (landing, of course, during the dark of night) the onboard computer searches for and identifies the dinosaurs you pass, none of which are the one you want. However, the one you least want seems to be following you. It's a huge, red, warty **Carnotaurus**, and its name gives you a hint as to what it eats (meat, meaning you). This can't be good!

To make matters worse, your Time Rover is having a bit of trouble navigating in the ancient muck and mire, and for a while it looks as if you're done for. If the Carnotaurus doesn't get you, the incoming meteor will (our money's on the dinosaur). In the split second before you become a barbecued dinner, the computer fixes on the iguanodon, and Dr. Seeker steals you back from the fiery jaws of death. If you can still see when you stumble out of your Time Rover and back to the Institute, look at the television screens that monitor the hallways. Seems your mission was successful!

As you might expect from a tour that whisks you back 144 million years, the ride jolts and bumps and generally tosses you around (wear those seatbelts). This is serious thrill-seeker territory, not for the faint of heart.

ROOKIE MISTAKES | It's tempting to soft-sell an attraction so that the timid rider in your group comes along, but these little white lies generally backfire. Being scared silly tends to cause youngsters to balk at even the most benign attraction afterward. Just because a young'un wants to opt out of a ride doesn't mean you have to line up twice. See Chapter 1 for details on using Rider Swap.

 MISS-ABLE   IF YOU HAVE TIME   WORTH MAKING TIME FOR   NOT TO BE MISSED!

 WILL ONLY WORRY YOUNG CHILDREN   MAY SCARE MANY YOUNG CHILDREN; FEW ADULTS   WILL SCARE MOST YOUNG CHILDREN; SOME ADULTS   MAJOR SCARE FACTOR

 VISUAL DISORIENTATION MILD PHYSICAL MOVEMENT INTENSE FEELING OF MOTION  EXTREME PHYSICAL SENSATIONS AND VISUAL DISORIENTATION

THE BONEYARD

 (UNDER 10)

Although the first big find was discovered in 1947, **DinoLand U.S.A.** is still producing fossils, much to the delight of the students who are working at various dig sites around town. The professors at the institute have opened one of the main sites to the public as a means of inspiring children to become researchers, but in keeping with their prankster ways, the students have added elements that make a serious topic fun. Now, the "boneyard" almost seems like a playground! Open doors and crates, explore caves, stomp on dino footprints . . . this site is interactive, with surprises at every turn. A great place to take youngsters while others in your group experience the Dino Institute's secret mission.

HIDDEN MAGIC That enormous shoulder blade that acts as a sign for the Boneyard is a casting of an authentic stegosaurus bone. In fact, all of the fossils you see around DinoLand have been cast from real dinosaur bones.

THE DIG SITE

 (UNDER 7)

The students are working at a dig site, and **budding paleontologists** can help uncover the latest find (which is looking a lot like a mammoth). Youngsters can grab a bucket and a shovel or just dig with their hands and feet. Happily, 4-million-year-old sand doesn't stick; a quick brush-off and you're good to go!

FINDING NEMO—THE MUSICAL

Oddly placed, the **Theater in the Wild** doesn't fit into either of the lands it borders, but it is officially a part of **DinoLand**. Let's just say that's because fish have been around for a long, long time.

The front rows here don't necessarily give the best view of the show. The whole theater is used, so the rows in the back half of the theater offer a fuller experience.

The show features live performers, puppetry, animation, and original songs, telling the story of Nemo, who is lost yet again. It begins in the **Great Barrier Reef** with clownfish Coral and Marlin choosing names for their offspring (lots of Marlin Juniors and one Nemo), when suddenly a tragedy befalls the family and Marlin is left to protect his only remaining son.

Nemo's excitement at exploring his underwater world is symbolized in the bright colors of the reef and its creatures as masterful puppeteers make gently waving corals, anemones, and other creatures come alive. But despite Marlin's best efforts to teach Nemo to be wary of the ocean's dangers, the curious clownfish and his pals dare each other to venture into the dreaded dropoff, where Nemo is captured in a scuba diver's net.

Interacting directly with the audience, Marlin meets Dory, the forgetful blue tang who agrees to help him in his quest to find his son. She can read the address on the mask the diver has dropped, and they head for Sydney, Australia. The pair meet Bruce and his shark friends, navigate exploding underwater mines, survive a forest of jellyfish, and surf the East Australian Current with the sea turtle Crush.

Nemo has been sold to a dentist with a niece who has kindness issues, but with the help of his aquarium friends and the unrelenting determination of his dad, Nemo is rescued, and Marlin finally acknowledges his son's abilities, encouraging him to allow life to be an adventure.

Performers are dressed to represent the puppet they manipulate, the sets are beautifully evocative, and the impact of seeing it as a musical makes a familiar tale seem new again.

HIDDEN MAGIC While its location in Animal Kingdom is suspect, its tie to Epcot is clear; the signature musical number, "In the Big Blue World," can also be heard at the end of the Finding Nemo attraction in the Seas with Nemo & Friends pavilion.

★ MISS-ABLE
☺ WILL ONLY WORRY YOUNG CHILDREN
⌇ VISUAL DISORIENTATION

★ IF YOU HAVE TIME
☺ MAY SCARE MANY YOUNG CHILDREN; FEW ADULTS
⌇ MILD PHYSICAL MOVEMENT

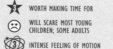
★ WORTH MAKING TIME FOR
☹ WILL SCARE MOST YOUNG CHILDREN; SOME ADULTS
⌇ INTENSE FEELING OF MOTION

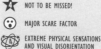
★ NOT TO BE MISSED!
☺ MAJOR SCARE FACTOR
⌇ EXTREME PHYSICAL SENSATIONS AND VISUAL DISORIENTATION

Shopping in Dinoland

CHESTER AND HESTER'S DINOSAUR TREASURES

This store, once a gas station, is now a gift shop for **Dino-Rama**, but signs of its previous life are everywhere. The **floor** tells much of the story here. The former garage floor was yellow, blue, and black, and the red area was muddy ground. Notice the big doors on the right side as you face the back of the shop. That's where mechanics pulled cars in for repairs. Now it's a snack shop with dino souvenirs.

Dining in Dinoland

TRILO-BITES

$

This quick service kiosk sells turkey legs, but we think it's more fun to call them raptor legs.

RESTAURANTOSAURUS

★★★ $

The story at Restaurantosaurus is one of the best. When the Dino Institute opened and began accepting students, they needed somewhere to live. The owners of the town's restaurant, which had become a fossil preparation lab, switched gears again and became a dormitory and commissary. There are signs of student infestation everywhere, including the roof before you even enter the building. Obviously, the undergrads have a real sense of humor! Find burgers, sandwiches, and salads here.

Asia

Welcome to **Anandapur**, the "place of all delight!" Nestled comfortably at the feet of the **Himalayas**, this village lives in agreement with the natural world around it. Technology is making small inroads here, as seen at **Shangri-La Trekkers Inn & Internet Cafe**, but people still rely on bikes and feet to get where they're going, as seen in the prints left in the dried mud you're walking on. Superstition plays a large role in the everyday lives of most villagers.

Prayer flags fly as requests are made, and thanks are given in the form of small bells when requests are granted. Here, nature has its way with the ruins of ancient towns and temples, making the man-made elements subservient to their surroundings.

MAHARAJAH JUNGLE TREK

Deep and mysterious, this is the former Royal Hunting Palace of the rajahs. It is weathered, worn, abandoned; the animals of the jungle now make it their home. Bats live in the courtyard off of a gathering place now used by the villagers for movies and lectures; tigers have taken over the gardens; Bantangs, the sacred cow of India, graze amid the ruins, and even the tomb of Anantah, the first ruler of Anandapur, has become a refuge for wild animals. Black and white tiles and central columns are the only remnants of a once-magnificent ballroom as the jungle slowly takes over.

As you enter the palace grounds, **murals** tell the story of the **four maharajahs** who ruled here. The ruler on the left of the first archway is a hunter, who believed it was his right to control the animals around him. The prince on the right had some interest in the natural world but was primarily motivated by material things. A third king attempted to regain control as the palace began to deteriorate, and the final king, surrounded by birds, fled the palace to live in nature, returning the formerly private hunting grounds to the people. Now, all may enjoy its beauty.

 MISS-ABLE

 WILL ONLY WORRY YOUNG CHILDREN

VISUAL DISORIENTATION

 IF YOU HAVE TIME

 MAY SCARE MANY YOUNG CHILDREN; FEW ADULTS

MILD PHYSICAL MOVEMENT

WORTH MAKING TIME FOR

WILL SCARE MOST YOUNG CHILDREN; SOME ADULTS

INTENSE FEELING OF MOTION

 NOT TO BE MISSED!

 MAJOR SCARE FACTOR

 EXTREME PHYSICAL SENSATIONS AND VISUAL DISORIENTATION

HIDDEN MAGIC

The story of the conflict of man and nature is beautifully told in five large **bas relief carvings** just after the bridge filled with prayer flags. The first scene is a creation story, and the second shows nature in harmony, with animals gathered around the Tree of Life (see photo insert). The third represents human influence, symbolized by a man cutting the tree down. In the fourth carving, the balance of nature has been upset, and chaos ensues. Finally, humans realized they must protect the world around them for balance to be restored.

FLIGHTS OF WONDER

As you travel the ancient trade route between Asia and Africa you have come across a **former preserve**, built by the maharajahs to house unusual animals, but now in ruins. You are on a tour focused on studying birds, some of which have remained after the preserve was abandoned and are now protected by conservation-minded researchers. But today's lesson is interrupted by **Guano Joe**, a tour guide with a profound fear of birds. Only through meeting these beautiful creatures and understanding their role in nature's balance will Guano Joe conquer his phobia and find a new appreciation for our avian friends.

Although today's lecture has been interrupted, you still get to meet a grape-chasing hornbill, a parrot with amazing math skills, and several other birds whose natural behaviors make them incredibly important in maintaining the balance of nature.

Joe eventually agrees to feed **Frasier (the) Crane**, finally understanding how beneficial birds are and promising to help protect them. The story here has changed a number of times (it was once a caravan stop along the trade route, hence the theater's name, **Caravan Stage**), but the conservation message remains strong.

There is a small stage to the right of the attraction's entry where animal encounters occur several times daily.

★ POOR	★★ FAIR	★★★ GOOD	★★★★ EXCELLENT	★★★★★ GOURMET
$ UNDER $10	$$ $10–15	$$$ $15–$20	$$$$ $20–$25	$$$$$ $25+

 B BREAKFAST   **L** LUNCH **D** DINNER  **CS** COUNTER SERVICE **TS** TABLE SERVICE   **TS2** TABLE SERVICE (TWO CREDITS)

ROOKIE MISTAKES

Staying at a Disney resort? The Extra Magic Hours perk is not always a big timesaver, especially in the evenings at Magic Kingdom. Because it is so popular, evening wait times can still reach an hour during peak periods, making a slow day at the park a better option. However, Disney's Animal Kingdom's evening Extra Magic Hours are well worth seeking out!

KALI RIVER RAPIDS

Essential Information: 3 feet, 6 inches, some rafts have child seats; Fastpass

Remember the royal hunting grounds of **Maharaja Jungle Trek**? The royal family had a hunting lodge here, too, and as you make your way toward the **Kali River Expeditions'** boarding area for your rafting tour of **Chakranadi River**, you pass the ruins of the palace walls and its grounds, just beyond a **Tiger Temple** shrine, tour outfitters, and the **Expedition office**.

The river's serenity is punctuated by gentle rapids and scenic waterfalls, ancient ruins dot the riverbanks, and the surrounding forest is home to endangered animals, including the revered Asian tiger, which can be heard growling in the underbrush. But deforestation has taken a huge toll and, as you float along, the sounds of chainsaws alert you to the fact that all is not well here.

HIDDEN MAGIC

As you reach the top of the lift hill, look at the **rock formation** straight ahead of you. Notice how it looks like a tiger face? Originally, the attraction was going to be called Tiger River Rapids, with real animals along the banks of the river. Just as the live animal idea was scrapped at Magic Kingdom's Jungle Cruise, here too the story changed as the attraction developed.

Things turn worrisome when you come upon a logging truck sliding into the water as the ground it stands on erodes. Great piles of burning trees litter the ground, and destruction is everywhere. The animals have all fled.

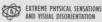

Because human impact has upset the natural order, it is as if **Kali, the Hindu goddess of transformation** who lends her name to the rapids here, is taking her revenge, casting you down a waterfall created by the erosion from irresponsible clear-cutting practices.

As the water cascades over your head (or as you watch the people across from you get soaked to the skin) be thankful you got off easy. Kali is also the goddess who creates a fear of death in people, so bear her lesson in mind. You may even want to plant a tree when you get home.

REALITY CHECK | Two of the main causes for emergency room visits in Orlando are dehydration and sunstroke. You will need far more water than you are probably used to (soda and beer are not water!), especially in summer, and it's easy to forget to reapply sunblock when you're having fun.

EXPEDITION EVEREST—LEGEND OF THE FORBIDDEN MOUNTAIN

Essential Information: 3 feet, 8 inches; Fastpass

In this story, you've reached the foothills of the **Himalayas** for the experience of a lifetime: climbing to the summit of **Mount Everest**. Your journey begins in **Serka Zong**, the first stop on your way to the mountain. If you need climbing gear or supplies, **Gupta's Gear** and **Tashi's Trek and Tongba Shop** have them. Want to pray for a safe journey? The **Yeti Mandir** is nearby. A visit to the Yeti Museum shows how seriously the villagers take the **Protector of the Mountain**, and offers a grim warning: Not all expeditions have returned safely. With that in mind, it's time to check in with **Norbu and Bob's Himalayan Escapes**. They're the relatively new (and controversial) company that will be handling your tour today.

You have probably heard the legend of the Yeti prior to arriving, but what you consider a folksy myth is very real here, and it's clear you've arrived during

a time when the villagers are on edge. References to the Yeti abound and swaths of red paint are everywhere, meant to ward off evil spirits but also a sign of the local belief in the sacredness of the mountain's protector, who has been riled up by all of the activity on the **Forbidden Mountain**. And that's exactly where you're going.

HIDDEN MAGIC | As you walk through Serka Zong, notice the **wood** piled on top of some of the buildings. It's a sign of wealth in a place where wood is scarce. Where do the villagers get it? They harvest it from those gnarly trees you see in the courtyard near the tea plantation's warehouse.

Climb aboard the steam train, formerly used by the **Royal Anandapur Tea Company**, that will take you to the Forbidden Mountain on your way to **Base Camp**. Wind your way over and around the foothills, then make the first big trek up to the mountain. As you ascend, your train comes across a shrine, a reminder that the villagers don't fear the Yeti, they revere him. Once through the shrine you make the first big push toward the summit, where an ice cave leads to the snow-capped mountain and your first big hint the Yeti is not pleased by your presence.

In fact, his displeasure is so evident that you are forced to re-route— backward! Cue the darkness and the screaming (and a surprisingly powerful descent)! But you're only halfway down, and now you have a choice: stay where you are or find another route up. When the Yeti appears in the distance, your choice is absolutely clear. He is not happy, and you'd better beat a hasty retreat down and away from the Forbidden Mountain.

But you're not getting away that easily. If you weren't convinced by the Yeti from afar, maybe a face-to-face encounter will seal the deal. And that's exactly what you're getting next!

Norbu and Bob have named their tours well, but after your near-disaster, you have to wonder if they're escaping to the mountain, or from it!

 MISS-ABLE
WILL ONLY WORRY YOUNG CHILDREN
VISUAL DISORIENTATION

 IF YOU HAVE TIME
MAY SCARE MANY YOUNG CHILDREN; FEW ADULTS
MILD PHYSICAL MOVEMENT

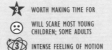 WORTH MAKING TIME FOR
WILL SCARE MOST YOUNG CHILDREN; SOME ADULTS
INTENSE FEELING OF MOTION

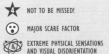 NOT TO BE MISSED!
MAJOR SCARE FACTOR
EXTREME PHYSICAL SENSATIONS AND VISUAL DISORIENTATION

You may not have noticed it when you arrived in Serka Zong, but now that you've made your escape, those **stone tablets** sitting along a wall near the exit from the train station take on new meaning. They're prayer tablets, and when grouped together as they are here, they indicate there is something many villagers feel is worth praying about.

Shopping in Asia

MAGICAL MERCHANDISE

Mandala Gifts has clothing and jewelry, and **Serka Zong Bazaar** is the place for all your Yeti-wear needs.

Dining in Asia

YAK & YETI RESTAURANT

★★★★ $$$$

What's the story here? You're visiting a home-turned-hotel in response to the popularity of tours going up the Forbidden Mountain. Walls have been knocked out to make comfortable gathering places for the villagers, who graciously bring their own chairs (notice they are all different). But these villagers are not superstitious. You won't see any red slashes of paint on the building's façade. Entrees include ribs, steak, chicken, fish, and curry, plus noodle and stir-fry dishes.

HIDDEN MAGIC The homeowner has employed a traditional decorative technique at Yak & Yeti, hand-painting **scenes on the walls** in place of artwork (see photo insert). Wander through the restaurant and see how many you can find.

★ POOR	★★ FAIR	★★★ GOOD	★★★★ EXCELLENT	★★★★★ GOURMET
$ UNDER $10	$$ $10–15	$$$ $15–20	$$$$ $20–$25	$$$$$ $25+
B BREAKFAST	L LUNCH	D DINNER	CS COUNTER SERVICE	TS TABLE SERVICE	TS2 TABLE SERVICE (TWO CREDITS)

YAK & YETI LOCAL FOOD CAFES

★★★ $ 🍴(L) 🍴(D) 🍴(CS)

These small cafes are local-owned food stalls where busy villagers or tourists can grab a quick meal, then sit outside to enjoy the scenery. They serve stir-fries, sandwiches, and egg rolls.

ANANDAPUR ICE CREAM TRUCK

$

Intricately detailed, Anandapur Ice Cream Truck is the real deal. It was actually shipped over from Nepal, and all of the scenes except the mural of Kali River Rapids and the siamang ape towers are original. Pick up an ice cream or a soda here.

HIDDEN MAGIC | As you depart Asia, look at the **shrine along the water** that faces Expedition Everest. Notice how the turrets of the shrine mimic the peaks of the Himalayas (see photo insert).

Rafiki's Planet Watch

Most of the attractions at Animal Kingdom tell their story indirectly, through thematic elements and the overall experience you have as you enjoy them. Rafiki's Planet Watch is the exception; hosted by **Rafiki**, the wise old mandrill from *The Lion King*, the exhibits here practically shout their message, which is one of conservation and humans finding a balance with nature.

With an understanding of the challenges that face the animal kingdom, move on to the rewards of making a difference in the world and in your own backyard. Hope and optimism combine with knowledge in this place of inspiration, reminding us that our actions count.

 MISS-ABLE   IF YOU HAVE TIME   WORTH MAKING TIME FOR   NOT TO BE MISSED!

WILL ONLY WORRY YOUNG CHILDREN MAY SCARE MANY YOUNG CHILDREN; FEW ADULTS WILL SCARE MOST YOUNG CHILDREN; SOME ADULTS MAJOR SCARE FACTOR

VISUAL DISORIENTATION MILD PHYSICAL MOVEMENT INTENSE FEELING OF MOTION EXTREME PHYSICAL SENSATIONS AND VISUAL DISORIENTATION

WILDLIFE EXPRESS TRAIN

Eastern Star Railways offers several daily departures from the **Harambe Railway Station** to various locations across Africa, including **Conservation Station**, which is where you're headed today. With luggage loaded on top of the train (you're going to be there for a while, studying the unique needs of susceptible and endangered animals), you're off on a journey of discovery that just happens to provide some neat backstage views of the animal's nighttime homes.

HABITAT HABIT!

Acting as a symbolic transition bridge between the train station and the learning facility, this lush pathway sets the stage for thinking of conservation in a new way, which includes your own efforts toward a better world.

HIDDEN MAGIC | Stand in front of **the sign for Conservation Station** and notice where the animals' eyes are looking. They're looking directly at you. Their gaze is intended to engage you in a silent appeal for conservation-mindedness.

CONSERVATION STATION

Your first hint that this is going to be a positive experience comes when you reach the colorful train depot at Conservation Station. No stuffy schoolrooms or preachy messages at this learning facility. Instead, your classes include **hands-on encounters** with small animals, picture windows with views into the laboratories and treatment rooms where researchers and veterinarians do their work, and **Sounds of the Rainforest**, a cautionary tale told by **Rafiki**. But even that message is hopeful, highlighting animals whose stories were nearly tragedies until human behavior changed and things now look brighter. **Song of the Rainforest listening booths** allow you to experience the rainforest at night through its mysterious natural "music."

AFFECTION SECTION

 (UNDER 6)

Now that you know how to care for nature in your own community, it's time to **cuddle a critter**! Most here are of the farmyard variety but the impact of interacting with living creatures is powerful for young children, who are the main focus of this petting setting.

Young conservationists can also enjoy an **entertaining stage show** highlighting interesting animal behaviors, and keepers are on hand to answer questions about their charges. The story here is, in some ways, the ending of a fable, where the final words are, "and they lived happily ever after."

Africa

Ecotourism has come to the East African coastal village of **Harambe**, thriving in post-British times with modern conveniences such as Internet access and satellite television. The story elements here hint at former British occupation in the village; the remains of fortress walls can be seen in the pavement, an old British mailbox is still in use, there are signs referencing **Smythe-Wallis British East Africa Livestock Ltd**, a former cattle shipping concern, and **Uhuru**, the Swahili word meaning "freedom and unity" can be seen in various locations. According to the sign near **Tamu Tamu Refreshments**, Harambe earned its independence in 1961, an important date in Africa's real history as it is also the year **Tanganyika** (now Tanzania) shed the cloak of British rule.

Harambe Wildlife Preserve was established in 1971, and several touring companies have sprung up in response to this newfound source of income (notice the advertisements on several buildings). But **Kilimanjaro Safaris** is the most successful. In fact, as an ecotourist visiting this little village, it's likely you already have a reservation for an excursion with them. As successful as the village has become, there are still issues to be resolved. Signs warning of poaching are everywhere, a reminder that the villagers are diligent about protecting the animals they once shot for sport, but that imbalance still exists.

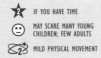
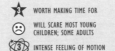
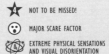

KILIMANJARO SAFARIS

Essential Information: Fastpass

There was a time when shooting wild game in **Harambe** didn't involve a camera, but with conservation now a hot topic, this former hunting ground has become the **Harambe Wildlife Reserve**. You're on a two-week photo safari onboard **Simba One**, while **Wilson Mutua**, an airborne game warden, patrols overhead, maintaining radio contact throughout your expedition.

Start your safari in the **Little Uturi Forest**, where rhinos wander freely. Next, cross a bridge over the **Safi River** and its resident hippos, leading to one of many washed-out roads within the reserve. Further along, another rickety bridge spans the Safi River, but there is a worrisome Nile crocodile menace here, so hang on tight!

ROOKIE MISTAKES There are no bad seats for viewing the animals, but if possible the photographer in your group should try to sit on the end. And remember, it *is* going to be bumpy, so you may want to use your neck or wrist strap as you're taking pictures.

Wilson, still patrolling overhead, tells your tour there is elephant activity ahead, and as you enter the savanna giraffes, gazelles, wildebeests, and antelope may roam right across the path you're traveling. But Wilson has another message: A baby elephant is lost, and your tour can help by looking for its mother. This is the first indication **poachers** may be present.

Passing **Monkey Point,** the truck's radio picks up a local station playing the beautiful **Baba Yetu** (it's a modified version of the Lord's Prayer in Swahili). But yikes! The bridge you are crossing is the worst so far! If you make it across you'll be in elephant territory, and because the savanna is also home to Africa's big cats, you might also see cheetah under the trees or lions among the rocks of a nearby kopje.

But Wilson radios again, this time warning you there are poachers in the area. Your tour is eager to help as you detour out of the preserve and into

★ POOR   ★★ FAIR   ★★★ GOOD   ★★★★ EXCELLENT   ★★★★★ GOURMET
$ UNDER $10 $$ $10–15 $$$ $15–$20 $$$$ $20–$25 $$$$$ $25+
B BREAKFAST   L LUNCH   D DINNER   CS COUNTER SERVICE   TS TABLE SERVICE   TS2 TABLE SERVICE (TWO CREDITS)

Magadi hot springs through a gate the poachers have broken. You're hot on their tail, passing their deserted camp filled with ivory tusks, and Wilson thanks you for driving them straight toward his patrol. The baby elephant will be reunited with his mother, so it's "Kwaheri"—go well—as your tour ends. Strange . . . it didn't feel like two weeks!

PANGANI FOREST EXPLORATION TRAIL

Pangani is the "place of enchantment." In this part of the story, you're visiting a research facility and wildlife sanctuary that helps support conservation efforts in **Harambe Wildlife Reserve** and other preserves throughout the world. **Dr. Kulunda**, founder and director of **Pangani Forest Conservation School**, urges students to observe so they can help solve forest animals' problems, and today you have the opportunity to do the same.

The walking trail that winds through Pangani forest has several observation points, mini-classrooms with study materials used for research, and stations where instructors and students have left field notes about what they've observed.

Dr. Kulunda's research station is here too, giving the students a place to observe smaller animals whose behavior can't be observed easily in the wild. Outside there is an aviary for the study of native birds. Beyond that is an underwater hippo-viewing area where students are researching hippo sounds, and further along is the savanna, with its meerkat colony and an overlook into **Gorilla Valley**, affording an up-close view of the forest's gorilla family and bachelor groups.

HIDDEN MAGIC

There are some living things Dr. Kulunda isn't eager to study. Notice the bright yellow can of **Super Acting DOOM insect killer** on the desk near the entry door. A humorous example of placemaking that quickly tells us something about the "reality" of where we are.

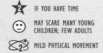
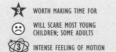
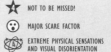

Some of the school's researchers will be present when you visit, so be sure to ask them questions. And when you get home, log on to *www.bushmeat.org* to support the Bushmeat Crisis Task Force in working against unsustainable hunting in Pangani Forest and around the world.

Shopping in Africa

MAGICAL MERCHANDISE

Duka la Filimu is the "last film before safari" shop and **Mombasa Marketplace** carries African crafts and clothes.

Dining in Africa

DAWA BAR AND KUSAFIRI COFFEE SHOP

$

Dawa Bar is the place villagers hang out, and there is evidence the residents staying in Hoteli Burudika enjoy its free concerts (look up at the roof). Nearby Kusafiri Coffee Shop and Bakery offers pastries, cakes, and drinks.

TAMU TAMU REFRESHMENTS

★★ $ 🍴B 🍴L 🍴D 🍴CS

Harambe Fort (established in 1420) is now Tamu Tamu Refreshments, serving up cheeseburgers and sandwiches, with seating in what is now a pleasant courtyard.

TUSKER HOUSE RESTAURANT

★★★★ $$$$ 🍴B 🍴L 🍴D

Tusker House Restaurant is Harambe's main restaurant, with a vast array of choices, much of it hinting at African flavors. While all meals are served buffet style, breakfast and lunch take on an added element of fun as **Donald's Dining Safari**, hosted by Donald and Daisy Duck dressed in their safari gear. Reservations are required, and it's a popular family choice.

Camp Minnie-Mickey

If you stretch your imagination a bit, Camp Minnie-Mickey is in keeping with the overall story in that we have learned to revere animals so much that we make them into celebrities. It also highlights our capacity to assign human attributes to animals, in some ways blurring the line between "us" and "them."

HIDDEN MAGIC

As you cross the bridge leading to Camp Minnie-Mickey, look over the right side and you'll see a rock formation in the shape of a dragon (see photo insert). That's **Dragon Rock**, a throwback to the time when this area was intended to be **Beastly Kingdom**, a land of mythical animals. You can also see a reference to this never-built land on signposts, above the ticket booths at the front entry, and as the Unicorn section in the parking lot.

The real story here is that you're at **summer camp** in the **Adirondacks** with the cartoon friends of your childhood. Hiking, fishing, picnicking . . . it's all here, set amid a scenic forest, rivers, and those all-important hiking trails. There is an arts-and-crafts style to the man-made elements, which are created from natural objects such as wood and stone.

Just like at summer camp, there is no nutritional value to the food on offer. Unlike summer camp, you'll be sorry when it's time to leave!

CHARACTER GREETING TRAILS

Hiking trails at summer camp usually lead to boredom. Here, they lead to Mickey Mouse, Minnie Mouse, and characters from the Winnie the Pooh stories, *The Lion King*, *The Jungle Book*, and *Song of the South*. It's a wonderful opportunity to meet some of the characters that are a bit harder to find, and to have your picture taken with Mickey and Minnie in their hiking outfits. There are signs at the entry to each trail telling you who is there, and don't forget your camera, autograph book, and a fat pen!

 MISS-ABLE
WILL ONLY WORRY YOUNG CHILDREN
VISUAL DISORIENTATION

 IF YOU HAVE TIME
MAY SCARE MANY YOUNG CHILDREN; FEW ADULTS
MILD PHYSICAL MOVEMENT

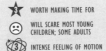 WORTH MAKING TIME FOR
WILL SCARE MOST YOUNG CHILDREN; SOME ADULTS
INTENSE FEELING OF MOTION

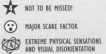 NOT TO BE MISSED!
MAJOR SCARE FACTOR
EXTREME PHYSICAL SENSATIONS AND VISUAL DISORIENTATION

FESTIVAL OF THE LION KING

At the end of a long day of swimming in the lake, fishing from the dock, and swatting flies off your hamburger in the mess hall, campers look forward to the evening story time. Tonight's gathering, inside the assembly hall, is put on by a troupe of traveling entertainers. Curiously enough, some of them are also characters from Disney's blockbuster movie, *The Lion King*.

The first entertainers to arrive perform a tribal dance to music from the movie, calling forth the lion king himself, Simba. Colorful floats carrying Timon and his warthog friend, Pumbaa, an elephant, and Simba arrive, and the festival is in full swing.

The wildly popular **Tumble Monkeys** perform trampoline tricks and gymnastics first, but things turn dark when a warrior arrives, and it's clear he's here to represent **Scar**, Simba's uncle, who wants to take over the pride. Drummers, dancers, and a fire-twirler reinforce the message that evil is afoot. But we are reminded there is harmony and balance in the world, as bright parrot dancers perform a gentle ballet on and above the stage.

All of the animals join together in a grand finale, celebrating the circle of life through song and dance. But it's not quite over yet. Simba invites all of the campers to join in a sing-along, each section adding its own part to "The Lion Sleeps Tonight." C'mon, join in—you know the words!

In a big **Hakuna Matata** sendoff, the troupe sings a montage of songs from the movie. Every childhood should include a summer camp like this!

ROOKIE MISTAKES If you want to be in the show (sit in the front row and wave wildly when asked) bear in mind there are four seating sections (Lion, Elephant, Giraffe, and Warthog) and you'll be making the sound of the animal in your section . . . in front of everyone in the theater. Choose wisely!

Dining in Camp Minnie-Mickey

CAMPFIRE TREATS

$

This food stand is just what it says; you'll find soft serve ice cream, soft-serve floats, funnel cakes, and hot dogs here.

Parades, Tours, and Special Events

MICKEY'S JAMMIN' JUNGLE PARADE

Showing once daily, this colorful cavalcade is a grand safari-style celebration of the diversity and "oneness" of nature. Villagers from all around have come together, parading their skills as artisans through the costumes they wear and the elaborate floats and puppets they have created. Characters from *The Lion King*, *Song of the South*, and *The Jungle Book* are on safari with Mickey, Donald, Minnie, Pluto, and Goofy, and several lucky families will be chosen to ride on the floats as special guests.

REALITY CHECK Everyone's a kid at Disney, even if they're over six feet tall and on the far side of fifty. If you want an unobstructed view of the parades or nighttime shows, stake out a spot an hour or more in advance in high season. You cannot show up ten minutes before the show and expect people to let your children stand in front of them.

BACKSTAGE SAFARI

Essential Information: Mon., Wed., Thurs., Fri.; ages 16 and up, ID required; meet at Guest Relations outside the park

 MISS-ABLE
 IF YOU HAVE TIME
 WORTH MAKING TIME FOR
 NOT TO BE MISSED!
 WILL ONLY WORRY YOUNG CHILDREN
 MAY SCARE MANY YOUNG CHILDREN; FEW ADULTS
 WILL SCARE MOST YOUNG CHILDREN; SOME ADULTS
 MAJOR SCARE FACTOR
 VISUAL DISORIENTATION
 MILD PHYSICAL MOVEMENT
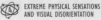 INTENSE FEELING OF MOTION / EXTREME PHYSICAL SENSATIONS AND VISUAL DISORIENTATION

Go behind the scenes for a three-hour insider view into how Disney's Animal Kingdom is run. See the animal care facilities and meet some of the keepers who provide for their charges' nutritional and veterinary needs.

WILD BY DESIGN

Essential Information: Mon., Wed., Thurs., Fri.; ages 14 and up; meet at Guest Services outside the park.

Ever wonder how Africa and Asia were recreated here in central Florida? This is your chance to find out. This three-hour tour tells you the story of the park's design and how artifacts and crafts were used to create realistic settings.

WILD AFRICA TREK

Essential Information: Daily; ages 9 and up, limit 350 pounds; meet at Dawa Bar in Africa

Safari into the wilds of **Harambe Wildlife Preserve** in this amazing three-hour tour around and above the animal habitats. Part of the trek involves crossing rope bridges on foot; part is onboard a safari truck. The tour ends at a private camp within the preserve.

Holidays at Animal Kingdom

HOLIDAY CELEBRATIONS

The whole park will be decorated, but Camp Minnie-Mickey takes on an especially festive feel starting in mid-November, with **Santa Goofy's Wild Wonderland**. The daily parade becomes **Mickey's Jingle Jungle Parade**, with a Christmas theme. Santa Goofy is in attendance.

Write Your Own Story

Write Your Own Story

Write Your Own Story

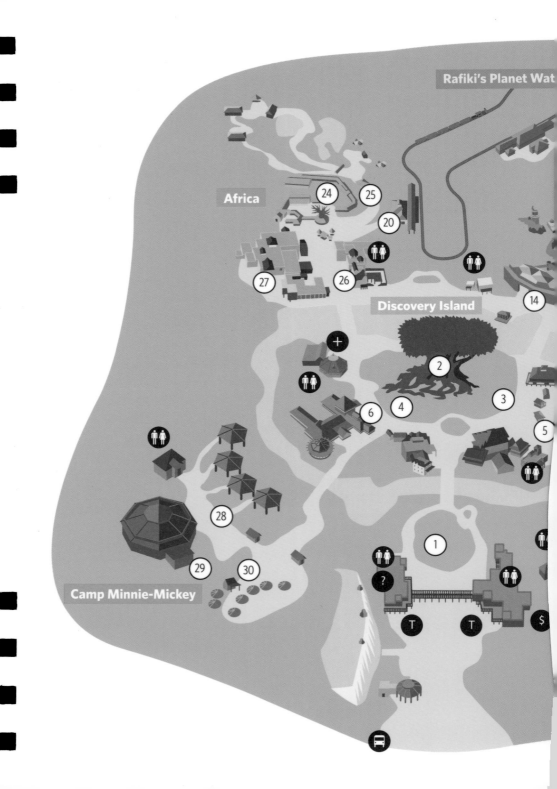

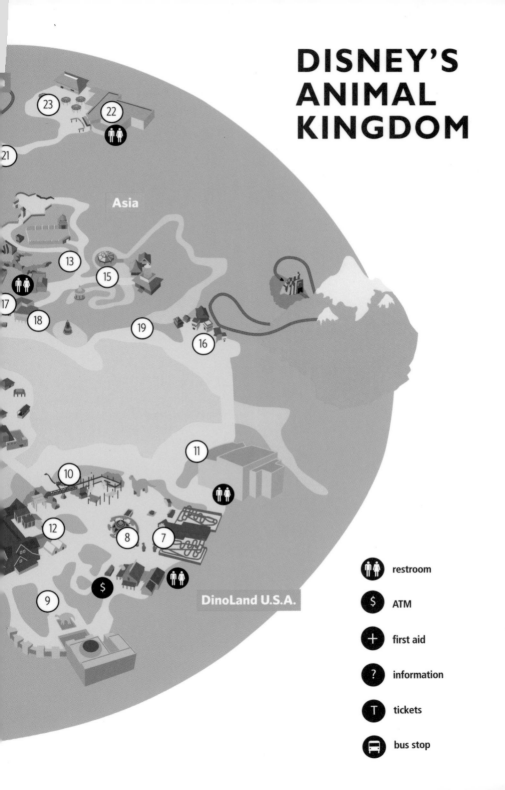

DISNEY'S ANIMAL KINGDOM

Asia

DinoLand U.S.A.

restroom

$ ATM

+ first aid

? information

T tickets

bus stop

DISNEY'S ANIMAL KINGDOM

① THE OASIS

DISCOVERY ISLAND
② The Tree of Life
③ "It's Tough to Be a Bug!"
④ Discovery Island Trails
⑤ Flame Tree Barbecue
⑥ Pizzafari

DINOLAND USA
⑦ Primeval Whirl
⑧ TriceraTop Spin
⑨ Dinosaur
⑩ The Boneyard
⑪ Finding Nemo—The Musical
⑫ Restaurantosaurus

ASIA
⑬ Maharajah Jungle Trek
⑭ Flights of Wonder
⑮ Kali River Rapids
⑯ Expedition Everest—Legend of the Forbidden Mountain
⑰ Yak & Yeti Restaurant
⑱ Yak & Yeti Local Food Cafés
⑲ Anandapur Ice Cream Truck

RAFIKI'S PLANET WATCH
⑳ Wildlife Express Train
㉑ Habitat Habit!
㉒ Conservation Station
㉓ Affection Section

AFRICA
㉔ Kilimanjaro Safaris
㉕ Pangani Forest Exploration Trail
㉖ Tamu Tamu Refreshments
㉗ Tusker House Restaurant

CAMP MINNIE-MICKEY
㉘ Character Greeting Trails
㉙ Festival of the Lion King
㉚ Campfire Treats

Chapter 7

Enhancing the Story:
Water Park Fun and More

IN KEEPING WITH THE FOUR GREAT THEME PARKS, there is plenty more to experience with the many alternative attractions within Walt Disney World. From golf to NASCAR, weddings to water parks, and high school sports to Major League Baseball, there is an amazing array of superbly themed diversions. And, once again, there are more stories to enjoy along the way; tales of typhoons and blizzards, sports and romance, all told with the immense imagination you have come to expect from the master storytellers at Disney Imagineering.

Typhoon Lagoon

When this 61-acre park was first announced in 1985, it was going to be called **Splash**, after the big Tom Hanks–Darryl Hannah movie of the previous year. Thankfully, more imaginative heads prevailed and Typhoon Lagoon opened on June 1, 1989.

According to Disney legend, a Pacific village was struck by an enormous **typhoon**, leaving it with permanent reminders of this chaotic event (not to mention a host of outrageous Imagineering puns, ranging from hilarious to "ouch!"). The Placid Palms Resort was now the **Leaning Palms** and a small harbor had been cut off by the immense storm, leaving an upturned boat surrounded by thousands of **tropical fish**—and a few **sharks**!

To top off its landscape-changing achievement, the typhoon threw the shrimp boat **Miss Tilly** up on to the neighboring volcano, impaling it on the very peak of the craggy mountain. To this day, **Mount Mayday** tries in vain to dislodge its unwelcome visitor with great geysers of water every half-hour. Mount Mayday is the focal point of the park, with most of the rides and flumes descending its slopes, which legend says were created when the mountain was hit by an **earthquake**. Then, the locals ingeniously turned the gulleys and ravines into slides!).

HIDDEN MAGIC | See those nautical flags strung over the park entrance (see photo insert)? That isn't a random sequence, of course. Check out the International Code on the side wall and you'll see it spells "Welcome to Typhoon Lagoon."

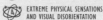

HUMUNGA KOWABUNGA

Essential Information: 4 feet

Start with **Humunga Kowabunga**, the main high-speed body slide, which zips riders down one of three identical enclosed flumes at up to 30 mph, featuring a five-story drop down through the mountain!

STORM SLIDES

Not as steep as Humunga Kowabunga, but equally fun are the Storm Slides, a trio of open **flumes** for riders to descend Mount Mayday in watery fashion. The drop is only 30 feet down three contrasting, twisting, turning tracks that encounter caves, waterfalls, and geysers on the way, with a big splashdown at the end! Lines do build up at both of these but move fairly steadily.

GANG PLANK FALLS

The left side of the beautifully landscaped mountain offers three tube rides, starting with the big **Gang Plank Falls**, a "medium intensity" family raft experience taking up to four riders at a time down 300 feet of flume. Beware the sudden waterfalls, rapids, and other wet ambushes that the Mount has up its sleeve! Start at the bottom by collecting your tube and then climb the steps to the ride.

MAYDAY FALLS

Mayday Falls offers the single-rider version from the shadow of *Miss Tilly* to another big splashdown. The longest and highest tube ride, it is also more dynamic and turbulent with its "rapids" and small drops. Again, you'll find tubes at the bottom before you ascend the stairs.

KEELHAUL FALLS

Keelhaul Falls is a rather more gentle experience down this sculpted part of Mount Mayday, with the ability to spin you round as well. Don't forget to pick up your tube at the bottom before you head up the stairs!

SURF POOL

 (UNDER 12)

The *big* attraction at Typhoon Lagoon is the Surf Pool. The world's largest at 2.5 acres, and with waves to match (permanently agitated by the storm!), it offers a regular two-hour sequence of pounding surf and more child-friendly bobbing waves. But make no mistake—this is a wild stretch of water when the **Big Waves** are unleashed (every ninety seconds for a ninety-minute period) and the 6-foot rollers have the power to knock adults off their feet—let alone pint-sized paddlers—so parents should be extra careful with young'uns here (better still, keep them in **Ketchakiddee Creek**).

SURF SCHOOL

$ (FEE DOES NOT INCLUDE PARK ENTRY, BUT SPECTATORS CAN WATCH FOR FREE PRIOR TO PARK OPENING)

Children eight and older can sign up for Surf School at the **Surf Pool** before park opening on select mornings. Here, professional instructors take groups on a learn-to-surf program that includes thirty minutes of instruction and two hours in the water. It usually starts at 6:45 A.M. Call 407-939-7529 up to ninety days in advance to reserve.

CASTAWAY CREEK

If you're looking for something more gentle than the wave action over at the Surf Pool, try Castaway Creek, where the continuously flowing lazy river meanders around a 2,100-foot course that takes in caves, open grottoes, waterfalls, tropi-

 MISS-ABLE   IF YOU HAVE TIME   WORTH MAKING TIME FOR   NOT TO BE MISSED!

 WILL ONLY WORRY YOUNG CHILDREN   MAY SCARE MANY YOUNG CHILDREN; FEW ADULTS   WILL SCARE MOST YOUNG CHILDREN; SOME ADULTS   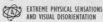 MAJOR SCARE FACTOR

 VISUAL DISORIENTATION   MILD PHYSICAL MOVEMENT   INTENSE FEELING OF MOTION   EXTREME PHYSICAL SENSATIONS AND VISUAL DISORIENTATION

cal rainforests, and a dilapidated water supply system, abandoned by **Typhoon Waterworks**. Grab a tube, swim, or just bob along with this slow-moving current.

KETCHAKIDDEE CREEK

 (UNDER 8)

Set aside specifically for children under 4 feet tall, Ketchakiddee Creek is a mini-playground of small-scale pools, slides, fountains, bubble-jets, and more, tucked away to the left of **Mount Mayday**. All children must be supervised, so head here first if you have kids of the requisite age.

BAY SLIDES

For those who are just a little too tall for Ketchakiddee Creek (but still under 5 feet tall), **Bay Slides** offer a variety of **scaled-down body slides** for those unable to try the likes of Humunga Kowabunga or who find the Storm Slides too forbidding.

SHARK REEF

One of the most unusual features is Shark Reef, one of the "pools" created by the infamous typhoon. Tropical fish and a handful of harmless sharks were among the seagoing denizens caught by the storm, and this now creates a **unique snorkeling opportunity** in the chilly waters. Snorkel equipment is free (you cannot bring your own). For those not brave enough to try it, the shipwreck provides a perfect view into the reef. For an additional fee, you can try the thirty-minute Supplied Air Snorkeling program, a reef tour with a customized scuba tank and buoyancy vest. See the Dive Shop at the entrance to Shark Reef.

HIDDEN MAGIC

Look for the fruit company's broken sign, Tropical Amity, now reading **"Tropi Calamity!,"** and the tractor dropped through the roof!

 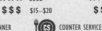

Hideaway Bay

Hideaway Bay is a subsection of Typhoon Lagoon and offers some lovely white-sand beach—albeit without a lot of shade—and the park's other five-star thrill, the "water-coaster" **Crush 'n' Gusher**. This adds a wonderful twist to the Lagoon story, a **fruit-packing factory** that was devastated by the typhoon but which the locals revived with some clever re-theming.

CRUSH 'N' GUSHER

The story here is that the fruit conveyor belts and wash chutes in Tropical Amity's former produce washing facility have become Banana Blaster, Coconut Crusher, and Pineapple Plunger—the three flumes of Crush 'n' Gusher. You can "ride the factory" in **one-, two-, or three-person rafts** that whiz along, down and even *up* the chutes. Powerful bursts of water keep the rafts moving and the 420-foot ride ends with an impressive splashdown into the main pool. Riders must be able to hold the raft handles and substantial lines do build up here by late morning but they usually move fairly steadily.

Dining in Typhoon Lagoon

You'll find a variety of kiosks serving ice cream, cold drinks, and turkey legs throughout the park. However, you can bring your own picnic with you if you'd prefer. Just be sure to leave any glass articles or alcohol at home.

LEANING PALMS

If you don't bring a picnic, you can grab a burger, hot dog, sandwich, pizza, or salad from quick service **Leaning Palms**.

 MISS-ABLE   IF YOU HAVE TIME   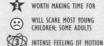 WORTH MAKING TIME FOR   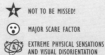 NOT TO BE MISSED!

😊 WILL ONLY WORRY YOUNG CHILDREN   🙂 MAY SCARE MANY YOUNG CHILDREN; FEW ADULTS   😟 WILL SCARE MOST YOUNG CHILDREN; SOME ADULTS   😧 MAJOR SCARE FACTOR

🌀 VISUAL DISORIENTATION   🌀2 MILD PHYSICAL MOVEMENT   🌀3 INTENSE FEELING OF MOTION   🌀4 EXTREME PHYSICAL SENSATIONS AND VISUAL DISORIENTATION

TYPHOON TILLY'S

This snack bar offers decent snacks and drinks. You can tell Typhoon Tilly's is the only lagoon business owned by a woman, by the way—it is the only one decorated with potted plants for that feminine touch.

LOWTIDE LOU'S

★★

Lou's snack station may be humble, but if you're hankering for a good old-fashioned peanut butter and jelly sandwich, this is the place to find it. Also find ice cream, sandwich wraps, and drinks here.

Shopping in Typhoon Lagoon

MAGICAL MERCHANDISE

Singapore Sal's is the eclectic park shop, with a suitably tropical array of beach-wear, gifts, and sundries, while towels and life vests can be rented at the **High 'n Dry** shack.

HIDDEN MAGIC | See the **empty chair and telescope** set up at the front of Singapore Sal's (see photo insert)? That's where Captain Sal returns each evening to survey his stretch of tropical beach, looking for things to sell in his store!

Blizzard Beach

With **Typhoon Lagoon** a huge success and often reaching capacity, the call had gone out for another water park with a whole new theme. Once again, the Imagineers went to town with the backstory of a **freak winter snowstorm** that inspired the locals to create the state's first ski resort, in true Alpine style. Of course, the snow started to melt and the resort was in danger of looking as

out of place as, well, a snowman in the Sunshine State. Faced with the loss of their newly built business, the residents were ready to call it a day when a cry of "Yah-hoo" was followed by the sight of an **alligator** whooshing down one of the ski runs and splashing down into a pool of water.

"Aha!" said the locals. Here's the answer—we'll turn our ski resort into a water resort. And Blizzard Beach was born.

Mount Gushmore is the resort icon, its melting snow, having formed **Melt-away Bay** and **Cross Country Creek**. The **ski jump** and **mogul run** were converted into body slides and the bobsled and ski runs became tube slides. **Ski Patrol Training Camp** has become a preteen play area; Snow Joe's Ski Rental is now **Snowless Joe's Locker & Towel rental** and snow plows have been transformed into ice cream and cold drink kiosks!

SUMMIT PLUMMET

Essential Information: 4 feet

While Blizzard Beach doesn't boast the great wave pool of Typhoon Lagoon, it does offer a better array of slides, including fearsome Summit Plummet, the **world's tallest body slide** at 120 feet. Designed as the **resort's ski jump**, it still offers all the fear factor of a jump into oblivion down a near-vertical chute that will test your swimsuit material to the max at speeds up to 60 mph!

SLUSH GUSHER

Essential Information: 4 feet

If Summit Plummet is just too terrifying (as we would attest), Slush Gusher—the **converted mogul run**—is a better alternative. With two distinct "jumps" on the drop, it isn't nearly as steep but still reaches almost 50 mph.

 MISS-ABLE IF YOU HAVE TIME WORTH MAKING TIME FOR NOT TO BE MISSED!

 WILL ONLY WORRY YOUNG CHILDREN MAY SCARE MANY YOUNG CHILDREN; FEW ADULTS WILL SCARE MOST YOUNG CHILDREN; SOME ADULTS MAJOR SCARE FACTOR

 VISUAL DISORIENTATION MILD PHYSICAL MOVEMENT INTENSE FEELING OF MOTION 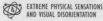 EXTREME PHYSICAL SENSATIONS AND VISUAL DISORIENTATION

The mythical alligator that set the ball rolling is now immortalized as the park mascot, with tributes to **"Ice Gator"** throughout the park—and one memorable "accident." Look at the side wall of the Beach Haus shop (in direct line from the ski-jump). Yes, that's a **gator-shaped hole and skid-marks** where Ice got carried away. Now turn and look at the building opposite—and you can see Ice's ski tracks in the remaining snow!

DOWNHILL DOUBLE DIPPER

Essential Information: 4 feet

Speed junkies will also want to try out the Downhill Double Dipper. These two **side-by-side "ski runs"** are now a fun-but-fast tube ride that is **timed on a stopclock** at the bottom of the run (just like the Winter Olympics!). Racers line up two at a time and then launch themselves down a two-part, 50-foot-tall flume that arrives at the bottom much faster than most expect.

TEAMBOAT SPRINGS

Okay, we're on to the tube rides, so hold tight here! Teamboat Springs is the biggest of its kind, originally the ski resort's **1,200-foot bobsled run** but now a watery family raft ride with several big dips and drops. The "finishing gate" offers riders an ice-cold shower but it is more fun than scary. Long lines do build up from late morning but they usually move fairly steadily.

SNOW STORMERS

Kids adore Snow Stormers, a **"ski slalom test"** face-first on mats, down one of three twisting, turning **flumes**. You probably won't notice the **ski gates** as you whiz down but they are indicative of a typical slalom course in this snowy world. In truth, it's more like a bobsled ride but is guaranteed fun for almost everyone.

TOBOGGAN RACERS

Right next door to the Snow Stormers is the equally child-friendly Toboggan Racers, an eight-lane **toboggan run** down a 250-foot slope. Grab your mat and go headfirst as you race friends and family (is the winner the one who goes under the Finish Line first or goes furthest?).

RUNOFF RAPIDS

Runoff Rapids is the only one of the big slides on the backside of Mount Gushmore. You start at the bottom by collecting your **one- or two-person tube** and carrying it up the steps to the ride itself. The three-part **"slalom run"** consists of two similar open tubes and one enclosed tube (single riders only) completely in the dark. Great fun if you also like **Space Mountain**! There is no strict height limit but children must be able to sit properly on the tube and hold on to the handles.

CROSS COUNTRY CREEK

Cross Country Creek is the highlight of the Blizzard Beach story for many guests. This ride is a **3,000-foot float around the park** on the "current" provided by the melting snow flowing off the mountain. It is one of the most **elaborate lazy river** features anywhere, featuring a trip through an "ice cave" under the mountain and several waterfalls. There are seven entrances/exits where you can grab a tube and simply bob along (which will take around thirty minutes for a full circuit), or you can swim/float under your own power. On your travels, look out for abandoned **snowmaking machines, geysers**—and **Ice Gator**. Yes, he still lives at Blizzard Beach and his house can be found on an island in Cross Country Creek. But he's not a well gator—he suffers permanently from a head cold and his explosive "sneezes" rocket from the chimney!

 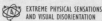

HIDDEN MAGIC The history of Blizzard Beach goes back—*way* back—to prehistoric times. Keep your eyes open while you traverse the ice cave along Cross Country Creek and you may spot **petroglyphs** carved into the walls (see photo insert), hinting at a previous ice age and the presence of a **Yeti**!

MELTAWAY BAY

Meltaway Bay is where most of the melting snow has accumulated (thankfully, considerably "warmed" under the Florida sun!) to form a **one-acre wave pool**. Body-surfing à la Typhoon Lagoon is not on the menu here, though, which means that younger children can play quite happily.

SKI PATROL TRAINING CAMP

 (6- TO 12-YEAR OLDS)

Children under 5 feet tall should head for Ski Patrol Training Camp—formerly where the ski resort trained its guides and rescue folk, but now an **adventure playground** of scaled-down slides, **T-bar drop** (a T-bar is usually a type of ski lift, but here it has been adapted for watery pursuits), **Thin Ice walk**, and even their own "bobsled" ride (a tube flume called **Cool Runnings** after the 1993 Disney movie about the Jamaican bobsled team). Although there is no minimum height requirement at Ski Patrol Training Camp, many of the area's elements are too high or too intense for most preschoolers.

TIKE'S PEAK

(UNDER 6)

Those not tall enough for Ski Patrol have Tike's Peak, a junior-sized playground offering **miniature versions** of the Mount Gushmore rides and an imaginative snow-castle fountain pool, all with suitably shallow water. Parents with preschoolers often spend most of their time at Tike's Peak but seating is limited. Head here *first* if you think this could be for you!

★ POOR	★★ FAIR	★★★ GOOD	★★★★ EXCELLENT	★★★★★ GOURMET
$ UNDER $10	$$ $10–15	$$$ $15–$20	$$$$ $20–$25	$$$$$ $25+

 B BREAKFAST   **L** LUNCH   **D** DINNER   **CS** COUNTER SERVICE  **TS** TABLE SERVICE   **TS2** TABLE SERVICE (TWO CREDITS)

Dining at Blizzard Beach

GENERAL DINING

Grab a meal at the renamed **Lottawatta Lodge** (the resort's former hostelry), where the hearth now goes unused and sports red plants instead of an open fire. Then there are **Avalunch** and the **Warming Hut**, plus four kiosks serving ice creams and drinks.

Shopping at Blizzard Beach

BEACH HAUS

You can shop at the **Beach Haus** (another funny combination of Alpine and Floridian naming), where skis, ski boots, and sleds are still in stock, alongside the more obvious swimsuits, T-shirts, and sunscreen.

ESPN Wide World of Sports Complex

ESPN Wide World of Sports (originally known Disney's Wide World of Sports) opened in March 1997 and the "cast list" of star guests and performers was impressive. It was hugely varied, if not wildly eclectic. The problem was that no one really knew what it was for. There weren't any full-time sports and guests couldn't just turn up and play. Then it joined forces with **Disney's prime TV sports channel** in 2010 to create a more coherent story, with signature ESPN elements, and things now make more sense.

The architectural style of the complex—hugely popular for **Atlanta Braves' spring training games** each March—uses tall towers and seemingly endless archways to give the venues a dynamic retro quality that is designed to inspire all the athletes who enter, whether they are established MLB stars or high school greenhorns.

The two big indoor complexes are **HP Field House** (with information touch-screens and a photo-printing station), and the **Jostens Center**, hosting college

  MISS-ABLE

 WILL ONLY WORRY YOUNG CHILDREN

 VISUAL DISORIENTATION

 IF YOU HAVE TIME

MAY SCARE MANY YOUNG CHILDREN; FEW ADULTS

MILD PHYSICAL MOVEMENT

 WORTH MAKING TIME FOR

 WILL SCARE MOST YOUNG CHILDREN; SOME ADULTS

 INTENSE FEELING OF MOTION

 NOT TO BE MISSED!

 MAJOR SCARE FACTOR

EXTREME PHYSICAL SENSATIONS AND VISUAL DISORIENTATION

basketball, high school volleyball, World Cheerleader championships, and the X Games. The extensive **Hess Playing Field** accommodates a variety of sports, while tennis, baseball, softball, and track are also catered for, and you'll find merchandise and snack kiosks during major events.

It's also fun just to wander the fields and facilities and dine at the **ESPN Grill** (soups, sandwiches, burgers, pizza) ★★ $ 🍴🅛 NOT DDP. An imaginative cafeteria-style diner full of ESPN themes that makes a neat venue for lunch or dinner (as well as a great photo opportunity, with a **replica Sports Center desk**). Or try out the **PlayStation Pavilion**—a battery of sports-related video games in a super-cool, high-tech setting. And coming soon is a **100-lane bowling center**. Due to be built next to the Jostens Center, this will cater to the country's biggest bowling events and, unlike **Splitsville at Downtown Disney**, will be geared for serious competition rather than recreation. Construction could begin as early as 2012.

The Wide World of Sports has its own general entry fee and is included as a Water Park Fun & More option with the Magic Your Way tickets (not applicable for special events and spring training baseball games). Parking is free.

Disney Golf

While water parks and sports centers may not have been on the original blueprint for Walt's World, golf certainly was. In a state boasting hundreds of courses, it was only natural Disney had to have its own. For all Disney golf, call 407-939-4653. Select tee times are reserved for Disney resort guests while fees are reduced after 3 P.M. and for same-day replays. Resort guests may book ninety days in advance; nonresort players can book sixty days in advance. Appropriate attire is required.

HIDDEN MAGIC | That Mickey Mouse–eared bunker you see in many promotional videos is actually on the par-three sixth hole at the Magnolia course.

 ★ POOR   ★★ FAIR   ★★★ GOOD   ★★★★ EXCELLENT   ★★★★★ GOURMET

$ UNDER $10 $$ $10–15 $$$ $15–20 $$$$ $20–25 $$$$$ $25+

🅑 BREAKFAST   🅛 LUNCH   🅓 DINNER   🅒🅢 COUNTER SERVICE   🅣🅢 TABLE SERVICE   🅣🅢2 TABLE SERVICE (TWO CREDITS)

MAGNOLIA AND PALM GOLF COURSES

Magnolia—named for the 1,500 magnolia bushes sprinkled through the landscaping—is rated the toughest of the two courses. It's a long (7,500 yard) challenge for power hitters. Palm—named for the rich use of Florida palm trees—is a shorter but more scenic test. Overtly "Disney" touches are light and fanciful (Mickey tee-box markers and occasional marble plinths tucked among the trees offering playful golf instruction) and the accent is more on nature than animation.

OAK TRAIL GOLF COURSE

The nine-hole Oak Trail course is another Water Park Fun & More option (pre-booking is necessary and golf club rental is extra). It's a walking course—no carts allowed—meant more for beginners than experts, and with family play in mind, it still features some intriguing golf and picturesque woodland.

LAKE BUENA VISTA GOLF COURSE

Golf was also originally at the heart of the Downtown Disney area, with the adjacent Lake Buena Vista course intended to be the residential community's recreational opportunity. Today, it threads its way between the **Old Key West** and **Saratoga Springs** resorts, a more straightforward course than Palm and Magnolia but still with plenty of challenges.

OSPREY RIDGE GOLF COURSE

Disney's final course, Osprey Ridge, opened in 1992, and is another championship-quality eighteen holes. With rolling sandhills and undulating fairways, it is unlike any of the others. It is also recognized by the Audubon Society for its wetland conservation areas, with raised boardwalks among the thick pine forests.

 MISS-ABLE   IF YOU HAVE TIME   WORTH MAKING TIME FOR   NOT TO BE MISSED!

 WILL ONLY WORRY YOUNG CHILDREN   MAY SCARE MANY YOUNG CHILDREN; FEW ADULTS   WILL SCARE MOST YOUNG CHILDREN; SOME ADULTS   MAJOR SCARE FACTOR

 VISUAL DISORIENTATION   MILD PHYSICAL MOVEMENT   INTENSE FEELING OF MOTION   EXTREME PHYSICAL SENSATIONS AND VISUAL DISORIENTATION

Mini Golf

Okay, it's not quite the "real thing" but mini golf is a sure-fire family hit and Disney has two of the best courses in Orlando.

FANTASIA GARDENS

Located near the Swan and Dolphin resorts, Fantasia Gardens is a two-part challenge of **eighteen-hole mini golf** and **eighteen-hole putting course.** The course, which includes popular icons from the 1940 classic *Fantasia*, will probably appeal most to kids, and it comes in five sections: the music-themed **Toccata and Fugue** (including musical notes when you get it right!); **The Nutcracker Suites** (with dancing mushrooms and a frost-covered pond); **Pastoral Symphony** (featuring a pipe-playing faun and a trip inside "Mount Olympus"); **Dance of the Hours** (with the challenge of a pirouetting hippo!); and **The Sorcerer's Apprentice** (with various ways to get you wet).

WINTER SUMMERLAND

Winter Summerland (next to Blizzard Beach) is a more straightforward but magnificently themed array of two eighteen-hole "elf-sized" courses with a great story. Tying into the Blizzard Beach story, Santa noticed the snow-themed water park one Christmas Eve and decided it was the perfect vacation spot for his off-duty elves. The only thing it lacked was a golf course but the elves couldn't agree if they wanted a winter or summer theme, so they split into two groups. One built the "snow" course and the other the "sand" course, with festive theming on both. The visual jokes fly thick and fast and each course maintains its winter/summer style superbly, with **"Squirty the Snowman"** a hazard on the former and a **real smokin' campfire** on the latter.

★ POOR   ★★ FAIR   ★★★ GOOD   ★★★★ EXCELLENT   ★★★★★ GOURMET
$ UNDER $10 $$ $10–15 $$$ $15–$20 $$$$ $20–$25 $$$$$ $25+
(B) BREAKFAST   (L) LUNCH   (D) DINNER   (CS) COUNTER SERVICE   (TS) TABLE SERVICE   (TS2) TABLE SERVICE (TWO CREDITS)

HIDDEN MAGIC

Finish either course at Winter Summerland and receive a special greeting from Santa on his home computer courtesy of the **"winternet"** (groan!). Santa's **"winterbago"** has been converted to serve as the starter kiosk, gift shop, and snack stand.

Walt Disney World Speedway

Disney and motorsports don't seem like an obvious fit, but the Walt Disney World Speedway opened with much fanfare in January 1996. And then proceeded to prove why it wasn't a good fit! Designed and built on a tight budget, **the Mickyard** (a play on the famous Brickyard of the Indy Speedway) was intended to stage races for the Indy Racing League, but enormous parking snarl-ups, the lack of permanent seating and other facilities, problems with scheduling, and three major accidents in practice combined to spell the end for Disney's Indy 200.

HIDDEN MAGIC

At the groundbreaking ceremony for the speedway in June 1995, Indianapolis Speedway chairman Mari Hulman George presented the Disney circuit with one of the **original paving bricks** from their famous Brickyard. This is now buried under the start-finish line.

Happily, the Disney Speedway found alternative use from the **Richard Petty Driving Experience,** which arrived in 1997 and became a full-time opportunity for fans to try NASCAR racing, either as a driver or passenger. Ever since, the sound of stock cars zipping around at up to 130 mph can be heard every day, with six different programs to choose from.

Most people opt for the **Ride Along experience** which runs most days from 9 A.M.–4 P.M., but other driving experiences must be pre-booked. **The Indy Experience** runs 350 days a year (not Easter, Thanksgiving, Christmas Eve, Christmas Day, New Year's Eve, and New Year's Day) from 4 P.M.–dusk.

 MISS-ABLE   IF YOU HAVE TIME   WORTH MAKING TIME FOR   NOT TO BE MISSED!

☺ WILL ONLY WORRY YOUNG CHILDREN   ☺ MAY SCARE MANY YOUNG CHILDREN; FEW ADULTS   ☹ WILL SCARE MOST YOUNG CHILDREN; SOME ADULTS   MAJOR SCARE FACTOR

 VISUAL DISORIENTATION   MILD PHYSICAL MOVEMENT   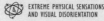 INTENSE FEELING OF MOTION   EXTREME PHYSICAL SENSATIONS AND VISUAL DISORIENTATION

Disney's Wedding Pavilion

Disney's Wedding Pavilion opened in 1995 and hosts up to six weddings a day in true fairy-tale splendor. If ever there was a place where a true romance story could be written, it's here amid a beautifully evocative setting where brides and their grooms vow to live happily ever after. There is no wedding story so fanciful that Disney cannot make it come true.

Disney's Wedding Pavillion is built on the shore of Seven Seas Lagoon, and it offers two iconic views of **Cinderella Castle**—through a window behind the altar, and through a hedge arch outside the chapel—to provide the perfect photographic backdrop. Couples can also plan their special day at **Franck's Bridal Studio**, a re-creation of the Victorian summerhouse of Franck Eggelhoffer (Martin Short) from the movie *Father of the Bride*. Select from three ceremonies: **Escape**, a complete wedding and honeymoon package with up to eighteen guests, a cake, and champagne toast; **Wishes**, a more personalized version with a minimum of eighteen guests; and **Couture**, a deluxe package with truly exquisite touches. Disney characters, a herald trumpeter, private fireworks, confetti cannons, or Cinderella's Coach can also be hired to enhance the experience.

Want a wedding with a unique twist? Disney can arrange "special guests"—actors who can be hired as **Tacky Tourists** or **Uninvited Guests**, ready to play out roles with improvised comedy and other themed fun!

Of course, the Wedding Pavilion isn't the only venue to stage marriage ceremonies throughout the World. There are another twelve locations where you can tie the knot in true Disney style, including the **Magic Kingdom**, the **pavilions of the World Showcase in Epcot**, the **BoardWalk Resort**, and the **Yacht and Beach Club** resorts. But, when a venue is this perfectly situated for that genuine fairy-tale occasion, why look further for your dream Disney day?

Write Your Own Story

Write Your Own Story

Chapter 8

The World by Night

JUST WHEN YOU THINK YOU HAVE SEEN (and done) everything there is to do in this amazing World, along comes Mickey with that "something extra" to add still more fun, excitement, magic—and stories. Want a whole downtown district of shops, dining, and entertainment? Check. How about a world-class show from some of the most famous performing artists on the planet? Got that, too. Dinner shows with great food and even more family fun? You can count on it. More live entertainers and boardwalk games? All part of the story. Somewhere to go dancing? Got that as well! The one snag? You may end up exhausted just trying to "do it all" in this vast playground of imagination and creativity. If your story could use one more chapter, you'll find plenty of inspiration in Walt Disney World once the sun goes down.

Downtown Disney

When the original plans for Epcot were drawn up in the late 1960s, the "working city of tomorrow" wasn't properly defined. Many elements ended up in the park, but some found their way into the **Lake Buena Vista Shopping Village**, which was later named **Walt Disney World Village**, and then **Disney Village Marketplace**. In 1989, the nightclub complex of **Pleasure Island** was added and, six years later, this still-evolving area was dubbed **Downtown Disney**. Downtown Disney is festive at any time of day, but is at its most captivating in the evening. Spend time strolling under the fairy lights in the trees, enjoying the breeze off of Village Lake; there is magic in the air here, and it's worth making time for a visit.

Marketplace

This is primarily the shopping heart of Downtown, along with the restaurants of Rainforest Café, **Cap'n Jack's**, **T-Rex Café**, and **Earl of Sandwich** (see Chapter 9). For a quick snack, there is the choice of **Ghirardelli's** (wonderful ice cream and sundaes), **Pollo Campero** (a counter service, Latin-influenced chicken restaurant), and a **Wolfgang Puck Express**. Artisans mix with **hairbraiders**, **silhouette artists**, a **kiddie train**, and a **classic carousel**. Need a personalized wooden nameplate? This is the place for you!

The architecture is old-world European in style, inviting guests to wander the streets and stop frequently to admire the scenery. **The Dock Stage** hosts school-age performers, while the **Marina** has boating options and bass fishing excursions (for reservations call 407-939-7529). Or, grab an ice cream treat from **Ghirardelli's** and sit and enjoy the village-y hustle-bustle.

SHOPPING IN THE MARKETPLACE

MAGICAL MERCHANDISE

Shopping is the key feature, though, and there is plenty of retail therapy available. Kids will make a beeline for the recently revamped **LEGO Imagination Center**, with its hands-on activities and amazing models; **Once Upon a Toy**, a wonderful Disney-Hasbro collaboration of classic games and collectibles; **Design-A-Tee**, a chance to design and print your own personalized Hanes shirt; and **Goofy's Candy Co.**

Grownups will enjoy the more distinctive style of **Basin**, for blissful bath and facial products; **The Art of Disney**, with its fabulous array of Disney artwork and artists-in-residence; **Arribas Brothers**, a crystal specialty shop; **Team Mickey**, featuring sporting apparel; ESPN-branded goods; and a Rawlings kiosk for personalized baseball gear; plus the new Ridemakerz (customizable radio-controlled cars); **Disney's Days of Christmas**, for all things festive; and **Tren-D**, a women's treasure trove of clothing, handbags, jewelry, lotions, and perfumes. Stop to admire the eclectic décor and artwork in Tren-D and you might notice **Edna 'E' Mode** (from the movie *The Incredibles*) by the dressing rooms, telling prospective buyers they look "fabulous, darling." Other highlights include a huge **Pin Traders** indoor/outdoor pin-trading station, **LittleMissMatched** (for young fashionistas), **Marketplace Fun Finds** (Disney gifts for $25 or less), **Mickey's Pantry** (notably for some great specialty teas), and **Disney's PhotoPass Studio.**

HIDDEN MAGIC

Anyone thinking **Cap'n Jack's Marina** and restaurant are themed after the iconic Captain Jack Sparrow of *Pirates of the Caribbean* fame would be way off beam. Like twenty-eight years off. Yes, there is a strong nautical theme, but the Downtown Disney Cap'n Jack was named in 1975 for Walt's former king of merchandise at Disneyland (and then Disney World), Jack Olsen. The Johnny Depp character didn't arrive until 2003.

THE WORLD OF DISNEY

The big draw, in every sense, though, is the **World of Disney**, a 51,000-square-foot palace of Disney merchandise of all kinds, from clothing to home décor and jewelry to DVDs, all set in themed rooms from classic Disney movies. Also here, in the suitably princess-themed section, is the **Bibbidi Bobbidi Boutique**, a magical salon for little princesses and rock-star wannabes ages three and up (immensely cute but beware the prices—up to $200!).

Pleasure Island/Hyperion Wharf

In story terms, the original "island" was home to Merriweather Adam Pleasure, an eccentric inventor and adventurer who "discovered" the island in 1911 and turned it into his own private recreation and industrial center. It thrived for many years until the owner was lost at sea, his children proved less able managers, and a major storm left much of it in ruins. Disney Imagineers "rediscovered" it and turned many of the old, ramshackle buildings into nightclubs, shops, and restaurants.

Disney management decided it needed to change and announced the closure of the clubs in 2008 to make way for **Hyperion Wharf**, a nostalgic yet modern take on an early twentieth-century port city and amusement pier, with more shops, dining venues, and an open-air amphitheater for small-scale live entertainment, plus amazing lighting effects. At least this was the story in November 2010. By summer 2011, Hyperion Wharf was officially "being re-evaluated" and rumors persisted that the plan would be shelved. Now no one really knows what to expect. In late 2011, Disney still referred to it as Pleasure Island; press releases insisted Hyperion Wharf remained on the horizon, but a completion date of late 2012 looked highly optimistic. Taking the status quo as the best guess-timate, it remains a mix of shops and restaurants, notably the Irish pub-and-entertainment style of **Raglan Road** (with its Cookes of Dublin fish and chip shop), Latin-tinged **Paradiso 37**, the authentic Italian fare of **Portobello**, and some fine seafood at **Fulton's Crabhouse** (see Chapter 9).

Shopping opportunities are provided by **Apricot Lane**, a new outlet of women's celebrity-inspired clothing, jewelry, and accessories; surf shop **Curl by Sammy Duval**; and, arguably the only "adult" venue left on Pleasure Island, the tobacco emporium **Fuego by Sosa Cigars** (with a lounge offering fine wines,

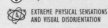

beers, cordials, tea, and coffee). The latter is a genuine family business from the Sosa family, exiled from Cuba in 1962 and now one of Florida's finest names in hand-rolled cigars. Live entertainment here can be a bit hit and miss, from some loud open-air disco "parties" to strolling musicians and talented duos playing to backing tracks.

West Side

The newest part of Downtown Disney opened in a blaze of publicity in 1997 and introduced a whole new world of nighttime fun. A few stores have changed in the intervening years but it is still largely the same as when it made its debut.

While the Marketplace has a more village style and Pleasure Island a winding interior promenade, the West Side features an **expansive grand boulevard**, with iconic buildings at either end (**Planet Hollywood** and **Cirque du Soleil**) and a vibrant mood of motion and light. The architecture is eclectic and ultra three-dimensional (witness the giant pineapple at one end of Bongo's Café!), utilizing elements of California Crazy, Floridian motifs (with lots of palm trees), and even classic boardwalk styling. The West Side is all about unique, individual experiences, though, and delivers some of the most "grown-up" offerings in Walt's World.

LA NOUBA

Without doubt, the highlight of the West Side is La Nouba, the amazing theatrical extravaganza by the world-famous Cirque du Soleil company. The exterior design is a **Grand Chapiteau**, the famous "Big Top" tent that many traveling Cirque shows use, while the set is reminiscent of a well-traveled, rustic setting. The auditorium features seven cloud-like "Fabulous Figures" that decorate the ceiling while the seats are reminiscent of grand old theaters of the past. And then there's the show, a multi-sensory kaleidoscopic array of talent that dazzles and amazes in equal parts. From a high-wire act, flying trapeze, diabolos, and jugglers, to the mind-boggling trampoline artists, it's

 MISS-ABLE   IF YOU HAVE TIME   WORTH MAKING TIME FOR   ☆ NOT TO BE MISSED!

☺ WILL ONLY WORRY YOUNG CHILDREN   ☺ MAY SCARE MANY YOUNG CHILDREN; FEW ADULTS   ☹ WILL SCARE MOST YOUNG CHILDREN; SOME ADULTS   ☻ MAJOR SCARE FACTOR

 VISUAL DISORIENTATION   MILD PHYSICAL MOVEMENT   INTENSE FEELING OF MOTION   EXTREME PHYSICAL SENSATIONS AND VISUAL DISORIENTATION

a feast that draws your attention in different directions all the time. Add live musicians and superb vocalists, and you have a performance that leaves its audience in awe five nights a week, two times each night. In story terms, La Nouba is the dream-like meeting of two worlds: the brightly colored realm of a circus and that of the dour Urbains (urbanites) in dark, monochromatic outfits. When the two collide, the magic of the one sparks the imagination of the other, with the Urbains all sporting brilliant white at the end.

Descriptions like "breathtaking" and "mind-boggling" are too tame for Cirque du Soleil, and La Nouba is even harder to describe. It is one of the most startling shows you will see anywhere in the world and appeals to all ages. Tickets start at $76, but it is worth every cent.

CHARACTERS IN FLIGHT

Another ultra-cool feature is Characters In Flight, a wonderful six-minute **tethered balloon ride** 400 feet above Downtown Disney, weather permitting. It takes up to thirty people in a circular, hollowed-out basket (imagine a giant doughnut ring!) for fantastic views over Disney and the surrounding area. Obviously the best views are by day, but it also flies at night and the lighting effects are stunning.

HOUSE OF BLUES

★★★ $$$$

This joint restaurant/music venue offers live music in the dining room and full-scale concerts in its main hall. You can also sample the wonderfully entertaining ninety-minute **Gospel Brunch** here each Sunday (with performances at 10:30 A.M. and 1:00 P.M.), a soul stage-show extravaganza accompanied by a stomach-stretching buffet. Not only will you eat enough food to sink a battleship, the lively forty-five-minute show will have you singing along and bouncing to the beat long after it's all over! Book tickets up to six months in advance at *www.houseofblues.com* or call 407-934-2583.

★ POOR   ★★ FAIR   ★★★ GOOD   ★★★★ EXCELLENT   ★★★★★ GOURMET
$ UNDER $10 $$ $10–15 $$$ $15–$20 $$$$ $20–$25 $$$$$ $25+

 BREAKFAST   LUNCH   DINNER   COUNTER SERVICE   TABLE SERVICE   TABLE SERVICE (TWO CREDITS)

DISNEYQUEST

A great family diversion (especially with children ages 6–18) is DisneyQuest, a five-story "theme park in a box" full of arcade games, with one-of-a-kind gaming experiences, classic video games, virtual reality rides, and much more. Once through the turnstiles, you enter the **Cybrolator** (a special-effect–laden elevator accompanied by Genie from *Aladdin*) that delivers guests to **Ventureport**, leading to the four zones that make up DisneyQuest. Choose from the **Explore Zone**, a virtual adventure in exotic and ancient destinations; **Score Zone**, a chance to test your game-playing skills in superhero competition; **Create Zone**, an Imagineering studio with the chance to create your own toys, rides, and animation; and the **Replay Zone**, an extravaganza of retro-futuristic games, from golden oldies like Pac-Man and Space Invaders to air hockey and pinball.

HIDDEN MAGIC | Think the "**Invasion**" game sounds a bit familiar? Yes, it is named after the now defunct Alien Encounter attraction in Magic Kingdom (now Stitch's Great Escape). It also borrows from that mythology by introducing more futuristic technology from the mythical X-S Tech company that ran the Alien Encounter show.

AMC DOWNTOWN DISNEY 24

The final original element of the West Side is **AMC Downtown Disney 24**, recently remodeled to include **six dine-in theaters** at the cinema complex. The "Fork & Screen" adaptations allow guests to select from a full food and beverage menu while they watch a movie, with table service throughout the screening. If you'd like to try the AMC cinemas' Dine-In option, enter at the Planet Hollywood end of the complex. If you want the traditional movie experience, go to the entry opposite Wolfgang Puck's Café. Dine-in guests must be at least 18, unless accompanied by a parent or guardian.

HIDDEN MAGIC | To avoid as much meal noise as possible, many of the food items at the Dine-In theaters are prepared for ease of eating, while the **plates are made of bamboo**, which reduces the sound of cutting!

 MISS-ABLE   IF YOU HAVE TIME   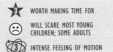 WORTH MAKING TIME FOR   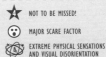 NOT TO BE MISSED!

☺ WILL ONLY WORRY YOUNG CHILDREN   ☺ MAY SCARE MANY YOUNG CHILDREN; FEW ADULTS   ☹ WILL SCARE MOST YOUNG CHILDREN; SOME ADULTS   ☹ MAJOR SCARE FACTOR

↻① VISUAL DISORIENTATION   ↻② MILD PHYSICAL MOVEMENT   ③ INTENSE FEELING OF MOTION   ⊕ EXTREME PHYSICAL SENSATIONS AND VISUAL DISORIENTATION

This is the first movie theater of its kind in central Florida and a real novelty hereabouts, while all the cinemas have been upgraded to the new-tech **Enhanced Theater Experience** (ETX), which features a larger screen with full 3-D capability, twelve-channel audio, and the latest digital projectors.

HIDDEN MAGIC According to the Pleasure Island legend, the site of the AMC 24 cineplex was originally part of the **sailmaking business** of Merriweather Adam Pleasure, who then gave it to son-in-law Raoul Manzanera for a secret government project to create a new train propulsion system. When the funding was withdrawn in 1940, Manzanera rigged a huge explosion to blow up his work. All that was left was the central superstructure and some outbuildings. AMC and Disney then rebuilt it in 1988. Which explains the steel "warehouse" look to one end of the building. Neat, huh?

SPLITSVILLE LUXURY LANES AND DINNER LOUNGE

(opening in late 2012)

More entertainment fun is due to arrive with the opening of Splitsville Luxury Lanes and Dinner Lounge with a smart retro-1950s look. It will be home to fourteen lanes of ten-pin bowling, a billiards parlor, bar, restaurant, and lounge with dance floor. And Disney aims to make it so smart and chic you may not even want to go bowling—just turn up to hang out or have a meal!

GENERAL DINING

Wonderland Café serves desserts and drinks, and **FoodQuest** serves basic burgers, chicken, wraps, and sandwiches. Like all good attractions, you exit through the gift shop on the ground floor. Also check out the **House of Blues**, **Bongos Cuban Café**, **Planet Hollywood**, and **Wolfgang Puck Café** (see Chapter 9), plus the snacks of Wetzel's Pretzels and Häagen-Dazs ice cream.

★ POOR   ★★ FAIR   ★★★ GOOD   ★★★★ EXCELLENT   ★★★★★ GOURMET
$ UNDER $10 $$ $10–15 $$$ $15–$20 $$$$ $20–$25 $$$$$ $25+
🅑 BREAKFAST   🅛 LUNCH   🅓 DINNER   CS COUNTER SERVICE   TS TABLE SERVICE   TS2 TABLE SERVICE (TWO CREDITS)

SHOPPING ON THE WEST SIDE

Shopping is fairly upscale and eye-catching, including the massive new outlet for the **Harley-Davidson Store**, with an amazing range of products, like their customized design-a-vest and photo studio; chic **Hoypoloi**, offering a wonderful range of original glass and ceramic artwork; **Pop Gallery**, an eclectic mix of art gallery and pop art museum; **Magic Masters**, an elegant magic shop inspired by Harry Houdini's personal library; a signature **Sunglass Icon** store; **Sosa Family Cigars**; and **Candy Cauldron**, a sweet magnet for kids of all ages dressed up like a candy kitchen (where you can watch some of the fare being made). There are also gift shops for **House of Blues**, **Planet Hollywood**, **Cirque du Soleil**, and **Bongos**, plus vendor carts and more live musical entertainment in the evenings, when the West Side pulsates with bright, vibrant life.

Disney's BoardWalk

While it may not be a nightlife district on the same scale as Pleasure Island used to be, the BoardWalk's extensive array of evening entertainment is well worth considering. Amazingly, many people don't give it a thought as they believe it is "only" a resort (see Chapter 2), but this homage to the great early twentieth-century attractions like **Coney Island** and **Atlantic City** is a genuine extravaganza of nighttime fun.

Along with several excellent table-service restaurants (see Chapter 9) there are snack kiosks and other quick-service options, like the **BoardWalk Bakery** (fresh cakes, pies, and pastries from their own oven), **Seashore Sweets** (typical boardwalk candy, like saltwater taffy, fudge, and cotton candy), and the **Pizza Window**. You'll also find another seven shopping outlets—notably the chic **Wyland Gallery**, featuring the art, conservation, and nature of various well-known marine artists, the **ESPN Club Store**, and the fine apparel of **Thimbles & Threads**—as well as an enticing selection of boardwalk midway games, caricature artists, and hair-braiding stands.

  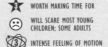 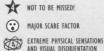

Live entertainment is provided by a series of **BoardWalk buskers** who turn up unannounced from 6:30–10:30 P.M. and provide some terrific family fun, from rope-tricks to juggling, magic acts, comedy, and music. But don't get too close—you might end up as part of the act!

The more energetic will want to try the **Surrey Bikes** (canopied two- or four-seat bicycles) that can be pedaled around the near one-mile circuit of Crescent Lake that includes the Yacht and Beach Club resorts and the Swan and Dolphin resorts. Walk around to the **Yacht/Beach Club Bayside Marina** and you can hire a variety of boats, take a fishing excursion, or try one of the specialty cruises (must be booked up to ninety days in advance; call 407-939-7529). You can also catch a boat to Epcot or Disney's Hollywood Studios. You'll also find the live music of Jellyrolls, a dueling piano bar, and Atlantic Dance Hall, with DJ-spun music and large-screen videos.

JELLYROLLS

This dueling piano bar is open every night from 7:00 P.M. (music from 8:00 P.M.) until 2:00 A.M. The two pianists take turns to perform well-known tunes, inviting the audience to suggest songs and sing along, and it makes for a lively, entertaining evening, with a lot of humor as they interact with the crowd and play with the lyrics from time to time. Special occasions can be celebrated, friends made fun of, and audience participation is encouraged, hence it can be a raucous evening out. It is hugely popular and you need to arrive early to get a table (otherwise it is standing room only). Entry is strictly twenty-one and up.

HIDDEN MAGIC Jellyrolls is named for **Ferdinand Joseph LaMothe**, otherwise known as Jelly Roll Morton, the famous ragtime pianist and jazz musician who lived from 1904–1941. His is a fitting name as a lot of his early material was distinctly ribald and Jellyrolls' pianists can get a bit bawdy late at night!

★ POOR	★★ FAIR	★★★ GOOD	★★★★ EXCELLENT	★★★★★ GOURMET
$ UNDER $10	$$ $10–15	$$$ $15–$20	$$$$ $20–$25	$$$$$ $25+
BREAKFAST	LUNCH	DINNER	COUNTER SERVICE	TABLE SERVICE

 TABLE SERVICE (TWO CREDITS)

ATLANTIC DANCE HALL

The Atlantic Dance Hall has gone through several changes since it opened in 1996, initially as a classic early twentieth-century dance club, with a live band playing the songs of yesteryear and a cover charge, and now as a modern nightclub. Parts of its original **art deco** interior remain, hinting at the romantic atmosphere of the 1920s and '30s—which is a touch at odds with the modern DJs and their video screens—but it remains an original venue for a dance club. It opens five nights a week (Tues.–Sat.), and is free to enter (twenty-one and up only) apart from special events, like their New Year's Eve Party.

Dinner Shows

You might be surprised to learn there are three major dinner shows open to Disney guests—and not just hotel guests—in two of the resorts, tucked away in corners of the Polynesian Resort and Fort Wilderness. They've been here a while, too, and make for a great night out. Food-wise, they are a cut above most of the dinner shows in the rest of Orlando, and all come with that essential Disney "magic," as well as a great story.

SPIRIT OF ALOHA

 $$$$$

The **Polynesian Resort's** luau show dates back to the hotel's official opening on October 24, 1971, when the occasion was marked by a grand luau feast along the **Seven Seas Lagoon** shoreline. Today, the show is a full ninety-minute **South Seas extravaganza**, telling the tale of a native girl who has lost her cultural roots but gradually rediscovers them through a series of traditional acts, dances, and ceremonies that feature the spirit of Hawaii, Tonga, Tahiti, New Zealand, and Samoa.

 MISS-ABLE
 IF YOU HAVE TIME
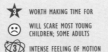 WORTH MAKING TIME FOR
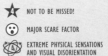 NOT TO BE MISSED!

WILL ONLY WORRY YOUNG CHILDREN   MAY SCARE MANY YOUNG CHILDREN; FEW ADULTS   WILL SCARE MOST YOUNG CHILDREN; SOME ADULTS   MAJOR SCARE FACTOR

VISUAL DISORIENTATION   MILD PHYSICAL MOVEMENT   INTENSE FEELING OF MOTION   EXTREME PHYSICAL SENSATIONS AND VISUAL DISORIENTATION

The buffet dinner features live music in a tropical setting, and the show culminates with the amazing **Samoan Fire-Knife Dance**. Other highlights include the **Maori Poi Dance**, the graceful **Hawaiian hula**, and the traditional **'ote'a** from Tahiti. It has genuine Polynesian charm and the atmosphere is wonderfully laid-back. The Spirit of Aloha usually runs twice nightly at 5:15 and 8:00 P.M. (Tues.–Sat.). The second show is often better, especially in summer, as it benefits from the darkening nighttime backdrop.

HOOP DEE DOO REVUE

★★★ $$$$$ 🍽️ⓓ 🍽️Ⓣ🅂

Step back in time with the **Pioneer Hall Players at Fort Wilderness** for this song-and-dance parody of nineteenth-century fun. Vaudeville meets frontier comedy and typical wholesome Disney family entertainment in an authentic 1820s Northwest Territory setting.

HIDDEN MAGIC One of the original scriptwriters for **the Hoop Dee Doo** was Tom Adair, a successful TV sitcom writer from the 1960s and '70s. This was perfect period territory for him as he already had one big hit from the cowboy era, the comedy series *F Troop*.

Pioneer Hall, opened in 1974, was not part of the original Fort Wilderness resort. It was originally a Davy Crockett–themed restaurant, but the need for more revenue-earning activities led to the creation of the revue as a summer space-filler, with college program kids performing the six roles. It proved so popular that Disney made it part of the full-time repertoire and now, almost thirty years later, it has performed to more than 10 million guests and is one of the most beloved shows anywhere in the World.

Six performers arrive on the "stagecoach," mingling with the audience before taking to the stage for a ninety-minute show with well-known songs like "Oh My Darling, Clementine" and "They Call the Wind Mariah." "Song of the States" gives the cast a chance to ad lib and have fun with the audience while the closing song, "Mammoth Historical Pageant", is a gag-filled extravaganza paying tribute to Davy Crockett and bringing down the curtain in style. All together now: "Yeehaw!"

A "cowboy favorites" dinner is served on metal plates and from metal buckets, which kids really enjoy, and beer, wine, tea, coffee, and soft drinks are all included. The show runs three times a night, usually at 5:00, 7:15, and 9:30 p.m. You need to allow plenty of time to arrive if you are not staying at Fort Wilderness. Catch a boat from Magic Kingdom, Contemporary Resort, or Wilderness Lodge, or catch a bus to the campground's Settlement Depot, then walk to Pioneer Hall. All three categories of seating are good, although category one provides the best chance of cast interaction.

HIDDEN MAGIC   Ever since 1974, the opening number had been "Hoop Dee Doo," based on the 1950 **Perry Como polka** but, in 2011, the original authors of the song came calling on Disney, demanding royalties for using "their" song. However, rather than give in to the demand, Disney simply wrote a new opening number.

MICKEY'S BACKYARD BBQ

★★ $$$$$

More Western-themed fun can be found with this lively buffet dinner show, in the outdoor (but covered) **Fort Wilderness Pavilion**, March–December only, weather permitting. Aimed more at children for its character interaction and style, it is as much a country and western experience as anything else, with a live band, hosts **Cyclone Sally** and **Tumbleweed Will**, and **Mickey and the gang** in their cowboy costumes. **Chip and Dale** greet guests on arrival, while **Mickey and Minnie** are available for photos at the end. In between, the characters all come out to dance—children are invited up to dance with them, which can be a touch chaotic—and there is an eye-catching rope act and plenty of music, plus "activities" like the Electric Slide, Macarena, and Chicken Dance (ugh!), and a flag-waving grand finale hoedown.

★ MISS-ABLE   ★ IF YOU HAVE TIME   ★ WORTH MAKING TIME FOR   ★ NOT TO BE MISSED!

☺ WILL ONLY WORRY YOUNG CHILDREN   ☺ MAY SCARE MANY YOUNG CHILDREN; FEW ADULTS   ☹ WILL SCARE MOST YOUNG CHILDREN; SOME ADULTS   ☹ MAJOR SCARE FACTOR

VISUAL DISORIENTATION   MILD PHYSICAL MOVEMENT   INTENSE FEELING OF MOTION   EXTREME PHYSICAL SENSATIONS AND VISUAL DISORIENTATION

The help-yourself food is simple but hearty, with salad, smoked chicken, stuffing, ribs, hot dogs, burgers, corn-on-the-cob, cornbread, baked beans, coleslaw, watermelon, Mickey ice cream bars, and marble cake, while the kids' offerings include mac and cheese. Beer, wine, tea, coffee, and soft drinks are again all included. All dinner shows can be booked online or by calling 407-939-3463, with pre-payment required.

And There's More. . . !

We couldn't finish without pointing out two of the best free activities in Walt's World. And you don't have to be a resort guest to enjoy them.

FORT WILDERNESS CAMPFIRE PROGRAM

Every night, Chip and Dale host a regular campfire get-together at the resort's **Meadow Trading Post**, with a great chance to meet your favorite chipmunks and get your autograph book signed. It begins at 8:00 P.M. (7:00 P.M. in fall and winter) with a Disney host opening the campfire to a traditional marshmallow roast (bring your own or buy them from the handy Chuck Wagon) and sing-along, with the two mischievous 'munks then coming out for a typical meet-and-greet. After thirty–forty minutes of character fun, a classic Disney movie is shown on the big outdoor screen, with bleacher and bench seating (or bring your own blanket to spread out on the ground). **The Chuck Wagon** also serves drinks and snacks—including pizza, hot dogs, sodas, coffee, and beer—or you're welcome to bring your own refreshments.

ELECTRICAL WATER PAGEANT

If you enjoy the **Magic Kingdom's Main Street Electrical Parade**, you should definitely watch out for the waterborne equivalent, which occurs every night on Bay Lake and Seven Seas Lagoon in front of Magic Kingdom. Here, on fourteen specially created floats, an eight-minute maritime procession passes in

 ★ POOR $ UNDER $10   B BREAKFAST
 ★★ FAIR $$ $10–15   L LUNCH
 ★★★ GOOD $$$ $15–$20   D DINNER
 ★★★★ EXCELLENT $$$$ $20–$25  CS COUNTER SERVICE
★★★★★ GOURMET $$$$$ $25+ TS TABLE SERVICE
 TS2 TABLE SERVICE (TWO CREDITS)

front of the Polynesian Resort, Grand Floridian, Wilderness Lodge, Fort Wilderness, Contemporary Resort, and Magic Kingdom itself (during extended hours) from 9:00–10:15 P.M. (with a slight delay when the Magic Kingdom fireworks are at 9:00 P.M.).

You could be forgiven for thinking it is King Triton (from *The Little Mermaid*) coming to pay us humans a visit; in reality the series of oceangoing characters, from dolphins and turtles to an octopus and whale, are actually overseen by **Neptune, the Roman god of the sea**. A new musical score was added in 1996 that includes songs from *The Little Mermaid*. In a dramatic finale, all the floats change to a patriotic stars-and-stripes theme (just as they did back in 1971), to the tune of "You're a Grand Old Flag," "Yankee Doodle," and "America the Beautiful." Classic Disney heart-tugging nostalgia.

HIDDEN MAGIC | The **Electrical Water Pageant** made its debut as part of the dedication ceremony for the Polynesian Resort on October 26, 1971. It was so successful, Disney management looked to create a version for the Disneyland park in Anaheim—and the Main Street Electrical Parade was born, using the same original music, "Baroque Hoedown." So, yes, the Pageant predates the Parade!

 MISS-ABLE   IF YOU HAVE TIME   WORTH MAKING TIME FOR   NOT TO BE MISSED!

 WILL ONLY WORRY YOUNG CHILDREN   MAY SCARE MANY YOUNG CHILDREN; FEW ADULTS   WILL SCARE MOST YOUNG CHILDREN; SOME ADULTS   MAJOR SCARE FACTOR

VISUAL DISORIENTATION   MILD PHYSICAL MOVEMENT   INTENSE FEELING OF MOTION   EXTREME PHYSICAL SENSATIONS AND VISUAL DISORIENTATION

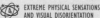

Write Your Own Story

Chapter 9

Discovering Dining

JUST BECAUSE WE'VE LEFT THE THEME PARKS and other attractions behind doesn't mean the story stops. There is plenty more to discover when you turn to Disney's amazing array of fine dining opportunities! You've already learned about dining in the parks in Chapters 3–6 and all about the quick counter-service options located in the food courts at the resorts (Chapter 2), but here you'll find an in-depth look at the many great table-service options both in the resorts and Downtown Disney.

Keep in mind that the key to booking a table-service restaurant is the Advance Dining Reservation (or ADR). You can make ADRs up to 180 days ahead (180 plus the length-of-stay for resort guests) and this is highly advisable. The growth of the Disney Dining Plan (see Chapter 2) is largely responsible as more people are taking the plan and booking all their meals in advance. You can book by calling 407–939–3463 from 7:00 A.M.–10:00 P.M. EST; by dialing *55 on any resort phone; at any Guest Relations office; or—much better—online at *www.disneyworld.com/dining*.

Armed with the information needed to make a dining reservation, the next step is to choose where you will dine. Some of the best restaurants are located outside the theme parks, and we highlight them here.

Character Meal Line-Up

For many guests, the highlight of a Disney trip is a visit with the beloved characters that inhabit their earliest childhood memories. From **Mickey Mouse** to **Mary Poppins**, these are friends we've grown up with, whose stories are part of our own story. And while you can meet them for free in the parks, there is nothing quite so special as having your favorite friends show up at your table for some genuine one-on-one time. It is truly the stuff of magical memories.

Everyone has their favorite characters, and while you may know "who" you want to meet, you may not know where to find them. The handy chart below will help make selecting a character meal easier.

LOCATION	RESTAURANT	MEAL	CHARACTERS
MAGIC KINGDOM	Crystal Palace	B L D	Winnie the Pooh, Piglet, Tigger, Eeyore
	Cinderella's Royal Table	B L D	Cinderella, Sleeping Beauty, Snow White, Mary Poppins, Fairy Godmother
	Restaurant Akershus	B L D	Some combination of Sleeping Beauty, Ariel, Belle, Snow White, Jasmine, Mary Poppins
	Garden Grill	D	Farmer Mickey, Pluto, Chip 'n Dale
DISNEY'S HOLLYWOOD STUDIOS	Hollywood & Vine	B L	Little Einsteins, Handy Manny, Oso
ANIMAL KINGDOM	Tusker House	B	Safari Mickey, Goofy, Donald, Daisy
GRAND FLORIDIAN	1900 Park Fare	B D	Alice in Wonderland, Mad Hatter, Mary Poppins, Winnie the Pooh
	Wonderland Tea Party (CHILDREN ONLY)	TEA	Alice in Wonderland, Mad Hatter
	My Disney Girl's Perfectly Princess Tea	TEA	Sleeping Beauty
CONTEMPORARY RESORT	Chef Mickey's	B D	Chef Mickey, Goofy, Pluto, Minnie, Donald
BEACH CLUB	Cape May Café	B	Goofy, Donald, Chip 'n Dale
POLYNESIAN RESORT	'Ohana	B	Mickey, Pluto, Lilo, Stitch
SWAN RESORT	Garden Grove	B (SAT & SUN ONLY) D	Goofy, Pluto; Rafiki and Timon (Mon. and Fri. only)
FORT WILDERNESS	Mickey's Backyard BBQ	D (SEASONAL)	Mickey, Minnie, Goofy, Pluto, Chip 'n Dale

Resorts

Port Orleans Riverside

BOATWRIGHT'S DINING HALL

★★★ $$$$

This restaurant is home to the legacy of the legendary artisans who once worked within its wooden structure. Its walls are adorned with the tools of their trade and, hanging from the rafters, is the **Louisiana Lugger**, one of the flat-bottom boats that brought **Dixie Landings** its fame. Southern-style cuisine is the name of the game here, with entrees like jambalaya and blackened red snapper, plus traditional fare like prime rib, pasta, and filet mignon. Southern sides and pecan pie complete a well-rounded dining experience.

ROOKIE MISTAKES

While character dining is an undoubted highlight for most, it is wise to give young children a chance to meet the characters around the parks *before* you rush them into the restaurant experiences. Some youngsters find the size of Goofy, Pluto, and co. intimidating and the atmosphere a bit frenzied, and can end up spending the meal under the table!

Caribbean Beach

SHUTTERS

★★ $$$

Designed like a series of small dining rooms with faux outdoor views through lots of window shutters, its menu has a veneer of **Caribbean spiciness** but otherwise stays in fairly safe territory serving steak, ribs, prime rib, and pasta. The **open kitchen** is a nod toward Disney's more adventurous streak, but there is better fare elsewhere.

 ★ POOR   ★★ FAIR   ★★★ GOOD    ★★★★ EXCELLENT   ★★★★★ GOURMET

$ UNDER $10 $$ $10–15 $$$ $15–$20 $$$$ $20–$25 $$$$$ $25+

B BREAKFAST   L LUNCH   D DINNER   CS COUNTER SERVICE   TS TABLE SERVICE   TS2 TABLE SERVICE (TWO CREDITS)

Coronado Springs

MAYA GRILL

★★★★ $$$$$ 🍴B   🍴D   🍴TS

You are supposedly dining inside a Mayan pyramid here, with murals of Mayans at work, mapping the universe, and so on, but the **Nuevo Latino cuisine** is a delight, with genuine South American flair and gusto. Seafood, steaks, chipotle chicken, pork, and outstanding Kobe-style burgers.

Fort Wilderness

TRAIL'S END RESTAURANT

★★★ $$$$ 🍴B   🍴L   🍴D   🍴TS

Tucked away in the rustic heart of **Disney's camping resort** is this little gem which offers good value and reliable, hearty fare. Its frontier-style includes a pot-bellied stove, beamed ceiling, split-log walls, and flagstone floor, and the **evening buffet's "pioneer fare"** (way better than Davy Crockett ever imagined, and probably more sanitary!) should please most palates. The buffet includes soups, salad bar, peel-and-eat shrimp, smoked pork ribs, fried chicken, pasta, pizza, fresh-carved meats, fish, and a wonderful fruit cobbler.

Old Key West

OLIVIA'S CAFÉ

★★★ $$$ 🍴B   🍴L   🍴D   🍴TS

Drop into the casual world of the **Conch Republic** (otherwise known as Key West) and discover a splendidly laid-back menu and ambience. Wicker fans, eclectic wall art, and bright lighting make this an ideal, relaxed lunch venue, with that "Floribbean" cuisine influence from the mix of Florida and the Caribbean. Conch chowder, conch fritters, and other seafood items dominate the menu (although you can also get a good burger and prime rib), while the **Key Lime Tart** is a signature dessert.

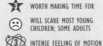
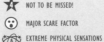

★ MISS-ABLE	★ IF YOU HAVE TIME	★ WORTH MAKING TIME FOR	★ NOT TO BE MISSED!
😊 WILL ONLY WORRY YOUNG CHILDREN	😐 MAY SCARE MANY YOUNG CHILDREN; FEW ADULTS	😟 WILL SCARE MOST YOUNG CHILDREN; SOME ADULTS	😨 MAJOR SCARE FACTOR
↻ VISUAL DISORIENTATION	MILD PHYSICAL MOVEMENT	INTENSE FEELING OF MOTION	EXTREME PHYSICAL SENSATIONS AND VISUAL DISORIENTATION

Saratoga Springs

TURF CLUB BAR AND GRILL

★★★ $$$$ 🍴L 🍴D 🍴TS

Horse-racing fans will be right at home in this casual offering right opposite Downtown Disney, with great views by day and by night. A surprisingly versatile menu runs from simple burgers and chicken to New York strip steak and a **Sustainable Fish of the Day**. Sports fans can enjoy the bar-style atmosphere, or just play pool, while horse-racing memorabilia decorates the walls.

Beach Club

CAPE MAY CAFÉ

★★★ $$$$$ 🍴B 🍴D 🍴TS

You might be tempted to bring your swimsuit here, as the bright, nautical "at the beach" theme is all-encompassing and highly enjoyable. Both meals are all-you-can-eat affairs from the central buffet, with a highly child-friendly (and often-overlooked) **Character Breakfast** with Goofy, Minnie, and Chip and Dale, and a **New England Clam Bake** for dinner. The food won't win any awards but it is usually very fresh, with plenty of seafood in the evening, and it is often easy to get an ADR. Interesting factoid? It is not a New England theme here—Cape May, America's oldest seaside resort, is actually in New Jersey.

Yacht Club

CAPTAIN'S GRILLE

★★★ $$$$ 🍴B 🍴L 🍴D 🍴TS

Formerly the Yacht Club Galley, this is the resort's more casual restaurant and features both buffet and à la carte choices for breakfast and a prix fixe selection for dinner. The more formal nautical style of the resort takes a bit of a break here, with brighter décor and more playful motifs, while the "Captain" hangs around the ceiling scanning the horizon. A great array of soups, salads,

---

and sandwiches highlights the lunch selection while the dinner menu boasts a rich mix of seafood and steaks, plus a daily pasta dish.

YACHTSMAN STEAKHOUSE

★★★★ $$$$$

The Yacht Club's formal restaurant is a genuine mecca for **meat lovers**, with some of the best hand-cut steaks in Orlando. Anyone who has been to Newport, Rhode Island, or Martha's Vineyard, Massachusetts, will be familiar with the **New England nautical club styling** here, a rich blend of warm woods, brass, and leather. You're not exactly setting sail but the posh seagoing ambience is definitely an adventure!

Polynesian Resort

'OHANA

★★★ $$$$$

"Ohana"—as we learn in *Lilo and Stitch*—means "family," so it should come as no surprise to learn the big dinner meal here is served **family style**, with huge amounts of grilled chicken, barbecued pork loin, marinated sirloin, and spicy shrimp. It's not cheap, and it can be quite raucous as there is live music, hula lessons, and coconut races, but the big central **firepit**, extravagant Polynesian styling, and spirit of the islands ensures this is as much an experience as a meal. The **Character Breakfast** also features **Lilo and Stitch**, as well as **Mickey** and **Pluto**, and there is a neat tropical twist to some standard menu items like the fruit juice and sausages.

KONA CAFÉ

★★★★ $$$$

In Hawaiian, "**Kona**" means "leeward" (and you thought we were going to say "coffee"!) and this modest restaurant in one corner of the Polynesian is very much in the lee (calm side) of signature diner **'Ohana**—which is a shame

 MISS-ABLE   IF YOU HAVE TIME   WORTH MAKING TIME FOR   NOT TO BE MISSED!

 WILL ONLY WORRY YOUNG CHILDREN   MAY SCARE MANY YOUNG CHILDREN; FEW ADULTS   WILL SCARE MOST YOUNG CHILDREN; SOME ADULTS   MAJOR SCARE FACTOR

VISUAL DISORIENTATION   MILD PHYSICAL MOVEMENT   INTENSE FEELING OF MOTION   EXTREME PHYSICAL SENSATIONS AND VISUAL DISORIENTATION

as its **Asian fusion twist** on American cuisine is well worth trying while its big brother dazzles with more show and pizzazz. The open pastry kitchen indicates its other specialty, with genuinely decadent desserts—including the resort's signature **Tonga Toast**—and yes, it does serve a good cup of coffee.

Contemporary Resort

CALIFORNIA GRILL

★★★★★ $$$$$

This beautifully stylish fifteenth-floor aerie atop the hotel proved that there really was a market for gourmet fare in the theme park world. The **California fusion cuisine** changes regularly and utilizes only the freshest in-season produce from an open kitchen featuring the superb creations of executive chef **Brian Piasecki**. The sharpest sushi and brick-oven flatbreads mingle with mouthwatering pasta and exquisite fish dishes, to ensure the food is as spectacular as the nighttime view over **Magic Kingdom**.

HIDDEN MAGIC

The California Grill's extensive—and outstanding—wine list from the Golden State includes several special hand-decorated bottles in the lobby with a strong Disney connection. Yes, those six Pixar-painted vintages are all signed by **John Lasseter**, chief creative officer of both Pixar and Walt Disney Animation, who has his own winery in Sonoma. Find out more at *www.lasseterfamilywinery.com*.

CHEF MICKEY'S

★★★★ $$$$$

You don't really come here for the food but the wonderful character interaction in the cavernous central lobby of the resort, where the monorail goes through at regular intervals and Mickey, Minnie, Goofy, Pluto, and Donald get everyone singing and dancing along (yes, and twirling napkins in the air—but, hey,

you're on vacation!). The breakfast and dinner buffets are standard but plentiful affairs, with fresh-carved meats and a signature sundae bar in the evening.

HIDDEN MAGIC

Chef Mickey's is the second-most popular character meal in Walt's World (after Cinderella's in Magic Kingdom) but that wasn't always the case. Mickey's character breakfast started in modest fashion at the old Empress Lilly restaurant at Downtown Disney (now Fulton's Crabhouse) and moved to the Village Restaurant (renamed Chef Mickey's in 1990). Five years later, Chef Mickey's was replaced by the Rainforest Café and Mickey and the gang moved permanently to the Contemporary Resort.

THE WAVE

★★★★ $$$$

If there was one thing lacking in the vast Disney repertoire of memorable dining in 2008, it was a restaurant that pushed the envelope of **avant-garde design**. Then along came The Wave, with its circular tunnel entrance, moody lighting, copper-colored metal ceiling, and sleek cocktail lounge, and we were genuinely wowed. The menu wasn't bad either, with world flavors added to contemporary American dishes and a **health-conscious** approach that promised enjoyable meals that wouldn't enlarge your waist.

The Dolphin Resort

SHULA'S

Essential Information: Not DDP

★★★★★ $$$$$

In the mood for a good steak? Go no further. Legendary Miami Dolphins head coach **Don Shula** started his own upscale steakhouse chain in 1989, themed for the famous "Perfect Season" of 1972 when his Dolphins went 17-0 and won

 MISS-ABLE
 IF YOU HAVE TIME
WORTH MAKING TIME FOR
NOT TO BE MISSED!

 WILL ONLY WORRY YOUNG CHILDREN
 MAY SCARE MANY YOUNG CHILDREN; FEW ADULTS
WILL SCARE MOST YOUNG CHILDREN; SOME ADULTS
 MAJOR SCARE FACTOR

VISUAL DISORIENTATION
 MILD PHYSICAL MOVEMENT
 INTENSE FEELING OF MOTION
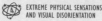 EXTREME PHYSICAL SENSATIONS AND VISUAL DISORIENTATION

the Super Bowl; hence it is also a football-lover's paradise. Menus are hand-painted on official NFL game footballs and signed by Shula himself. Hungry? One of the featured entrees is the 48-ounce porterhouse—finish it and you join **Shula's 48-Ounce Club**, which has more than 26,000 members!

TODD ENGLISH'S BLUEZOO

Essential Information: Not DDP

★★★★★ $$$$$

The Boston celebrity chef has made his mark with contrasting restaurants around the country, but few are as eye-catching as this collaboration with renowned architect and interior designer **Jeffrey Beers**. Like an underwater adventure in glass and light, bluezoo dazzles the senses and thrills the taste buds with a seafood extravaganza, from a **raw bar** and extensive fresh fish selection to the signature **Dancing Fish rotisserie**, a special grill over an open fire.

Swan Resort

GARDEN GROVE CAFÉ

Essential Information: Not DDP

★★★ $$$$$

This is primarily the **Swan/Dolphin's character meal** opportunity, with a lively weekend breakfast buffet featuring Pluto and Goofy and a nightly themed dinner buffet (from Southern barbecue to Mediterranean). With a genuine Central Park vibe from the garden décor and 25-foot-tall centerpiece oak tree, it also offers a pleasant light lunch alternative.

IL MULINO

Essential Information: Not DDP

★★★★ $$$$$

This **award-winning New York trattoria** came to the Swan in 2007 with its upscale Italian cuisine and ambience. It had to be good to replace the excellent Palio, and it was, bringing the Italian family experience to life along with a genuine flair for fresh pasta, veal, and risotto (plus equally appealing steaks, chicken, and fish). Live music on Fridays and Saturdays adds to the Big Apple state of mind here.

KIMONOS

Essential Information: Not DDP

★★★★ $$$$

If you're a fan of **sushi** you should make a beeline for this authentic Japanese seafood lounge/restaurant, where the dark teak wood décor and rich lighting provide the ideal setting for house specialties like gyoza, tempura platters, Kobe beef, and duck satay. True to form, **Kimonos** also features a nightly kara-oke sing-a-long, which is usually a hit with the late-night crowd.

Wilderness Lodge

ARTIST POINT

★★★★★ $$$$$

You are firmly in the **Pacific Northwest** in every sense in this large but refined restaurant in a quiet corner of the beautiful lodge. The artwork, décor, cuisine, and wines are all reminiscent of this former frontier region, which remains a haven of National Park splendor. Ornate iron lanterns suspended from rustic timber columns, huge picture windows framing the outdoor **Silver Creek Falls**,

  MISS-ABLE   IF YOU HAVE TIME   WORTH MAKING TIME FOR   NOT TO BE MISSED!

WILL ONLY WORRY
YOUNG CHILDREN

MAY SCARE MANY YOUNG
CHILDREN; FEW ADULTS

  WILL SCARE MOST YOUNG
CHILDREN; SOME ADULTS

MAJOR SCARE FACTOR

 VISUAL DISORIENTATION   MILD PHYSICAL MOVEMENT   INTENSE FEELING OF MOTION   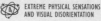 EXTREME PHYSICAL SENSATIONS
AND VISUAL DISORIENTATION

and authentic paintings of the rugged landscape are the perfect backdrop to a menu where the focus is on seafood, sirloins, and game, plus seasonal options and the kitchen's signature dish, cedar plank-roasted salmon. Not cheap but a memorable evening out.

WHISPERING CANYON CAFÉ

★★★ $$$$

In total contrast to the quiet backwoods feel of Artist Point, **Whispering Canyon Café** is the lodge's lively focal point, a rollicking family venue that offers fun for children and memorable food for adults. An extension of the cavernous—and highly appealing—hotel foyer, with its heavy wooden beams and heavy stone fireplace, it offers a hearty all-you-can eat skillet choice for each meal, as well as an à la carte menu. It can be a bit rowdy as the sassy waitstaff all get into the entertainment spirit here while the periodic **"pony races"** are a high-light for kids. Don't ask for the ketchup at Whispering Canyon Café—unless you want to set off a fun chain reaction around the restaurant!

Grand Floridian

1900 PARK FARE

★★★ $$$$$

In keeping with the hotel's **grand Victorian style**, this is a journey into a period fair, highlighted by the **authentic carousel horses** and whimsical décor. The food is largely standard buffet fare, with the addition of tasty baked ham, Lobster Benedict, and the signature strawberry soup at breakfast, and prime rib and chicken marsala at dinner. The real draw, though, is the character interaction—the **Supercalifragilistic Breakfast** with Mary Poppins and co. (usu-ally with Alice in Wonderland and the Mad Hatter) and **Cinderella's Happy Ever After Dinner**, with Cinderella and Prince Charming. The latter can be a good bet if Cinderella's Royal Table in Magic Kingdom is fully booked.

HIDDEN MAGIC   See that massive **band organ** in the alcove over the main dining room in 1900 Park Fare? That is Big Bertha—built in Paris in the nineteenth century and brought to the U.S.A. in 1909. It entertained amusement park guests in Grand Rapids, Michigan, until 1955 before falling into disrepair. Salvaged and repaired by Disney's Imagineers, it has been a Grand Floridian signature item since the hotel opened in 1988.

CITRICOS

★★★★   \$\$\$\$\$

This elegant dining room is distinctly more modern in décor and offers a fresh Mediterranean-inspired menu, with the likes of creative risottos, fresh pastas, seasonal seafood, and great steaks from their oak-fired grill. If the California Grill is already full, this is a handy alternative. Confused by the name? It is just Spanish for **citrus fruits**.

GRAND FLORIDIAN CAFÉ

★★★   \$\$\$\$

The more casual, all-purpose restaurant at the Grand Floridian is still a relatively pricey affair (despite the fact Disney calls it "moderately priced") but is a great breakfast venue in particular with its **Victorian conservatory ambience** and bright, airy feel. Looking for a different burger? The **Grand Floridian Burger** includes lobster, asparagus, and a horseradish-chive hollandaise sauce!

NARCOOSSEE'S

★★★★★   \$\$\$\$\$

Every good Victorian resort needs a fine seaside cottage and this is the Grand Floridian's. The all-wood styling, louvered shutters, and cathedral ceiling of this octagonal building ensure a memorable setting, and the food does the rest— superb fish, lobster, and scallops, plus filet mignon, lemon-oregano chicken,

---

 MISS-ABLE   IF YOU HAVE TIME   WORTH MAKING TIME FOR   NOT TO BE MISSED!

 WILL ONLY WORRY YOUNG CHILDREN   MAY SCARE MANY YOUNG CHILDREN; FEW ADULTS   WILL SCARE MOST YOUNG CHILDREN; SOME ADULTS   MAJOR SCARE FACTOR

 VISUAL DISORIENTATION   MILD PHYSICAL MOVEMENT   INTENSE FEELING OF MOTION   EXTREME PHYSICAL SENSATIONS AND VISUAL DISORIENTATION

and an excellent vegetarian dish. Once again, it's not cheap, but it is a beautiful setting and boasts a great **view of the Magic Kingdom fireworks** and **Electrical Water Pageant**. The name? It's a Muscogee (Creek) Indian word for "bear" (and also an abandoned nineteenth-century settlement in east Osceola County).

VICTORIA & ALBERT'S
Essential Information: Not DDP

★★★★★ $$$$$ 

Ready for a truly **regal dining experience** (as opposed to the faux style of Cinderella's Royal Table)? Disney's Imagineers created the perfect, small-scale palace of opulence with this homage to Britain's longest-reigning monarch and her consort. With a set seven-course meal (or ten to twelve if you choose the even-more-exclusive **Chef's Table** or **Queen Victoria's Room**), it features butler service, personalized menus, the finest linens, and Wedgwood tableware. The bill of fare changes according to the freshest produce available, but might include truffles from Italy, the finest caviar, beef from Japan, poulet rouge from North Carolina, and oysters from North Florida. It is not so much a meal as an exercise in culinary art under **master chef Scott Hunnel**. When you win the lottery, this is the place to celebrate—as long as you don't bring the kids. **Children under age 10 are not allowed**. It is also the only Disney restaurant with its own website: *http://victoria-alberts.com*.

    Don't even think of turning up at Victoria & Albert's without being dressed to the nines. The restaurant requires dinner jackets for men and a cocktail dress, or similar, for women.

Animal Kingdom Lodge

BOMA

★★★★★ $$$$$ 

The story-rich Lodge turns up another gem with its splendid **buffet restaurant**, where the theming is all-encompassing and the food is just as imaginative.

★ POOR   ★★ FAIR   ★★★ GOOD   ★★★★ EXCELLENT   ★★★★★ GOURMET
$ UNDER $10 $$ $10–15 $$$ $15–$20 $$$$ $20–$25 $$$$$ $25+
 BREAKFAST   LUNCH   DINNER   COUNTER SERVICE    TABLE SERVICE   TABLE SERVICE (TWO CREDITS)

"Boma" means "enclosure" in Swahili and there is a clever "fenced-in" aspect to the dining area, while the serveries are set out in marketplace style to provide an extensive African experience. The breakfast selection features more than forty-five items, while the dinner menu is even more impressive. And just in case the likes of coconut curry seafood soup, lentil kofta, fufu potatoes, and pepper-pot chicken don't appeal, there are still "home comforts" like chicken tenders, spaghetti and meatballs, and potato salad.

JIKO

★★★★★ $$$$$

As soon as you learn "jiko" is **Swahili for "cooking-place"** (as in cooker, or fireplace) you understand the intricacy of the storytelling at the Lodge's fine-dining restaurant. The two large ethnic wood-burning ovens are at the heart of the dining room, along with a smart show kitchen, while the lighting and coloring provides the effect of being out on the African savanna at sunset, with migrating birds (actually light fittings!) flying toward the setting sun—a Masai sign of good luck. The large brass rings around the pillars are indicative of the neck rings worn by women in several East African cultures, and the floor includes haystack motifs, a sign of wealth and prosperity. The menu is equally adventurous, with an African/Asian spin to classic dishes like filet mignon, short ribs, duck, and lamb, plus several specialized recipes such as spicy Peri-Peri Chicken and Durban Shrimp Curry. The fish dishes are another highlight, as are desserts (try the **Cape Malva Pudding**), while the wine list is completely South African and well worth trying.

HIDDEN MAGIC The exotic and **evocative lighting** of Jiko shouldn't come as any surprise to those familiar with Todd English's bluezoo. The interior décor is again all the work of Jeffrey Beers, the master of light and glass. Watch as the lighting gradually changes during "sunset."

  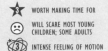 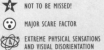

SANAA

★★★★ $$$$

Ready for another language lesson? "Sanaa" is **Swahili for "craftsmanship"** or **"artwork,"** hence this restaurant is another culinary adventure, albeit not quite as elaborate, menu-wise, as Boma or Jiko. The setting is novel, too; on the edge of the resort's animal savanna and given an interior design to make you feel you are outside, not just watching the giraffes and zebras, but among them. Exotically rustic and packed with authentic African art, the main dining room is made up of tree pillars that branch out to form the ceiling while rockwork adds to the outdoor vibe and the heavily woodworked tables are also works of art. The menu is Africa-meets-India with a lot of (mild) curries, fish dishes, and veggie dishes, but also recognizably Western offerings like short ribs, chicken, and a New York strip. However, with the great savanna views, you may not notice the food as much!

Downtown Disney

If the deluxe resorts offer an amazing range (and quality) of restaurant choice, Disney's nighttime district has caught up in recent years with an array of choice that varies from okay to outstanding, with even one counter-service restaurant worthy of note. While dining is more an experience than a story, some restaurants are so magnificently themed they're like stepping into the pages of an adventure novel. Others here tell travel tales of rural Tuscany, Cuba, and Louisiana, while still others bring to mind grand seafaring legends or the lush green hills of Ireland. One of them even takes you to another planet!

RAINFOREST CAFÉ

Essential Information: Not DDP

★★★ **$$$$**

Enter the "volcano" at **the Marketplace end of Downtown Disney** for a jungle adventure in best audio-animatronic style, where gorillas and elephants lurk in the undergrowth and periodic thunderstorms punctuate mealtimes. The interior is spectacular as diners are invited to go "on safari" among the tropical foliage and aquariums—just don't expect a quiet meal! The food is a mix of standard favorites and well-known dishes given a twist (like Pastalaya— jambalaya with pasta instead of rice), but it is really the scenery you are here for, so try not to look too hard at the prices!

CAP'N JACK'S RESTAURANT

★★★ **$$$**

The lone surviving original eating place at Downtown Disney, this nautical-themed diner would be at home at the Yacht or Beach Club resorts with its yacht club style. Dating back to October 1975, it was originally Cap'n Jack's Oyster Bar but was renamed in 2000 and maintains a fairly modest seafood-oriented menu. It is rarely overcrowded hence it remains a good last-minute choice for a relaxing sit-down in this area.

 HIDDEN MAGIC   Cap'n Jack's consists of two hexagonal-shaped ends connected by a rectangular mid-section, because the hexagon was the iconic shape of the original **Lake Buena Vista Shopping Village**, with its European chalet style. You also find the same shape for the Dock Stage, LEGO Imagination Center, and at the top of Disney's Pin Traders store (formerly the signature Captain's Tower).

EARL OF SANDWICH

★★★ **$**

★ MISS-ABLE   ★2 IF YOU HAVE TIME   ★3 WORTH MAKING TIME FOR   ★4 NOT TO BE MISSED!

☺ WILL ONLY WORRY YOUNG CHILDREN   ☺ MAY SCARE MANY YOUNG CHILDREN; FEW ADULTS   ☹ WILL SCARE MOST YOUNG CHILDREN; SOME ADULTS   ☹ MAJOR SCARE FACTOR

↻ VISUAL DISORIENTATION   ↻2 MILD PHYSICAL MOVEMENT   ↻3 INTENSE FEELING OF MOTION   ↻4 EXTREME PHYSICAL SENSATIONS AND VISUAL DISORIENTATION

Easily the best of the counter-service options in Downtown Disney is this founding restaurant for what is now an international chain. Opened in April 2004 and co-owned by Lord John Montagu, **the Eleventh Earl of Sandwich** (it was the Fourth Earl who is credited with inventing the "sandwich," hence the name, in 1762!), it maintains the building's original sense of style as The Gourmet Pantry with a series of excellent (and well-priced) gourmet hot sandwiches and salads using their own artisan-baked bread.

T-REX CAFÉ

Essential Information: Not DDP

★★★ $$$$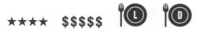

If Rainforest Café is your kind of place, you're going to *love* the prehistoric version! What the Rainforest does for the creatures of the jungle, T-Rex does for the dinosaur age, in dramatic fashion. The story is eye-catching, with an interior filled with bubbling geysers, a dino digsite, periodic meteor showers —and lurking dinos. Its five sections include the eerie **Ice Cave** and **Jurassic-era Fern Forest**, and a huge animatronic octopus hovers over the **Shark Bar** (featuring a 5,000-gallon shark tank). The food is above average, with dishes like **Cretaceous Chicken Fried Steak** and **Mega Mes-O-Bones** (slow-roasted ribs). Portions are suitably large, but dining here can be loud!

FULTON'S CRABHOUSE

Essential Information: Not DDP

★★★★ $$$$$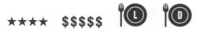

Although this iconic **Mississippi paddle-steamer** arrived in 1977, the **Pleasure Island Imagineers** retro-fitted it in 1989 as the boat Merriweather Adam Pleasure and his family arrived in to establish their new island home in 1911 (remember him? He's the guy whose story we told in the Pleasure Island section in Chapter 8). It remained moored alongside the island as a summer houseboat, to be reclaimed as a full-time restaurant under Disney ownership. **The Empress Lilly**—as it was when originally built—looked for all the world like a classic Mark Twain–era riverboat, named for Walt Disney's widow, **Lillian**. Taken over by Levy Restaurants in 1995, it was stripped of its twin smokestacks and stern paddlewheel and renamed. Happily, it does still offer some of the finest seafood in Orlando.

HIDDEN MAGIC Go to the reverse side of Fulton's Crabhouse, facing the lake, and you can still see the original **floating dock** used to welcome VIP guests aboard the Empress Lilly by boat.

PORTOBELLO

Essential Information: Not DDP

★★★★★ **$$$$**

Merriweather Adam Pleasure really got around, and his story applies here, too. Legend declares that, in 1918, the Pleasure family moved to "a Bermuda-style mansion overlooking Lake Buena Vista." Years later, it became the nautical-themed Portobello Yacht Club, on the edge of Pleasure Island, before becoming Portobello. It serves up a truly flavorful variety of Italian food with Tuscan overtones and it is often overlooked in this corner of Downtown Disney, hence dining reservations are usually available.

RAGLAN ROAD

★★★★ **$$$$**

Direct from Dublin, this huge **Irish pub-restaurant** offers live music and Irish dancing, a superb menu from Irish master chef **Kevin Dundon**, and a good craic (which is Gaelic for "a fun time"). The entire interior, with three separate bars and four dining areas, was all salvaged from pubs in Ireland and shipped to Orlando, where the Irish management continues to insist on doing things their way—including serving the Guinness just right—and with a great sense of humor (just read the menu). Two outside bars and their own Irish band complete an impressive picture here. The true story of Raglan Road in Dublin and the poet **Patrick Kavanagh** (whose bronze statue sits on the bench outside) can be found on *www.raglanroad.com*.

PARADISO 37

Essential Information: Not DDP

★★★ $$$

The tastes of the Americas (North, South, and Central) can be found here, along with a killer **tequila menu** and **live music** most evenings. This eye-catching bar-restaurant was the first thing to be built following the partial demolition of Pleasure Island in 2009 and the "37" in the name refers to the number of different tequilas they serve!

PLANET HOLLYWOOD

★★ $$$

Welcome to a whole new world; in fact, a whole new planet, where **alien spaceships** threaten to crash through the front door and giant alligators sit atop buildings. Yes, it is the loud, wacky, movie-oriented world of Downtown Disney's most popular restaurant, with a three-floor, in-depth adventure into film and TV memorabilia. Yes, the food is standard restaurant fare but you're here for the atmosphere—and the chance to have your picture taken next to the Terminator! However, if you've been to a Planet Hollywood elsewhere, there are much better dining choices in this area.

BONGOS CUBAN CAFÉ

Essential Information: Not DDP

★★★ $$$

Tropical Art Deco meets **South Beach** sizzle in this eye-catching Latin concoction from Cuban pop star **Gloria Estefan** and husband Emilio Estefan. The **Old**

★ POOR   ★★ FAIR   ★★★ GOOD   ★★★★ EXCELLENT   ★★★★★ GOURMET
$ UNDER $10 $$ $10–15 $$$ $15–$20 $$$$ $20–$25 $$$$$ $25+
 BREAKFAST   LUNCH   DINNER   COUNTER SERVICE    TABLE SERVICE   TABLE SERVICE (TWO CREDITS)

Havana architectural style was the first of several for the Estefans and they ensure the salsa beat stays consistent, from the sounds to the food. Those wary of trying traditional **Cuban fare** would do well to put aside any worries here and sample some great pork, chicken, and seafood.

WOLFGANG PUCK CAFÉ

Essential Information: Not DDP at Dining Room

★★★★★ $$$$$ 

If you can get past the zany pop art exterior to the slightly more calming and inviting three-part interior, you will discover a real dining gem—especially if you like sushi and a more European dining experience. The **Californian celebrity chef** fuses American and continental cuisine into a happy marriage of creative but recognizable elements. The **main Café** features great pizza, pasta, salads, and sandwiches, while the **Sushi Bar** is an absolute delight. Upstairs, the more exclusive (and expensive) **Dining Room** provides some new twists on **classic Austrian comfort dishes** in a stylish environment sprinkled with unique art.

HOUSE OF BLUES

Essential Information: Not DDP

★★★ $$$

Imagine an explosion in an old, rusty metal warehouse stacked full of American folk art. Then imagine it has been patched up enough to start a restaurant inside, which still reverberates with the sound of the blues. Finally, fill it with a timeless vibe of the rural South, from the talismanic candles on the bar to the Gospel Brunch every Sunday. The genuine **African-American folk art** is everywhere you look and is a nonstop celebration of the music era it came from. The food runs from simple burgers and sandwiches to a great rib-eye steak and sautéed salmon with eggplant stuffing, much of it with a Delta-inspired flavor. There is live music in the restaurant each Friday and Saturday, and in the outdoor courtyard every evening.

⭐ MISS-ABLE   ⭐ IF YOU HAVE TIME   ⭐ WORTH MAKING TIME FOR   ⭐ NOT TO BE MISSED!

😊 WILL ONLY WORRY YOUNG CHILDREN   😐 MAY SCARE MANY YOUNG CHILDREN; FEW ADULTS   ☹️ WILL SCARE MOST YOUNG CHILDREN; SOME ADULTS   😨 MAJOR SCARE FACTOR

🌀 VISUAL DISORIENTATION   🌀 MILD PHYSICAL MOVEMENT   🌀 INTENSE FEELING OF MOTION   🌀 EXTREME PHYSICAL SENSATIONS AND VISUAL DISORIENTATION

HIDDEN MAGIC

One of the most remarkable pieces of art in the House of Blues collection sits outside at the back. The **huge arch leading into the Voodoo Garden** is by Chicago folk artist Mr. Imagination and features all manner of bric-a-brac handed to him by Cast Members during construction, including name tags, photos, cups—and even an engagement ring.

BoardWalk Resort area

Disney's final gathering of dining delectation exists at **The BoardWalk Inn**, where the restaurant choice is just one more reason to spend some time here.

BIG RIVER GRILLE & BREWING WORKS

★★★★ $$$

Ever wondered what Tennessee tastes like? Well, to start with, it comes in a glass, is fairly full-bodied, and it originated in Chattanooga on the banks of the Tennessee River. And then there's the food—nothing fancy, but good American standards, freshly produced and flavored with some of their own liquid produce. Oh, did we mention this is a **microbrewery**, with an award-winning selection of ales and lagers? Well, we recommend the Rocket Red. And the Steamboat Pale Ale. And the Summer Wheat. Gosh darn it—just give any of them a try, it certainly beats drinking Bud!

ESPN CLUB

★★ $$$

It's a sports bar, what more is there to say? Okay, it's a *big* sports bar, full of all the stuff that makes sports fans whoop and holler and generally have a good time, like big-screen TVs, live sportscasting, big-screen TVs, video games, and more big-screen TVs (including in the bathrooms!). The food? Yes, there's food, but we're usually too busy watching the TVs to notice.

FLYING FISH

★★★★★ $$$$$

Taking the boardwalk theme into an artistic interpretation, this fine-dining restaurant takes classic amusement images like the **Ferris wheel**, **roller-coaster tracks**, **fun-house mirrors**, and **parachuting fish** and makes them the background to arguably the best seafood in Orlando. With a mouthwatering array of signature dishes like peekytoe crab cakes and potato-wrapped snapper, it also boasts a magnificent wine list, impeccable service, and a highly tempting **six-course prix fixe Chef's Wine Tasting Dinner**.

KOUZZINA

★★★★ $$$$

While it may seem a touch out of place in the American boardwalk line-up, this **Mediterranean-inspired eatery** is a well-established tradition hereabouts. **Kouzzina** is the brainchild of celebrity **Iron Chef Cat Cora** and brings a **Greek-influenced theme** to the cuisine, which remains perfect for the Mediterranean ambience. Enjoy one of **Cat's Wine Flights** as well as classic dishes like spanakopita (spinach phyllo pie), saganaki (flamed cheese), calamari, and pastitsio (a variation on lasagna). Or just try a New York strip steak or pan-roasted fish of the Day.

And now, with a full appreciation for the stories Disney Imagineers have so beautifully crafted, it's time for you to go out and make your own stories in this wonderful, magical place!

REALITY CHECK Don't assume this is a once-in-a-lifetime trip and you have to "do it all." You will be back!

 MISS-ABLE WILL ONLY WORRY YOUNG CHILDREN VISUAL DISORIENTATION

 IF YOU HAVE TIME MAY SCARE MANY YOUNG CHILDREN; FEW ADULTS MILD PHYSICAL MOVEMENT

 WORTH MAKING TIME FOR WILL SCARE MOST YOUNG CHILDREN; SOME ADULTS INTENSE FEELING OF MOTION

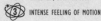 NOT TO BE MISSED! MAJOR SCARE FACTOR EXTREME PHYSICAL SENSATIONS AND VISUAL DISORIENTATION

Write Your Own Story

Index

ABC Commissary, 240–41
Accommodations, 41–90. *See also specific resorts*
  about: overview of, 42
  benefits, 43–45
  campground, 84–85
  deluxe villas, 77–83
  Dining Plans and, 44–45
  Extra Magic Hours privilege, 43, 87, 272
  outside Disney World, 88–90
  phone numbers, 33
  resorts, 45–77; deluxe, 60–77; moderate, 50–59; onsite non-Disney, 86–88; value, 46–49
Admission tickets, 21–22, 28–29, 33
Adventureland, 105–12
Affection Section, 278
Africa, 278–81
Africa Refreshment Coolpost, 190
Akershus Royal Banquet Hall, 186. *See also* Restaurant Akershus
Aloha Isle and Sunshine Tree Terrace, 112
AMC Downtown Disney 24, 314–15
American Adventure, 193–96
American Idol Experience, 229
Anandapur Ice Cream Truck, 276
Animal Kingdom
  about: holidays at, 285; overview of, 258; parades, tours, special events, 284–85; practical information, 258
  Africa, 278–81
  Asia, 270–76
  Camp Minnie-Mickey, 282–84
  DinoLand U.S.A., 263–69
  Discovery Island, 259–62
  The Oasis, 258–59
  Rafiki's Planet Watch, 276–78
Animal Kingdom Lodge, 74–77, 337–39

Animal Kingdom Villas, 82
Animation Courtyard, 244–46
Anniversaries, 30–31
Apps, for mobile devices, 31–32
Artist Point, 334–35
Art of Animation Resort, 49
Asia, 270–76
Astro Orbiter, 144
Atlantic Dance Hall, 318
Attractions. *See specific areas of park; specific attractions*

Baby care centers, 25–26
Backlot Express, 234
Backstage Magic, 153, 253
Barnstormer Hosted by the Great Goofini, 137
Bay Lake Tower at Contemporary Resort, 83
Bay Slides, 293
Beach Club and Yacht Club Resorts, 68–69, 326, 329–30
Beach Club Villas, 79
Beauty and the Beast–Live on Stage, 246–47
Behind the Seeds, 209
Be Our Guest Restaurant, 140
Bibbidi Bobbidi Boutique, 140
Biergarten, 191
Big River Grille & Brewing Works, 345
Big Thunder Mountain Railroad, 114–15
Birthdays, 30–31
Bistro de Paris, 203
Blizzard Beach, 33, 295–300
BoardWalk, 316–18, 345–46
BoardWalk Inn, 72–74
BoardWalk Villas, 79
Boatwright's Dining Hall, 327
Boma, 337–38
Bongos Cuban Café, 343–44
Boulangerie Patisserie, 202
Bowling, 315
Briar Patch Gift Shop, 120
Buzz Lightyear's Space Ranger Spin, 146–47

California Grill, 331
Campground, 84–85
Canada, 205–7
Candlelight Processional, 212
Cape May Café, 326, 329
Cap'n Jack's Restaurant, 340
Captain EO, 173–74
Captain Jack's Pirate Tutorial, 111
Captain's Grille, 329–30
Caribbean Beach Resort, 50–51, 327
Carousel of Progress, 143–44
Carrousel, 129
Casey Jr. Roundhouse, 137
Casey's Corner, 103
Castaway Creek, 292–93
Catalina Eddie's, 252
Celebrate a Dream Come True Parade, 149–50
Character greeting trails, 282
Character meal line-up, 325–26
Characters in Flight, 313
Chef Mickey's, 326, 331–32
Chefs de France, 202
Chester and Hester's Dino-Rama, 264
Chester and Hester's Dinosaur Treasures, 269
Children, considerations for, 24–26
China, 186–89
Christmas. *See* Holidays
Cinderella's Royal Table, 138, 326
Circle of Live–An Environmental Fable, 169–70
Cirque du Soleil, 33, 45, 312–13
Citricos, 336
Club Cool, 166
Columbia Harbour House, 125–26
Commissary Lane, 240–41
Conservation Station, 277
Contemporary Resort, 60–62, 326, 331–32. *See also* Bay Lake Tower at Contemporary Resort
The Coral Reef, 179–80
Coronado Springs, 57–59, 328

Cosmic Ray's Starlight Café, 147–48
Countries. *See* Dining (Epcot); Epcot, World Showcase; Shopping (Epcot)
Country Bear Jamboree, 117
Cross Country Creek, 298–99
Crowds, 24
Crush 'n' Gusher, 294
Crystal Palace, 326
Curtain Call Collectibles, 104

Diamond Horseshoe, 119
The Dig Site, 267
Dining. *See also specific areas of park (immediately below); specific establishments*
    character meal-line-up, 325–26
    resorts, 327–39
Dining (Animal Kingdom)
    about: character meal-line-up, 326
    Africa, 281
    Asia, 275–76
    Camp Minnie-Mickey, 284
    DinoLand U.S.A., 269
    Discovery Island, 262
Dining (BoardWalk), 345–46
Dining (Downtown Disney), 315, 339–45
Dining (Epcot)
    The American Adventure, 196
    Canada, 207
    China, 188–89
    France, 202–3
    Future World, 179–80
    Germany, 191
    Italy, 192–93
    Japan, 198
    Mexico, 182–84
    Morocco, 200
    Norway, 186
    The Outpost, 190
    United Kingdom, 204–5
Dining (Hollywood Studios)
    about: character meal-line-up, 326
    Commissary Lane, 240–41
    Echo Lake, 233–34
    Hollywood Boulevard, 228
    Pixar Place, 242
    Streets of America, 238–39

Sunset Boulevard, 250–52
Dining (Magic Kingdom). *See also specific establishments*
    about: character meal-line-up, 326
    Adventureland, 111–12
    Fantasyland, 138–40
    Frontierland, 118–19
    Liberty Square, 125–26
    Tomorrowland, 147–49
    Town Square and Main Street, 101–3
Dining (water parks)
    Blizzard Beach, 300
    Typhoon Lagoon, 294–95
Dining Plans, 44–45
Dinner shows, 318–32
DinoLand U.S.A., 263–69
Dinosaur, 265–66
Dinosaur Gertie's Ice Cream of Extinction, 234
Discovery Island, 259–62
Discovery Island Trails, 261
Disney Hotel Plaza, 86–87
Disney Junior–Live on Stage!, 245–46
DisneyQuest, 314
Disney's BoardWalk, 316–18
Disney's Family Magic, 152
Disney's Wedding Pavilion, 305
DiveQuest, 209
Dolphin and Swan Resorts, 66–67, 326, 332–34
Dolphins in Depth, 209
Downhill Double Dipper, 297
Downtown Disney
    about: dining, 315, 339–45;
    overview of, 309
    Marketplace, 309–12
    West Side, 312–16
Dream Along with Mickey, 129–30
Dumbo the Flying Elephant, 136–37

Earl of Sandwich, 340–41
Echo Lake, 229–34
The Electric Umbrella, 179
Emporium, 104
Emporium Gallery, 104–5
Enchanted Tiki Room (Tropical Serenade), 106–7

Epcot. *See also* Dining (Epcot); Shopping (Epcot); *specific attractions and establishments*
    about: holidays at, 211–12;
    overview of, 162; parades, tours, events, 208–12;
    practical information, 162
    Future World, 162–80;
        about: overview of, 162–78; attractions, 162–78;
        dining, 179–80; shopping, 180
    World Showcase, 181–207;
        about: overview of, 181;
        The American Adventure, 193–96; Canada, 205–7;
        China, 186–89; France, 201–3; Germany, 190–91;
        Italy, 192–93; Japan, 196–99; Mexico, 181–84;
        Morocco, 199–201;
        Norway, 184–86; The Outpost, 189–90; United Kingdom, 203–5
Epcot Seas Aqua Tour, 210
ESPN Club, 345
ESPN Wild World of Sports Complex, 300–301
Expedition Everest–Legend of the Forbidden Mountain, 273–75
Extra Magic Hours privilege, 43, 87, 272

Fairfax Fare, 252
Fantasia Gardens, 303
Fantasmic!, 239, 250
Fastpass system, 28–29
Festival of the Lion King, 283
Festivals. *See* Parades, tours, events
50's Prime Time Café, 233
Finding Nemo–The Musical, 267–68
Fishing, 33
Flag Retreat Ceremony, 100
Flame Tree Barbecue, 262
Flower and Garden Festival, 210
Flying Fish, 346
Food and Wine Festival, 210–11
Fort Wilderness, 84–85, 326, 328
Fort Wilderness Campfire Program, 321

Fountainview Café, 179
France, 201–3
Frontierland, 113–20
Frontierland Pin Trading, 120
Fulton's Crabhouse, 341–42
Future World. See Epcot

Gang Plank Falls, 291
Garden Grill, 180, 326
Garden Grove Café, 326, 333
Gaston's Tavern, 139
Germany, 190–91
Golden Oak Outpost, 119
Golf, 33, 301–4
Grand Floridian Café, 336
Grand Floridian Resort & Spa,
    64–65, 326, 335–37
Gran Fiesta Tour Starring the
    Three Caballeros, 182
The Great Movie Ride, 227–28
Group reservations, 33

Habitat Habit!, 277
Hall of Presidents, 121
Halloween party, 154
Handicapped visitors, 26–27, 33
Haunted Mansion, 122–24
Heritage Manor Gifts, 196
Hey Howdy Hey Take Away, 242
Hideaway Bay, 294
Holiday D-Lights (seasonal), 211
Holidays, 153–54, 211–12, 253,
    285
Hollywood & Vine, 233, 326
Hollywood Boulevard, 226–28
The Hollywood Brown Derby,
    228
Hollywood Studios
    about: holidays in, 253;
        overview of, 226;
        practical information, 226;
        tours and special events,
        252–53
    Animation Courtyard,
        244–46
    Commissary Lane (dining),
        240–41
    Echo Lake, 229–34
    Hollywood Boulevard,
        226–28
    Mickey Avenue, 242–43
    Pixar Place, 241–42
    Streets of America, 235–40

Sunset Boulevard, 246–52
Honey I Shrunk the Kids Movie
    Set Adventure, 236–37
Hoop Dee Doo Revue, 319–20
Hotels. See Accommodations
House of Blues, 313, 344–45
Humunga Kowabunga, 291

Illuminations: Reflections of
    Earth, 208–9
Il Mulino, 334
Imageworks, 173
Imagination!, 172–73
Impressions de France, 201–2
Indiana Jones Epic Stunt Spec-
    tacular!, 230–31
Innoventions East and Innoven-
    tions West, 165–66
Inspiration: Through Walt's Eyes,
    253
ISTC's Advanced Training Lab,
    177
Italy, 192–93
"It's a Small World," 127–28
"It's Tough to Be a Bug!," 260–61

Japan, 196–99
Jellyrolls, 317
Jiko, 338
Journey Into Narnia: Prince Cas-
    pian, 243
Jungle Cruise, 107–9

Kali River Rapids, 272–73
Keelhaul Falls, 292
Ketchakiddee Creek, 293
Keys to the Kingdom, 152
Kilimanjaro Safaris, 279–80
Kimonos, 334
Kona Café, 330–31
Kouzzina, 346
Kringla Bakeri og Kafé, 186

La Cantina de San Angel, 183
La Cava del Tequila, 183–84
La Hacienda de San Angel,
    182–83
Lake Buena Vista Golf Course,
    302
The Land, 168
La Nouba, 312–13
Leaning Palms, 294
Le Cellier, 207

Le Chapeau, 104
Liberty Inn, 196
Liberty Square Riverboat, 122
Liberty Tree Tavern, 125
Lights, Motors, Action! Extreme
    Stunt Show, 237
Living with the Land, 168–69
Lost & found, 33
Lotus Blossom Café, 188
Lowtide Lou's, 295

Mad Tea Party, 131
Maelstrom, 184–85
The Magic, The Memories and
    You!, 150
The Magic Behind Our Steam
    Trains, 153
Magic Carpets of Aladdin, 106
Magic Kingdom. See also specific
    attractions and establishments
    about: holidays at, 153–54;
        overview of, 98; parades,
        tours, events, 149–53;
        practical information,
        98–99
    Adventureland, 105–12;
        attractions, 105–11; dining,
        111–12; shopping, 112
    Fantasyland, 127–41;
        attractions, 127–37; dining,
        138–40
    Frontierland, 113–20;
        attractions, 113–17; dining,
        118–19; shopping, 120
    Liberty Square, 120–26;
        attractions, 120–24;
        dining, 125–26; shopping,
        126
    Main Street, U.S.A., 99–105;
        attractions, 100; dining,
        101–3; shopping, 104–5
    Tomorrowland, 141–49;
        attractions, 141–47; dining,
        147–49; shopping, 149
The Magic of Disney Animation,
    245
Magnolia Golf Course, 302
Maharajah Jungle Trek, 270–71
Main Street, U.S.A., 99–105
Main Street Bakery, 103
Main Street Electrical Parade, 150
Mama Melrose's Ristorante Ital-
    iano, 238–39

Many Adventures of Winnie the
    Pooh, 131–32
Marketplace, 309–12
Maurice's Cottage, 135–36
Maya Grill, 328
Mayday Falls, 291
Meltaway Bay, 299
Mexico, 181–84
Mickey Avenue, 242–43
Mickey's Backyard BBQ, 320–21,
    326
Mickey's Jammin' Jungle Parade,
    284–85
Mickey's Not So Scary Hallow-
    een Party, 154
Mickey's Philharmagic, 132–34
Mickey's Very Merry Christmas
    Party, 154
Min and Bill's Dockside Diner, 233
Mini golf, 302–4
Mission: Space, 175–77
Mitsukoshi, 198–99
Monorail, 60, 62, 64, 83, 152
Monsters, Inc. Laugh Floor, 147
Morocco, 199–201
Muppet*Vision 3-D, 235–36
My Disney Girl's Perfect Princess
    Tea, 326

Narcoossee's, 336–37
Night of Joy, 154
Nighttime at Disney. See also spe-
    cific attractions
    BoardWalk, 316–18
    dinner shows, 318–32
    Electrical Water Pageant,
        321–22
    Fort Wilderness Campfire
        Program, 321
    Marketplace, 310–12
    West Side, 312–16
Nine Dragons, 188–89
1900 Park Fare, 326, 335–36
Norway, 184–86

Oak Trail Golf Course, 302
The Oasis, 258–59
Oasis Canteen, 234
O Canada!, 206–7
'Ohana, 326, 330
Old Key West, 78, 328
Olivia's Café, 328
One Man's Dream, Walt Disney,
    243

Osborne Family Spectacle of
    Dancing Lights, 253
Osprey Ridge Golf Course, 302
The Outpost, 189–90

Palm Golf Course, 302
Pangani Forest Exploration Trail,
    280–81
Parades, tours, events, 149–53,
    208–12, 232, 252–53, 284–85
Paradiso 37, 342
Parkside Antiques, 239
Passholder info and bookings, 33
Pecos Bill Tall Tale Inn and Café,
    118–19
Peter Pan's Flight, 134–35
Phone numbers, 32–33
PhotoPass, 30
Pinocchio Village Haus, 139
Pirate and Pals Firework Voy-
    age, 153
Pirates League, 112
Pirates of the Caribbean, 109–10
Pixar Pals Countdown to Fun!
    Parade, 232
Pixar Place, 241–42
Pizzafari, 262
Pizza Planet Arcade, 239
Planet Hollywood, 33, 343
Plaza Ice Cream Parlor, 103
Plaza Restaurant, 101, 326
Polynesian Resort, 62–63, 326,
    330–31
Pop Century Resort, 47–48
Portobello, 342
Port Orleans Resort, 52–56, 327
Primeval Whirl, 264–65
Prince Charming Regal Carrou-
    sel, 129
Princess Fairytale Hall, 135
Project Tomorrow, 164
Puffins Roost, 186

Rafiki's Planet Watch, 276–78
Raglan Road, 342–43
Rainforest Café, 340
Ratings key, 11–17
Reflections of China, 187–88
Resorts. See Accommodations;
    specific resorts
Restaurant Akershus, 326
Restaurant Marrakech, 200
Restaurantosaurus, 269

Rider Swap, 26
Rock 'n' Roller Coaster Starring
    Aerosmith, 248
Rose & Crown, 205
Rosie's All American Cafe,
    250–51
Runoff Rapids, 298

Sanaa, 339
San Angel Inn, 183
Saratoga Springs Resort and Spa,
    80–82, 329
Sci-Fi Dine-In Theater, 240
Scuttle's Scavenger Hunt, 131
Sea Base, 167–68
The Seas with Nemo & Friends,
    166–67
Under the Sea–Voyage of the
    Little Mermaid, 130–31
Segway Tour, 210
Seniors, 27
Seven Dwarfs Mine Train, 136
Shades of Green, 86
Shark Reef, 293
Shopping (Animal Kingdom)
    Africa, 281
    Asia, 275
    DinoLand U.S.A., 269
    Discovery Island, 262
Shopping (Downtown Disney)
    Marketplace, 310–12
    West Side, 316
Shopping (Epcot)
    The American Adventure, 196
    Canada, 207
    China, 189
    France, 203
    Germany, 191
    Italy, 193
    Japan, 198–99
    Mexico, 184
    Morocco, 201
    Norway, 186
    United Kingdom, 205
Shopping (Hollywood Studios)
    Animation Courtyard, 246
    Echo Lake, 234
    Hollywood Boulevard, 228
    Streets of America, 239–40
    Sunset Boulevard, 252
Shopping (Magic Kingdom)
    Adventureland, 112
    Fantasyland, 140–41

Frontierland, 120
Future World, 180
Liberty Square, 126
Tomorrowland, 149
Town Square and Main
    Street, 104–5
Shopping (water parks)
    Blizzard Beach, 300
    Typhoon Lagoon, 295
Shula's, 332–33
Shutters, 327
Ski Patrol Training Camp, 299
Sleepy Hollow Refreshments, 126
Slush Gusher, 296–97
Snow Stormers, 297
Soarin', 170–72
Sommerfest, 191
Sounds Dangerous with Drew
    Carey, 230
Space Mountain, 141–42
Spaceship Earth, 163–64
Special events. See Parades,
    tours, events
Special needs, 26–27, 33
Special occasions, 30–31
Speedway, 304
Spirit of Aloha, 318–19
Splash Mountain, 113–14
Splitsville Luxury Lanes and Din-
    ner Lounge, 315
Starring Rolls Café, 250
Star Tours, 231–32
Star Wars: Jedi Training Acad-
    emy, 232
Star Wars Weekends, 252–53
Stitch's Great Escape, 145–46
Storm Slides, 291
Storybook Circus, 136
Streets of America, 235–40
Studio Backlot Tour, 237–38
Studio Catering Co., 239
Summit Plummet, 296
Sunset Boulevard, 246–52
Sunset Ranch Market, 251
Sunshine Seasons, 180
Surf Pool, 292
Surf School, 292
Swan Resort. See Dolphin and
    Swan Resorts
Swiss Family Treehouse, 105–6

Tamu Tamu Refreshments, 281
Tangierine Café, 200

Teamboat Springs, 297
Tennis, 33
Teppan Edo, 198
Test Track, 177–78
Tickets, 21–22, 28–29, 33
Tike's Peak, 299
Toboggan Racers, 298
Todd English's Bluezoo, 333, 338
Tokyo Dining, 198
Toluca Legs Turkey Co., 251
Tomorrowland Speedway,
    142–43
Tomorrowland Terrace, 148
Tomorrowland Transit Author-
    ity, 143
Tom Sawyer Island, 115–16
Tony's Town Square Restaurant,
    101
Tortuga Tavern, 111
Tours, 33. See also Parades,
    tours, events
Toy Story Midway Mania, 241–42
Trails, 261, 280–81, 282
Trail's End Restaurant, 328
Trains, 100, 114–15, 136, 153, 277
Travel
    arriving in Orlando, 34–35
    Disney's Magical Express, 35
Tree of Life, 259–60
T-Rex Café, 341
Triceratop Spin, 265
Trilo-Bites, 269
Tropical Serenade, 106–7
Turf Club Bar and Grill, 329
Tusker House Restaurant, 281,
    326
Tutto Italia, 193
Twilight Zone Tower of Terror,
    248–50
Typhoon Lagoon, 33, 290–95
Typhoon Tilly's, 295

Undiscovered Future World, 210
United Kingdom, 203–5
Universe of Energy, 174–75

Via Napoli, 192–93
Victoria & Albert's, 337
Villas, deluxe, 77–83
Villas at Disney's Wilderness
    Lodge, 79
Voyage of the Little Mermaid,
    244–45

Walt Disney One Man's Dream,
    243
Walt Disney World Railroad, 100
Walt Disney World Speedway,
    304
Water parks, 290–300
    about: lost & found, 33
    Blizzard Beach, 295–300
    Typhoon Lagoon, 290–95
Watersports, 33
The Wave, 332
Weather, 23–24, 33
Wedding Pavilion, 304–5
Weddings, 33
West Side, 312–16
Whispering Canyon Café, 335
Wild Africa Trek, 285
Wild by Design, 285
Wilderness Lodge, 69–72, 334–
    35. See also Villas at Disney's
    Wilderness Lodge
Wildlife Express Train, 277
Winter Summerland, 303
Wishes Dessert Party at Tomor-
    rowland Terrace, 148
Wishes Nighttime Spectacular,
    151–52
Wolfgang Puck Café, 344
Wonderland Tea Party, 326
The World of Disney (shopping),
    311–12
World Showcase. See Epcot
Wyndham Bonnet Creek Resort,
    87–88

Yacht Club and Beach Club
    Resorts, 68–69, 326, 329–30
Yachtsman Steakhouse, 330
Yak & Yeti Local Food Cafes, 276
Yak & Yeti Restaurant, 275
Yakitori House, 198
Ye Olde Christmas Shoppe, 126
Yong Fens Shandgian, 189
Yorkshire Country Fish Shop,
    204
Yuletide Fantasy (seasonal), 211

Skull rock outside of Pirates of the Caribbean (see page 109)

This way to Ghastly Mansion (see page 112)

Pirate plunderings outside Tortuga Tavern (see page 111)

Guess what's right across from Mr. Crane's voice lessons? (see page 126)

Imagineers keeping watch over their work (see page 127)

The one place no one wants to see their name (see page 192)

Jupiter's big red spot at Mission: Space (see page 176)

Tower of Terror blends perfectly with Morocco (see page 199)

Replica of the street sign at Walt Disney Studios in California (see page 243)

Mahjong game at Tower Hotel that will never be finished (see page 249)

Rosie's patriotic Victory Garden (see page 251)

Tiki Gods are everywhere! (see page 63)

Chester and Hester's lawn art (see page 264)

Mysterious cave art at Blizzard Beach (see page 299)

Anandapur's prayer shrine mimics the outline of the mountains (see page 276)

A reminder of the land that never was at Disney's Animal Kingdom (see page 282)

One of five storytelling bas reliefs in Pagani (see page 271)

Welcome to Typhoon Lagoon (see page 290)

Captain Sal's survey spot (see page 295)

Hand-crafted wall art at Yak & Yeti restaurant (see page 275)

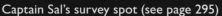